中国小学英语教材语法可学性评估

Learnability of Grammar: A Processability Perspective of Textbook Evaluation in English as A Foreign Language Settings

唐晓菲　著

武汉理工大学出版社
·武　汉·

内 容 提 要

本书运用当今国际第二语言习得研究领域具有重要影响力的理论——语言可加工性理论(Processability Theory)对中国国内小学英语教材的语法教学内容进行了较为系统地评估与分析，为教材的评估研究领域提供了以第二语言习得规律为基础的创新性方法，同时也对当前小学英语教材语法教学内容存在的局限性进行了较为系统地探讨，最后提出了一系列具有实际教学法意义的改进建议。本书既为我国小学英语教学及教材编写提供了科学理论依据，又将语言可加工性理论的应用进行了延伸，是一本兼具理论入门与实际应用作用的指导性学术专著。

图书在版编目(CIP)数据

中国小学英语教材语法可学性评估/唐晓菲著. —武汉：武汉理工大学出版社，2017.11
ISBN 978-7-5629-5671-6

Ⅰ. ①中… Ⅱ. ①唐… Ⅲ. ①英语-语法-小学-教学参考资料 Ⅳ. ①G624.313

中国版本图书馆 CIP 数据核字(2017)第 285800 号

项目负责人：田 高
责任编辑：王兆国
责任校对：徐 环
封面设计：许伶俐
出版发行：武汉理工大学出版社
地　　址：武汉市洪山区珞狮路 122 号
邮　　编：430070
网　　址：http://www.wutp.com.cn
经　　销：各地新华书店
印　　刷：武汉兴和彩色印务有限公司
开　　本：787×1092 1/16
印　　张：12.75
字　　数：326 千字
版　　次：2018 年 1 月第 1 版
印　　次：2018 年 1 月第 1 次印刷
定　　价：69.00 元

凡购本书，如有缺页、倒页、脱页等印装质量问题，请向出版社发行部调换。
本社购书热线：027-87515778 87515848 87785758 87165708(传真)

前　言

本研究基于第二语言(简称二语)习得规律对中国小学英语规定教材进行系统性评估。该评估旨在调查英语教材中的语法教学与目前国际二语习得领域重要理论之一的语言可加工性理论(Pienemann,1998,2005)所提出的第二语言习得顺序之间所存在的差异程度。

二语习得产生的前提条件是一定数量的语言输入。而在语言教学特别是外语教学的环境中,语言教材被视为学习者获得目的语语言输入的主要渠道。尤其在中国内地,英语学习者缺乏对目的语英语的自然习得环境,因而英语教材作为主要渠道为学习者提供了大量英语语言输入。因此,基于语言习得规律来编写教材显得尤为重要。

当前,主流研究对教材评估的调查分析主要集中在教材的潜在使用价值、教材对使用者的实际作用以及教材中会话文本的真实性或语用信息的充实性等领域。仅有几组研究采用第二语言习得理论来评估教材。因此,本研究试图从二语习得理论的角度对四套国内英语教材进行分析,并着重评估其中英语语素与关键句法结构所出现的顺序。

本研究首先对被调查的英语教材中被规定为教学目标的重点语素与句法结构进行系统性记录,其次依据语言加工性理论所提出的英语习得层级对相关教学目标进行科学分类,之后将分类后的教学目标与语言处理层级进行对比分析。研究结果显示:被调查的英语教材中所出现的语法教学目标的顺序与语言可加工性理论所提出的二语习得顺序存在部分一致。整体而言,位于习得层级初级阶段的语法结构在教材中出现的顺序符合其在语言可加工性理论中的科学假定。但是,位于中高级阶段的部分语法结构未按照其在语言加工性理论中的科学假定在教材中依次呈现。

研究者在对教材的进一步分析后发现:部分语法结构在教材中的过早出现可能与教材编写中所采用的以主题(话题)为基础的教学法相关。教材编写者更倾向于对语法结构在特定语境中有用性的考量,而非其在二语习得规律中的真实情况,即该语法结构对于现阶段学习者是否可学。对此,本研究基于语言输入、学习者二语发展规律以及二语教学课堂的差异性等方面对教材中的语法大纲编写以及教学法提出了一系列建议。

CONTENTS

Chapter 1

Introduction: Research Statement and Chapter Outline

1.1 Research statement: Aim, question, and motivations

This study aims to conduct an acquisition-based evaluation of four primary-school English textbook series including a total of 28 volumes. They are: *New Standard English* (Chen & Ellis, 2012; 8 volumes), *People's Education Press English* (Wu, 2012; 8 volumes), *Super Kids* (Liu, Krause, & Cossu, 2012; 4 volumes), and *Join in* (Zhang, 2014; 8 volumes). All are used on a nationwide scale in China. The textbook evaluation seeks to answer the research question: whether or not the sequencing of key grammatical structures introduced as the teaching objectives in the four textbook series is compatible with the sequenced development that the learners go through in acquiring English as a second language (L2) as stipulated in Processability Theory (Pienemann, 1998, 2005). The theoretical approach employed in this evaluation—Processability Theory—is a psycholinguistically-based second language acquisition (SLA) theory, developed by Manfred Pienemann (1998, 2005) to describe and explain a universal L2 developmental sequence from a language processing perspective.

L2 acquisition cannot take place without language input, and textbooks serve as one main form of language input for learners especially in a foreign language (FL) context. Textbooks provide instructional input that contains different components of the target language, such as grammatical rules, vocabulary, functions or notions, pronunciation, spelling, socio-cultural information, etc.

In FL settings such as those that prevail in China, learners of English have little or no opportunities to access the target language through natural exposure. Formal instruction in schools is the dominant environment where learners receive linguistic input. Indeed, textbooks are used as the main source of linguistic exposure to English and provide different modalities of language use (e. g., speaking, writing, listening, and reading) for the students. They also supplement and facilitate the teacher's instruction, by providing organized lesson plans and information on what kinds of teaching practice can be utilized in the classroom. As the use of textbooks in language classrooms is an almost inevitable component of formal instruction in EFL (English as a foreign language) settings (Hutchinson & Torres, 1994), an evaluation of textbooks for the purpose of more efficient teaching and effective learning is a worthwhile undertaking.

A review of existing research on textbook evaluation reveals that the majority of studies have been looking at the potential effectiveness of textbooks (e. g. , McDonough & Show, 1993; Mukundan, Hajimohammadi, & Nimehchisalem, 2011), the actual effects of textbooks on users (e. g. , Lan & Meng, 2009; Shi & Ji, 2011), and the pragmatic information and the authenticity of textbook contexts (e. g. , Petraki & Bayes, 2013; Wong, 2007). Only a handful of SLA-based studies (Lenzing, 2004, 2008; Zipser, 2012) have paid attention to the key issue concerning L2 learning, i. e. , how, in fact, L2 learners learn grammatical structures step-by-step. These studies take into account the developmental sequences of L2 grammar learning and explicate why, from a psycholinguistic perspective, some structures are more complex than others. They examine whether grammar instruction in the textbooks they assess is presented in a way that is learnable for L2 students.

To the best of my knowledge, the latter approach is not found in English textbooks compiled in mainland China. The present study therefore follows the line of SLA-based textbook studies to investigate whether the sequencing of grammar in English textbooks currently used in China conforms to a staged L2 development. It is guided by Processability Theory (PT), a psycholinguistic theory of SLA. Based on the psychological mechanisms underlying language information processing and spontaneous speech production, PT describes, explains and predicts the developmental sequence of L2 grammar. The plausibility of PT has been extensively tested and generally confirmed by a range of empirical studies on typologically diverse languages, such as German, English, Swedish, Chinese, Japanese, and Arabic (Jansen, 2008; Kawaguchi, 2005a; Mansouri, 2005; Pienemann, 1998; Zhang, 2005). Within its universal schedule of L2 development, PT describes and explains the sequence in which a certain range of grammatical structures is acquired in an ESL (English as a second language) setting.

In 2011, the Ministry of Education of China stipulated that the study of English was a compulsory subject in six-year primary-school education, starting at Grade Three (children aged eight or nine), as well as in three-year junior-secondary-school education. Among the most widely used L2 English learning materials in Chinese primary schools are the four textbook series *New Standard English*, *People's Education Press English*, *Super Kids*, and *Join in*. They were selected over a number of other publications, based on their authority and popularity in China. They are officially approved by the Chinese Ministry of Education for the teaching of English in primary schools from Grade 3 to Grade 6. They are published by two of the largest educational publishing companies in China, namely, the People's Education Press and the Foreign Language Teaching and Research Press. These textbook series are published in large numbers.

In this textbook analysis, the grammatical items that are introduced as teaching objectives will be documented and categorized according to the processability hierarchy as stipulated in Processability Theory. Their orderings throughout the textbook series will then be compared with the sequence of L2 English acquisition as outlined in the processability hierarchy. The cross-check of the degree of correspondence between the two sequences (in the textbooks and in the processability hierarchy) contributes to depicting whether learnability of grammatical structures has been considered in the language textbooks under investigation.

1.2 Chapter outline

The later content is organized as follows. It begins with a discussion of the key issues related to the motivations behind and the significance of the present study, including the role of language input, grammar learning, grammar teaching, and sequence of grammatical structures (Chapter 2).

Chapter 3 provides a critical review of research on textbook evaluation. Four prominent approaches are reviewed: predictive evaluation, retrospective evaluation, Conversation Analysis/Discourse Analysis-based evaluation, and SLA-based evaluation. The review focuses more on SLA-based evaluation as it is directly relevant to the present study.

Chapter 4 gives an overview of the SLA theoretical approach adopted in the textbook analysis undertaken in this study—Processability Theory. It starts with a review of the theoretical background of L2 acquisition, focusing on L2 developmental sequences, as this forms a basis for the description of Processability Theory. A discussion of the general principles of Processability Theory is followed by an outline of the theory's hypothesized processability hierarchy for ESL morpho-syntactic development.

The research methods and the selected textbooks of the study are presented in Chapter 5, including a description of the analyses of the four ESL textbook series. The results act as the basis for the discussion in Chapter 6 of a series of issues related to the present study, such as the discrepancy between the textbook grading and the developmental path of L2 English acquisition as outlined in Processability Theory, the deviant introduction of grammatical items in the textbooks, the intentions or considerations of textbook writers, etc. Chapter 6 also proposes suggestions for developing an acquisition-based grammatical introduction in ESL textbooks, as well as pedagogical implications for textbook design and L2 teaching.

Chapter 7 concludes with a summary of the major findings from the textbook analysis, focusing on the compatibility between the grading of grammatical items in textbooks and the sequence of ESL acquisition. It also summarizes the key aspects and implications of proposed suggestions for developing a learnable grammatical introduction in ESL textbooks. It ends with a discussion of the limitations of the study. Possible future improvements include a further investigation into the actual effect of the proposed grammatical instruction on L2 learning and teaching.

Chapter 2

Why Do We Need to Consider Learnability of Grammar?

This chapter discusses the key issues that are crucial to shaping the rationale for the motivations of this study—Why is it necessary to take into account the learnability of grammatical structures in the textbook development? The discussion will provide an understanding of several issues: Why does L2 learning need input? Why do we need to learn grammar? Do we need to teach grammar? If so, how should we teach it?

2.1 The role of input in language learning

Early conceptualizations or theories of how language learning occurred highlighted the importance of the input provided to the learner. This was particularly the case within the behaviourist period of language research between the 1940s and the 1970s (Gass, 2003). Behaviourism aimed to explain animal and human behaviour without reference to internal processes (VanPatten & Williams, 2007). It claimed that learning relied heavily on the external environment—the so-called 'input', 'experience' or 'stimulus' the learner was exposed to when achieving learning (Skinner, 1968, pp. 6-7). Language acquisition was regarded as a stimulus-response process and the formation of new habits. Behaviourist theory (e. g. , Bloomfield, 1933; Skinner, 1957) asserted that the process of language acquisition could be controlled by presenting learners with right-sized doses of input and then reinforcing the learners' attempts to practice them to form a set of habits.

Later studies on language acquisition have not diminished the role of input, however they have concentrated on how individuals process the input and how the input interacts with other key constructs of language learning, such as output and interaction (Gass, 2003, p. 229). The importance of input has been variably characterized depending on different approaches to language acquisition, such as Universal Grammar and Krashen's theory on comprehensible input.

Universal Grammar (UG) (e. g. , Chomsky, 1981a, 1981b; Cook, 1991; Cook & Newson, 1996; Haegeman, 1991) was developed as a powerful solution to the issue of L1 acquisition—'how languages are acquired'. It was primarily based on the observations of the mismatch between the input that a child (L1 learner) accesses and the linguistic knowledge he or she finally attains (i. e. , the output). According to UG, input is seen as the "primary linguistic data" (Chomsky, 1965, p. 47) or "raw linguistic data" (Cook & Newson, 2007, p. 115) that learners are exposed to. UG advocates argued that language input acts as a necessary 'trigger' for the learner's internal language processor (the innate UG-based learning mechanism) to be activated (Cook & Newson, 2007; White, 1989). The input provides evidence for learners to determine the values of structures which are left unspecified by UG, namely, what is possible in the target language (Cook, 1991; White, 1989). There are two types of evidence that can potentially function as input: positive evidence and negative evidence (White, 1989, p. 141). Positive evidence shows what is possible in the target language, such as grammatically correct forms and complete utterances. Negative evidence indicates what is incorrect in a language; it is usually provided by instruction. Although input needs to be given as a necessary component for language acquisition, it does not need to be sufficient because the learner's internal language processor (present in the human being's mind) supplements the knowledge that we cannot get from the input. More specifically, for SLA, the effect of instruction (concerning negative evidence) is extremely restricted to the instances where positive evidence is not sufficient and informative on its own. L2 instruction may assist the learner to master certain properties of L2 which are not appropriate for L1 but its effect does not retain over a long time (White, 1991).

In contrast to UG, SLA scholar Stephen Krashen (1977, 1981, 1982, 1985) emphasized that not just any input but only abundant 'comprehensible input' can result in language acquisition. 'Comprehensible input' is defined as the input that can be understood by recipients (learners) (Krashen, 1982). Krashen (1982) claimed that 'comprehensible input' is a fundamental and necessary requirement for L2 acquisition and that we are not able to acquire language without receiving 'comprehensible input'. It should be noted that Krashen hold the similar position on the role of instructional input as with UG's SLA accounts, namely, the effect of L2 instruction is fairly limited. According to Krashen (1985, pp. 33-34), the only need for L2 instruction is to provide 'comprehensible input' that may not be accessible in the informal environment; compared to L2 classrooms, the informal settings supply more 'comprehensible input' and thus the learner is able to understand more of the target language and to progress.

Krashen took a strong stance on the necessity of exposure to 'comprehensible input' in the L2 acquisition process. He drew our attention to the importance of input and the extent to which acquisition relies on the learner (White, 1987). However, while acknowledging that, without input, the learner is unable to make connections between forms and meaning, Swain (1985) argued that Krashen's work overvalued the role of 'comprehensible input' and neglected output in L2 acquisition. For example, in the Canadian immersion programs, Swain (1985, 1988) provided evidence that exclusive reliance on 'comprehensible input' without forcing and correcting production did not result in full acquisition of the L2 system, including grammatical accuracy. Swain (1985) argued that comprehensible input was greatly necessary but was not sufficient to L2 acquisition. L2 learners need to be 'pushed' to produce the utterances that can more precisely deliver their intended meaning. During this process, a specific kind of L2 instruction, namely, corrective feedback (e. g., explicit correction, confirmation checks, clarification checks) is utilized by teachers as a necessary aid to guide students to repair the errors of their or other peers' output; thus it contributes to actively engaging students in L2 learning within immersion classes (cf. Brook & Swain, 2009; Lapkin & Swain, 1996; Lightbown, 1998; Lyster, 2001; Lyster & Ranta, 1997; Swain, 2000; Swain & Lapkin, 1998).

While there is a little consensus on specific characteristic of input such as what types of input benefit acquisition, the necessity of exposure to the target language has been commonly accepted, namely, L2 acquisition cannot occur without input.

2.2 The role of grammar in L2 learning

Language learning necessitates exposure to the target language, such as its sounds or written forms. To infer a meaning from these forms, the learners must build up grammatical representations of the speech they are hearing or reading (Carroll, 2001, p. 2). A knowledge of grammar is considered as a fundamental aspect of language learning, since it can assist learners with the construction of connections between form and meaning (VanPatten, Williams, Rott, & Overstreet, 2004).

Grammar is perceived as the set of rules governing form and meaning and their relation, or—in Chomsky's words—"the rules that specify the well-formed strings of minimal syntactically functioning units (*formatives*) and assign structural information of various kinds both to these strings and to strings that deviate from well-formedness in certain respects" (Chomsky, 1965, p. 3). To understand meaning conveyed from input and express meaning appropriately, learners must rely on their knowledge of grammar to recognize and produce well-formed phrases and sentences in accordance with those rules. Grammar plays a significant role in language learning.

A number of SLA scholars also highlight the role of grammar in L2 learning. Larsen-Freeman (2003, 2015) defines grammar in discourse as the tool allowing learners to understand which of two or more grammatical features conveying a similar or identical semantic meaning they should use. Larsen-Freeman (2003) explains the five specific effects of grammar on texts. Grammar contributes to the cohesion, coherence, texture, formation of discourse patterns, and discourse functions of a text (Larsen-Freeman, 2003, pp. 67-68). From the perspective of discourse, the role of grammar is regarded as a rich resource for making contextualized meanings in a cultural and language-specific way. It is not simply the meaning-making capacity of language through the use of correct grammatical forms, but it is also a key part of the skill to make appropriate meaning in interaction with others (Larsen-Freeman, 2015; Liamkina & Ryshina-Pankova, 2012).

2.3 Do we need to teach grammar?

While the majority of SLA research has highlighted that grammar is a compulsory part of L2 learning (e. g. , Carroll, 2001; Ellis, 2008; Larsen-Freeman, 2003, 2005, 2015; Liamkina & Ryshina-Pankova, 2012; Nassaji & Fotos, 2011; White, 1990, 1996), whether grammar should be taught through formal instruction has long been debated. Generally speaking, there are three mainstream positions on the role of grammar teaching among the established SLA studies: the 'zero-impact' position, the modest-impact position, and the potentially-beneficial position.

2.3.1 The 'zero-impact' position.

The starting point of the 'zero-impact' position was Krashen's (1981, 1982, 1985) research in the early 1980s, which hypothesized that teaching grammar was not necessary at all. He asserted that language should be acquired through natural exposure to abundant 'comprehensible input'. Krashen's claim was based on Corder's (1967) hypothesis and SLA empirical studies that were known as 'morpheme order studies' (see Krashen, 1985).

Corder (1967) emphasized that L2 learners' 'built-in syllabuses' might determine the order in which L2 grammar is acquired. This order is predictable—"the learner is using a definite system of language at every point in his development" (Corder, 1967, p. 166). That is, some grammatical rules are acquired early and others are acquired late. Subsequent studies between the early 1970s and the early 1980s were conducted to investigate the order of the acquisition of English morpho-syntactic structures by L2 learners of diverse L1 backgrounds (e. g. , Bailey, Madden, & Krashen, 1974; Dulay & Burt, 1973, 1974; Ellis, 1984; Hakuta, 1974; Krashen, Butler, Birnbaum, & Robertson, 1978; Rosansky, 1976). These cross-sectional and longitudinal studies offered empirical evidence for the existence of a natural acquisition order in which L2 learners acquire certain grammatical morphemes and syntactic structures. Based on an extensive review of such studies, Krashen (1977) proposed a 'natural order' for L2 acquisition (Figure 2. 1).

Krashen (1982) pointed out that, given the existence of the natural order, L2 learners can progress from their current stage to the next one by understanding input that contains structures at the next stage. Krashen (1985) further stressed that:

If input is understood, and there is enough of it, the necessary grammar is automatically provided. The language teacher need not attempt deliberately to teach the next structure along the natural order—it will be provided in just the right quantities and automatically reviewed if the student receives a sufficient amount of comprehensible input. (Krashen, 1985, p. 2)

According to Krashen (1982, p. 59), the value of L2 classrooms did not rely on grammar instruction, but instead on providing comprehensible input such as teacher talk that focuses on meaning rather than forms. A number of SLA researchers subsequently advocated Krashen's claim that L2 learners only need to be exposed to naturalistic input in meaning-focused communication and do not require explicit grammar instruction (e.g., Prabhu, 1987; Schwartz, 1993).

However, the hypothesis that grammar instruction is not necessary was shown to be problematic when it was put to the test. A number of SLA empirical studies provided evidence that learners who were involved in a meaning-focused communicative environment without any grammar teaching always had problems in grammatical accuracy, namely, they could not use specific grammatical features accurately, despite the fact that they might develop a high level of comprehension skills and fluency (e.g., Harley & Swain, 1984; Lightbown & Spada, 1990; Lapkin, Hart & Swain, 1991; Swain, 1985, 1988).

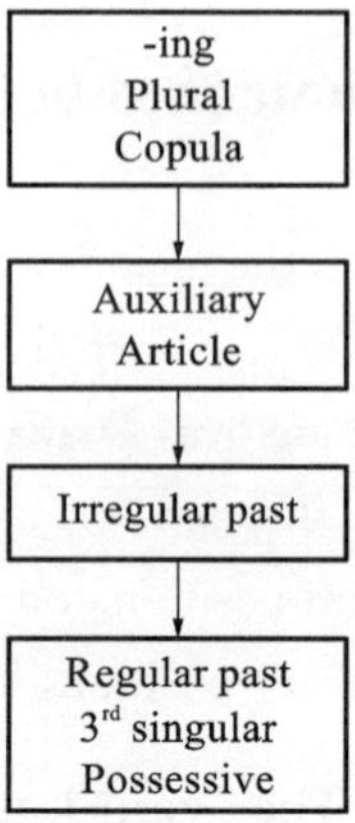

Figure 2.1: Krashen's (1977) proposed 'natural order' for SLA

For example, in the Canadian French immersion programs, the students of L1 English learned French through being exposed to an abundance of French-speaking input rather than being taught French grammar directly (Swain, 1985, 1988). The outcomes of the programs showed that the students became highly fluent and idiomatic in all skills, but their production did not have a high degree of grammatical accuracy even after six or seven years of meaning-focused communication (i.e., provision of 'comprehensible input' in French). Some students made constant errors in the use of even simple grammatical forms. Research on the Canadian French immersion programs shows, therefore, that exclusive reliance on 'comprehensible input' does not typically result in a high level of grammatical accuracy.

A similar finding was reported by Lightbown and Spada (1990) in their investigation of the spoken English of L2 learners taking intensive classes in a long-term project. The experimental group included 100 students enrolled in four intensive classes. The comparison group consisted of 200 students enrolled in regular classes. All students were native speakers of French aged 10-12 in either Grade 5 or 6 in elementary schools in Quebec, Canada. The learners in the intensive classes received meaning-focused communicative instruction with abundant 'comprehensible input', and they received little or no error correction from the teachers (Lightbown & Spada, 1990, p. 434). The results indicated that, after 5 months, students in the intensive classes achieved higher levels of comprehension ability, fluency and communicative confidence in L2 use than students in the regular classes. However, a further analysis of the intensive classes revealed that the meaning-focused approach without explicit grammar instruction did not lead to error-free English in the learners, even in simple structures. For instance, compared to the students in regular classes, students in the intensive classes merely achieved 37%-59% accuracy in their use of the morpheme *plural -s* and only 5%-28% accuracy in the case of *progressive -ing*.

Lightbown and Spada (1990) concluded that meaning-based communication contributes to the development of certain aspects of communicative skills such as fluency and communicative confidence in the use of a second language. However, this approach does not appear to increase the grammatical accuracy of learner production. Lightbown and Spada (1990) suggested that form-focused instruction should also be considered a necessary component within a meaning-based communicative context.

2.3.2 The modest-impact position

Later research in SLA has led to a reassessment of the role of grammar instruction in communicative language teaching, mostly asserting that grammar teaching has a modest impact on L2 learning within a classroom setting that primarily relies on communication (Larsen-Freeman, 2015). This position was derived from the question proposed in Long (1983), namely, whether or not L2 instruction makes a difference.

Long (1983) reviewed and analysed a number of established SLA empirical studies which investigated L2 acquisition with or without instruction (e. g., Fathman, 1975; Hale & Budar, 1970; Krashen & Seliger, 1976; Mason, 1971; Upshur, 1968). In general, those established studies were found to report on the comparison between natural exposure and L2 instruction from five aspects: first, the relative utility of the same amounts of exposure and instruction; second, the relative utility of varying amounts of exposure and instruction; third, the effect of differing amounts of instruction with the same amount of exposure; fourth, the effect of varying amounts of exposure with the same amount of instruction; fifth, independent effects of differing amounts of both exposure and instruction (cf. Long, 1983, pp. 116-119).

Based on a review of those research findings, Long (1983) concluded that despite no overwhelming evidence for the advantages of instruction over exposure, there was considerable empirical support for the benefits of instruction on L2 acquisition. Long (1983) revealed the varying effects of L2 instruction based on the different aspects above (the third aspect above was inconclusive due to the research results were ambiguous). Specifically, when the classroom was the only source of L2 input, instruction was effective. Under the circumstances of varying amounts of instruction with the same amount of exposure, more L2 instruction either benefited L2 acquisition or compensated for limited exposure. When differing amounts of exposure were added on to the same amount of instruction, more instruction could take more positive effects on L2 acquisition. Under the circumstances of varying amounts of both instruction and exposure, there was positive despite limited evidence that more instruction contributed to L2 acquisition.

While Long (1983) dose not take a strong position on the advantages of L2 instruction over exposure, his review of previous empirical studies highlights the potential effects of instruction on L2 acquisition, namely, L2 instruction does make a difference. Noteworthily, Long (1983) emphasized the review and categorization of research findings related to 'the effect of instruction' but he did not critically assess the research methodology of those studies with regards to some important issues that might influence on the results, such as what types of instruction provided in those studies, what specific SLA processes involved, and no investigation of control groups, etc. Nevertheless, Long (1983) draws our attention to reconsider the role of L2 instruction and to explore its implications for language teaching.

Later, Long (1991) went further in an investigation of effects of L2 instruction, focusing on grammar instruction in communicative classrooms. Long (1991) made a distinction between 'focus-on-form' (*FonF*) and 'focus-on-forms' (*FonFs*), and subsequently provided a detailed overview of the concept of FonF (Long & Robinson, 1998). Long (1991) defined FonFs as the traditional structural approach to language instruction, in which linguistic features such as grammar and vocabulary is presented to L2 learners without any communicative contexts. FonF was regarded as instruction that aimed to draw learner attention to grammatical forms once they made an error in meaning-focused communication. Long (1991) proposed a FonF approach to meaning-based communication—i. e., to use less formal intervention on grammar and more 'comprehensible input' by means of interactional modifications, such as comprehension checks (e. g., *do you understand what I mean*?), and by means of unnoticeable feedback, such as the case where teachers correctly recast or restructure learners' ungrammatical production (Larsen-Freeman, 2015).

The proposal by Long (1991) and Long and Robinson (1998) for FonF instruction has inspired a number of researchers to examine the effects of incidentally drawing learner attention to form during communicative activities. Some studies found that FonF instruction could facilitate learner comprehension and output (e. g., Gass & Varonis, 1994) and that such an effect could be maintained for some time (e. g., Mackey & Goo, 2007). Other studies have attempted to expand the impact of FonF instruction by integrating a pre-planned instead of incidental treatment of grammatical form into meaning-based communication (e. g., Nassaji, 1999; Nassaji & Fotos, 2010; Williams, 2005). For instance, FonF instruction can be used proactively in a predetermined way through a variety of input, output and consciousness raising tasks to help learners notice specific target structures (Keßler & Plesser, 2011; Nassaji & Fotos, 2010; Schmidt, 1990). Grammar instruction has been considered not only a reaction to grammatical problems, but also a pre-planned instructional strategy in meaningful language use (Ellis, Basturkmen, & Loewen, 2001; Larsen-Freeman, 2015; Nassaji, 2016).

2.3.3 The potentially-beneficial position

Over the past 30 years, growing empirical evidence from a large number of classroom and laboratory-based studies has showed a stronger position on the role of L2 grammar instruction (e. g., Akakura, 2012; Ellis, 2002, 2006; Housen, Pierrard, & Van Daele, 2005; Li, 2010; Liamkina & Ryshina-Pankova, 2012; Loewen, Li, Fei, Thompson, Nakatsukasa, Ahn, & Chen 2009; Norris & Ortega, 2000, 2001; Nassaji & Fotos, 2010). These studies not only have confirmed the necessity of grammar teaching, but also have suggested that explicit grammar instruction is potentially beneficial if it is provided appropriately.

For example, Liamkina and Ryshina-Pankova (2012) examined the acquisition of two German grammatical structures—clausal dative case and past tenses—by English-speaking learners of German as a second language. They argued that teaching grammar in meaning-based communication could help learners create a metalinguistic awareness that enabled them to make situationally appropriate linguistic choices in a native-like manner.

Akakura (2012) investigated the effects of explicit grammar instruction on the generic and non-generic use of English articles. 94 non-English-native speakers in New Zealand were taught the use of English articles *a*, *an* and *the*, through a variety of direct rule-giving activities. Four tasks were used to measure the level of acquisition, including elicited imitation, oral production, grammaticality judgements, and metalinguistic knowledge tasks. Three tests were conducted using these tasks: a pre-test, an immediate post-test, and a postponed post-test six weeks after the instruction. Akakura (2012) showed that durable effects for explicit grammar instruction were found in regards to improving oral production of certain grammatical rules and assisted learners in their acquisition of a self-corrective ability.

Norris and Ortega (2000, 2001) carried out a meta-analysis of 49 experimental and quasi-experimental studies on the effectiveness of L2 instruction published between 1980 and 1998, including explicit form-focused instruction (FonF and FonFs) and meaning-focused instruction. They found that the majority of studies on the effects of explicit grammar instruction measured the level of accuracy in learner production by comparing pre-test with post-test in regards to specific structures of the target language. Explicit grammar instruction usually includes rule presentation, description and exemplification, negative feedback, and rule review. Meaning-focused instruction may involve communicative exposure to target forms. Norris and Ortega concluded that, compared to meaning-focused instruction, explicit form-focused instruction resulted in considerable gains in acquisition of particular target forms, and found that these gains were durable. A similar conclusion was reached in Ellis's (1995) extensive review of SLA field studies and laboratory experiments. He pointed out that although form-focused instruction might not impact on sequences of acquisition, it contributed to enhancing the rate and the ultimate level of L2 learning.

2.4 How should we teach grammar?

If grammar teaching is necessary for the achievement of L2 accuracy and can contribute to successful L2 learning, the next logical question is how it should be taught. More specifically: should grammatical structures of L2 be sequenced and, if so, how?

Krashen (1982) asserted that input to classroom learners should not be grammatically sequenced. He claimed that there was no need to intentionally provide 'i+1' (i. e., any grammatical items that are slightly beyond the learner's current level of acquisition) in the input. As long as the input is comprehensible and delivers meaning successfully, 'i+1' will appear automatically. This argument against a deliberate attempt to sequence grammatical structures represented a considerable change of Krashen's stance since, in earlier work, he had called for grammatical rules to be provided along the 'natural order' as an input for L2 classroom learners (see Krashen, Madden, & Bailey, 1975; Krashen, 1976). Krashen's (1982, pp. 68-70) rationale for his revised stance is summarized below.

According to Krashen (1982), his earlier claim that classroom input could be grammatically sequenced was based on the assumption that every student in the class was at the same level of L2 development. However, individual differences such as the amount of exposure to the target language outside of class meant that students were unlikely to be at the same stage of acquisition. The alternative of unsequenced but abundant natural input would therefore provide a rich variety of grammatical items, so that 'i+1' would be present for everyone. Krashen (1982) further believed that sequenced input usually presented grammatical rules one at a time. Learners might miss the first presentation of a specific rule for different reasons. Unsequenced natural input could automatically present the appropriate rules in a repeated manner, so that learners would eventually have exposure to the target structures.

Krashen (1982) claimed that it was not necessary to build up the grammatically-based syllabus—the selection and grading of grammatical structures. Sequenced input would reduce the quality of comprehensible input and compromise the focus of meaning-oriented communication. Krashen (1982) also indicated that sequenced input intentionally predicted the order of L2 acquisition. However, given that the 'natural order' revealed the underlying process of language acquisition, there was no need to deliberately teach according to this order, because comprehensible input would automatically follow the 'natural order', both in formal and informal language environments.

Krashen's position of unsequenced grammatical input primarily relies on two cornerstones. First, a number of SLA researchers applied his meaning-based communicative approach to experimental studies, and the results revealed this method facilitated certain aspects of L2 learners' communicative skills such as fluency and confidence in L2 use (e. g., Prabhu, 1987). These studies suggested that L2 classroom input should merely focus on content-delivery or negotiation of meaning rather than the presentation of grammatical structures. Second, the well-known 'morpheme order studies' (e. g., Dulay & Burt, 1974) provided empirical evidence that the 'natural order' existed in L2 acquisition of specific grammatical rules. Other studies on the comparison between L2 instructed and naturalistic learners (e. g., Pica, 1983; Makino, 1979) also confirmed that there was no significant difference in the order of L2 acquisition between informal and formal language environments. This strengthened Krashen's belief that, since grammar instruction had no effect on the order of L2 acquisition, there was no need to deliberately sequence the grammatical input.

However, Krashen's advocacy of unsequenced grammar in classroom input did come under criticism from SLA researchers. Pienemann (1984, 1985) challenges Krashen's claims from three perspectives: their theoretical basis, their logical weakness, and their negative consequences (Pienemann, 1985, pp. 47-49).

First, Pienemann (1985) stated that the fundamental theoretical basis of the input hypothesis is extremely conjectural. He claimed that Krashen did not explicitly define the meaning of 'i' in 'i+1'. How do we determine stage 'i' in interlanguage development? Its lack of operationality led to little or no 'direct' empirical evidence in support of its assumption. The input hypothesis postulates that comprehension and production as two aspects of speech processing develop in an interrelated manner. The L2 learner is able to acquire and produce the target language only when he or she is exposed to 'comprehensible input' and understands the underlying meaning. However, Pienemann (1985) points out that there is evidence that comprehension does not always result in production. For instance, a learner may articulate the utterances before he or she understands them.

Pienemann's second criticism was aimed at the logical weakness in the relationship between 'comprehensible input' and sequenced grammar. Krashen asserted that, since 'comprehensible input' could provide 'i+1' for L2 learners with individual differences, there was no need to sequence grammatical input. However, there is little or no direct evidence to support the existence of the 'i+1' input and the positive correlations between it and acquisition. According to Pienemann (1985, p. 47), due to that the fundamental theoretical basis of the input hypothesis (i. e., input containing 'i+1' facilitates L2 acquisition) is rather speculative, Krashen's strong claim against sequenced grammar which is based on the input hypothesis appears to be logically weak. Pienemann (1985) further argued that grammar instruction could be distinguished according to different groups of L2 learners, as learners could be grouped in line with stages of L2 acquisition.

Third, Pienemann (1985) indicated that the avoidance of grammar intervention will potentially lead to the simplification of the interlanguage. Exclusive reliance on 'comprehensible input' only emphasizes message transmission. Learners are at risk of simplifying their interlanguage to achieve meaning-delivery and to avoid making grammatical errors when they use complex forms. Consequently, learners may not be able to develop their ability of using appropriate forms in a variety of social and cultural contexts.

A number of SLA researchers are also aware that grammatical sequencing is desirable for L2 acquisition in classroom settings. For example, as Larsen (1975) indicated, there is a consensus among practitioners of L2 classroom-based teaching—as exemplified in most ESL grammar textbooks—that grammatical input should be sequenced from the simple to the difficult (or complex). However, defining the concept of difficulty is a controversial issue (Larsen, 1975, p. 151). How do we determine that some structures are more difficult than others?

Based on a review of relevant studies in L2 acquisition undertaken by DeKeyser (2005), grammatical complexity is usually considered to be a reliable parameter for sequencing grammatical items according to difficulty. Grammatical complexity is generally measured using syntactic and morphological aspects (see also Bulté & Housen, 2012, 2014; Pallotti, 2014). Syntactic complexity, including sentence, clausal, and phrasal complexity, is usually determined by word length and subordination. Morphological complexity, including inflectional and derivational complexity, is determined by the number of forms taken by lexemes to express grammatical categories and functions. Structures that are morpho-syntactically less complex should be introduced before structures that require more operations for their grammatical realization. Take two sentences for example—'I believe' and 'I believe that you are right'. The first sentence is formed in accordance with the basic word order SV(O), while the second sentence consists of a main clause ('I believe…') and a subordinate clause ('…you are right'). According to grammatical complexity, the second sentence is more difficult due to its greater syntactic complexity compared to the first sentence.

In contrast, Manfred Pienemann states in his Processability Theory (1984, 1998, 2005) that grammatical complexity does not necessarily equate with learning difficulty. He considers that learning difficulty is best measured by processing constraints during actual L2 speech production. In other words, what matters is how difficult particular linguistic features are to process psycholinguistically, rather than how complex they are grammatically. For example, grammatically, the English morpheme 'third-person singular *-s*' is a straightforward item. In a sentence where the subject is a singular noun or a pronoun (such as *he*, *she*, *it*, *one*), the lexical verb needs to be suffixed by '-s' or '-es' to achieve the agreement between the subject and the verb. However, this 'simple' grammatical form is not easy and direct for L2 learners to process due to the related psychological constraints. Since the form of the verb is determined by the person and the number of the subject noun-phrase, the learner must hold this information (person and number) in his or her working memory until he or she produces the verb. In other words, there is a requirement for the learner to rely on his or her short-term memory during speech production; learning difficulty is created, not by the grammar but by psychological constraints such as the one referred to in the above example.

How do we sequence grammatical structures according to actual learning difficulty? Based on his criticism of Krashen's 'unsequenced grammatical input' and a range of empirical evidence on L2 instructed learning, Pienemann (1984, 1985, 1988, 1989, 1998) formulates the Teachability Hypothesis. The Teachability Hypothesis aims to deal with the issue of the influence of instruction on L2 acquisition. It highlights optimal timing of grammar teaching, namely, sequencing grammatical items in line with a staged L2 development.

There are two principles inherent in the Teachability Hypothesis (Pienemann, 1998, p. 250). First, stages of acquisition cannot be skipped through formal intervention; second, teaching will be beneficial if it focuses on grammatical structures belonging to 'the next stage'. The underlying logic of the Teachability Hypothesis is that teachability of target grammar is constrained by learnability—whether or not the learner is ready to acquire the structure at a given time in his or her L2 development. According to Pienemann (2015, p. 138), the principles of

Teachability Hypothesis can be formalized within Processability Theory (PT). PT provides a principled psycholinguistic developmental schedule for L2 acquisition, depicting the sequence of L2 learners' developmental readiness (the implicational acquisition stages) (Pienemann, 1998). A learner is considered developmentally ready to learn a given grammatical item when he or she is at the appropriate stage of the developmental sequence. At such a point, the learner has developed all those linguistic and procedural skills required to produce the structure. The learning of grammatical structures proceeds in a fixed order. The learner is capable of moving onto the next stage only after acquiring the previous stages.

Given that each stage necessitates processing procedures acquired during the earlier stages, it is not possible to 'miss out' a stage by means of instructional intervention (e. g. , the premature introduction of a structure that needs more complex processing procedures acquired only at a later stage). Grammar teaching may benefit L2 learning if L2 instruction focuses on 'the next stage' according to the sequence of the learner's developmental readiness. The predictions derived from the Teachability Hypothesis have been tested by a number of SLA empirical studies (e. g. , Bonilla, 2015; Boss, 1996; Dyson, 1996; Ellis, 1989; Pienemann, 1984; Spada & Lightbown, 1999; Zhang & Lantoff, 2015).

Pienemann (1984) is the first empirical research which tested the Teachability Hypothesis. It aimed to examine whether the process of natural L2 acquisition could be affected by formal intervention (Pienemann, 1984, p. 186). The informants were 10 Italian children of migrant workers aged 7-9 years who were enrolled in an Italian-language-class with supplementary L2 German instruction. In addition, they received a great deal of natural exposure to German language in their daily life. The interlanguage of those children was tape-recorded before and after a period of formal instruction with a focus on German word order. The data collection was achieved through 1) the pre-planned '*linguistic interview*' between the researchers and the informants; and 2) the '*hidden recording*' which collected the spontaneous oral production of the informants during their routine activities (e. g. , playground or backyard) (Pienemann, 1984, p. 191). The learning objective of the formal instruction was a German word order rule 'Inversion', which occurred at Stage X+3 of the developmental sequence of German as a L2 acquisition (cf. Pienemann, 1998, p. 45). The criterion to determine whether a structure is acquired is the *first systematic use* of the structure, namely, when the learner has—*in principle*—grasped the learning task (Pienemann, 1984, p. 191; cf. Meisel, Clahsen, & Pienemann, 1981). In order to investigate whether 'Inversion' could be taught before it was acquired naturally, the researchers tested the actual acquisitional stage of those children's interlanguage to make sure that all the informants had not acquired this word order rule prior to the formal intervention. The pre-test confirmed that the interlanguage of all the informants was at Stage X, Stage X+1 or Stage X+2 which was below 'Inversion' (Stage X+3).

The results of Pienemann's (1984) experiment showed that those informants whose interlanguage was at Stage X+2 before the formal instruction successfully acquired the Stage X+

3's structure 'Inversion'. However, the informants whose interlanguage was at Stage X or Stage X+1 at the onset of the L2 teaching did not acquire 'Inversion'. Therefore, Pienemann (1984) concluded that 1) L2 learners could not 'skip' the stage even through L2 formal intervention; but 2) a structure could only be learned under formal instruction if the learner's interlanguage had already reached a stage that was one step before the point where this structure was acquired in a natural setting (p. 205). These two claims were then formalized into the paradigm of the Teachability Hypothesis.

Pienemann (1984) makes a pioneering contribution to the formulation of the Teachability Hypothesis. The study is considered as the first empirical support for the validity of Teachability Hypothesis, namely, the teachability of German structures is restricted by the same processing constraints that determine the developmental sequence of natural acquisition of German as a L2. Nevertheless, it should be noted that Pienemann's (1984) explanation on the Teachability Hypothesis was based on the processing strategies approach while PT had not been conceptualized (cf. Clahsen, 1984; Pienemann, 1998). The strategies approach was developed on the basis of a large number of longitudinal and cross-sectional empirical studies carried out by ZISA group which investigated the acquisitional sequence of German word order (cf. Clahsen, 1978, 1980, 1981, 1982; Clahsen and Pienemann, 1981). This raises a further issue: whether the psycholinguistic constraints on the teachability of German addressed in Pienemann (1984) are also applicable to L2 acquisition of other languages.

Following Pienemann's (1984) project, the majority of subsequent studies have provided further empirical support for the Teachability Hypothesis regarding its cross-linguistic validity. For instance, Ellis (1989) reported on the classroom acquisition of three German word order rules 'Particle', 'Inversion', and 'Verb-final' in the interlanguage of 39 first-year university students aged 18-41 years from diverse L1 backgrounds, such as Spanish, English, French, Mauritian Creole, and Arabic. It sought to examine whether the sequence of acquisition of grammatical structures could be altered by L2 formal instruction. Pre- and post-tests were used to describe the sequence of classroom acquisition of the three German word order rules. Although the order in which these rules were instructed differed from the naturalistic order, a comparison of the acquisitional sequence for classroom learners with that reported for naturalistic learners of German showed no difference (Ellis, 1989, p. 305). This finding suggests that L2 formal instruction has no effect on the sequence of L2 acquisition. Ellis (1989) further emphasized the implication of his study, which shared a similar idea with Pienemann regarding L2 formal instruction on grammatical structures—"This, in turn, provides support for the view that instruction directed at a particular structure will not result in acquisition unless the learner is developmentally ready" (Ellis, 1989, p. 325).

A similar correlation between the effect of formal intervention and the learner's current status of L2 development was reported in Boss (1996) which looked into L2 German word order development of L1 English and Chinese speakers. In Boss (1996), the oral production of eight university students who were attending the beginner-level course of German in Australia was collected and analysed through the same research methodology employed among the previous SLA studies on German word order (cf. Ellis, 1990). The students' acquisition of five German word order rules (Stage X: SVO, Stage X+1: adverb-fronting, Stage X+2: verb separation, Stage X +3: inversion, Stage X+4: verb-end; cf. Pienemann, 1998) were compared with the taught syllabus in the coursebook and with the acquisitional stages as hypothesized in German word order studies (cf. Clahsen et al., 1983).

A preliminary comparison of word order rules revealed a discrepancy between the sequencing of those rules taught in the coursebook and their sequencing as proposed in German word order studies. Two differences were: 1) the feature 'adverb-fronting' (Stage X+1) was not taught in the coursebook due to that it was a non-standard form in the interlanguage; 2) 'inversion' (Stage X+3) was taught prior to the instruction of 'verb separation' (Stage X+2), which was opposite to their hypothesized sequencing; 3) 'SVO' (Stage X) and 'verb-end' (Stage X+4) were instructed in line with German word order studies (cf. Boss, 1996, pp. 94-95). The main results showed that despite the reversed instruction of 'inversion' (Stage X+3) and 'verb separation' (Stage X+2), seven of the eight students still acquired these two word order rules in the predicted order. The only student who produced 'inversion' first was found to have previous experience of learning German before the course (Boss, 1996, p. 99). As with Pienemann's (1984) and Ellis's (1989) studies, Boss (1996) reported that the grammatical structures specifically German word order rules were acquired in the hypothesized sequence for natural L2 development regardless of formal intervention. This finding adds another empirical evidence to the robustness of Teachability Hypothesis.

In the meantime, Dyson (1996) shifted her attention to ESL development through a small-scale study of three adult L1 Spanish speakers in Australia. Reliance on a two-year classroom observation, Dyson (1996) attempted to examine the influence of form-focused instruction on L2 acquisition of English word order 'do-fronting' (e.g., *Do you eat hamburgers?*). At the onset of the project, a pre-test was conducted through a communicative task in order to assess the learners' interlanguage status. Of the three informants, the first learner was at Stage 2, the second one was at Stage 3, and the third one was at Stage 5; none of them had acquired the target structure 'do-fronting' which was processable at Stage 3. A post-test was carried out a month after all the informants received a three-hour formal instruction on 'do-fronting' (approx. one hour per week during three weeks). Dyson's (1996) analysis of the post-test found that all the learners acquired the Stage 3 structure 'do-fronting' after the focal instruction. In particular, the two participants who were developmentally 'ready' for 'do-fronting' (one was previously at Stage 2 and the other one was at Stage 3) achieved progress in their ESL development. As a result, Dyson (1996) concluded that her study attested the predictions of Teachability Hypothesis, namely, "acquisitionally appropriate instruction can improve the rate by which learners move through the developmental stages, accelerating the learning process and making it more efficient" (p. 73). Dyson (1996) is considered as strong support for Pienemann's (1984) claims and empirical evidence for the pedagogical implication of Teachability Hypothesis on ESL development.

More recently, Teachability Hypothesis was also tested by Bonilla (2015) which explored the effect of instruction on L2 acquisition of a range of Spanish morpho-syntactic structures for beginning classroom learners in an American university. Similar to those established studies on SLA as mentioned above, Bonilla (2015) also employed the pretest-instruction-posttest design. The formal instruction focused on the Stage 3 structures 'XP-adjunction' and attributive number agreement, the Stage 4 features 'SV-inversion' and predicative number agreement, and the Stage 5 structure subordinate clause formation and subjunctive morphology (cf. Bonilla, 2014). The participants were assigned to one control group and two experimental groups; the experimental groups were exposed to a form-focused instruction on the target structures, whilst the control group did not receive any explicit explanation of those structures. The post-test of learner performance revealed that none of the learners skipped stages as a result of instruction and they gained progress in the hypothesized sequence as stipulated in PT. In addition, an interesting finding was reported that although the experimental groups did not show a significant advantage with regards to stage gains, they did perform increases in production frequencies compared to the control group (Bonilla, 2015, p. 226). It should be noted that Bonilla (2015) did not make an explicit explanation of the link between the effect of instruction and production frequencies since the Teachability Hypothesis concerns stage gains (e. g. , the emergence of stage) rather than production frequencies. Overall, Bonilla (2015) further confirms the validity of the PT-based processabilty hierarchy and the central claim of Teachability Hypothesis within the context of Spanish as a L2 acquisition.

In summary, the studies discussed above provide cross-linguistic evidence in support of the claims of Teachability Hypothesis that the learner cannot skip the stages in L2 development and that formal intervention cannot alter the acquisitional sequence. From a pedagogical perspective, those studies also suggest that the learner's developmental readiness should be taken into consideration in L2 formal instruction.

However, a few empirical studies have challenged the plausibility of the Teachability Hypothesis. One is the L2 classroom-based study conducted by Spada and Lightbown (1999). Their study attempted to examine the relationship between the learners' developmental readiness and formal intervention through the investigation into the formation of English questions by 144 French-speaking children aged at 11-12 enrolled in intensive ESL classes. The oral production of those informants was recorded and analysed before and after a two-week formal instruction that emphasized the use of English questions requiring Stages 4 and 5 through communicative activities. The pre-test and the post-test utilized both oral and written tasks to determine the children's developmental stages of acquisition of English questions. Noteworthily, since the claims of the Teachability Hypothesis only concern the oral production of L2 learners, thus only the results from the oral tasks are of interest here (cf. Spada and Lightbown, 1999, p. 14; Pienemann, 1989, p. 60). According to Spada and Lightbown (1999, pp. 9-10), at the beginning of the two weeks' intervention, the majority of the informants (over 82%) were found to be at Stage 2 or Stage 3; 79 informants were at Stage 2, 39 informants reached at Stage 3, 25 students were at Stage 4 and only one student was at Stage 5.

The results of the post-test showed that, after the two-week formal intervention, 29% of the informants who were at Stage 2 in the pre-test successfully moved to Stage 3, 7% of those students who reached at Stage 3 in the pre-test progressed to Stage 4, and none of the informants who were previously at Stage 4 went up to Stage 5 (Spada and Lightbown, 1999, pp. 9-10). Based on these findings, Spada and Lightbown (1999) asserted that their empirical evidence was contradictory to the predictions of the Teachability Hypothesis. One of their evidence against the Teachability Hypothesis is that the students who were at Stage 3 beforehand did not move to Stage 4, while most of those students who previously were at Stage 2 did progress to Stage 3 despite the formal instruction that was designed for the provision of the Stages 4 and 5 question forms (cf. Spada and Lightbown, 1999, p. 14). It appears that the learners who were developmentally 'ready' did not progress, whilst those who were not expected to benefit from the focal instruction did move on.

Nevertheless, it should be noted that Spada and Lightbown (1999) merely deals with one aspect of the Teachability Hypothesis, namely, whether the formal intervention is effective for the learners who are developmentally 'ready' in their L2 acquisition. In fact, the central claim of the Teachability Hypothesis is that L2 learners cannot 'skip' the stages through formal intervention (Pienemann, 1989, p. 250). Although Spada and Lightbown (1999) did not focus on this aspect, their study attested that the informants progressed in a sequenced development without skipping stages. As shown in the analysis of oral production tasks, almost all the Stage 2 learners who progressed afterwards went up to Stage 3 (not Stage 4) despite the teaching associated with those English questions requiring Stages 4 and 5 (Spada and Lightbown, 1999, p. 10). Therefore, it can be argued that Spada and Lightbown (1999) provides partial evidence for the Teachability Hypothesis, at least for its central claim.

The other critique against the Teachability Hypothesis derives from Zhang and Lantolf (2015). The aim of their study was to test the central claim of the Teachability Hypothesis, through examining whether learners were able to skip stages in the PT-based hierarchy for Chinese L2 topicalization by means of manipulated instruction. In their instructional design, Zhang and Lantolf (2015) selected four L1 English speakers from a beginning-level Chinese course at an American university. The pre-test prior to the instruction determined that those informants were located at Stage 2 (SVO, subject + verb + object) in their development of L2 acquisition of Chinese topicalization.

Based on Systemic Theoretical Instruction which emphasized explicit presentation of concepts related to a specific structure, three instruction sessions were organized to provide the instructional input that targeted the structures requiring Stages 3 and 4 such as 'ADJ (adjunct)+SVO' and 'OSV (objective+SV)' (Zhang and Lantolf, 2015, p. 163). Two post-tests were individually conducted one week after the first instruction session that targeted Stage 4 OSV structure and the second one that taught Stage 3 ADJ+SVO structure. In addition, a delayed post-test was made one month after the third instruction session that focused on the practice of those new structures. In order to elicit spontaneous oral production from the informants, Zhang and Lantolf (2015) utilized three kinds of tasks in the data collection; they were an elicited imitation task, a question-and-answer session, and an oral cartoon description task.

The main results of their study revealed that the informants did not progress through the PT-based learning sequence for L2 Chinese topicalization as reported in PT-based empirical studies such as Zhang (2007). Specifically, the first post-test showed that all the learners successfully acquired Stage 4 OSV structure after the focal instruction even though they were not previously taught Stage 3 structure; in the second post-test, all the informants demonstrated their abilities to produce Stages 3 and 4 structures after they received the focal teaching on Stage 3 ADJ+SVO; the delayed post-test confirmed the same case that all the learners acquired Stages 3 and 4 after the final instruction (cf. Zhang and Lantolf, 2015, pp. 165-172). It seems that the learners skipped Stage 3 and directly acquired the next stage—Stage 4 structure—through an artificially constructed instruction that went against the PT-based learning sequence. Therefore, Zhang and Lantolf (2015) concluded that "stages in the processing hierarchy for topicalization in Chinese can be directly taught without regard for the processing sequence predicted by general PT. Thus, the predictions of the TH (Teachability Hypothesis) corollary may not hold" (pp. 175-176).

Zhang and Lantolf's (2015) empirical evidence may draw our attention to reconsider the developmental pattern for Chinese topicalization. However, it should be noted that their study merely investigated three structures hypothesized to entail three corresponding processing stages. Although the informants in Zhang and Lantolf (2015) seemed to successfully produce a single structure OSV (Stage 4) without the prior instruction of Stage 3 structure, it might not be convincing that the learners had acquired all the procedural skills required for Stage 4 and skipped Stage 3. Conversely, another empirical study—Liu (2016) which provides a broader insight into L2 Chinese acquisition of syntax—investigated six word order patterns and three complex structures over a one-year longitudinal project by six L2 Chinese learners of three proficiency levels. Liu (2016) found two sequences for the acquisition of Chinese word order and complex structures, and both were consistent with the PT-based processing hierarchies (p. 164). Thus, the claims of Zhang and Lantolf (2015) against the Teachability Hypothesis and PT need to be verified by more reliable evidence.

Although a few studies provide some empirical evidence that challenges the predictions of the Teachability Hypothesis (e. g., Spada and Lightbown, 1999; Zhang and Lantolf, 2015), its claims particularly the crucial claim that stages cannot be skipped through instructional input have been supported by numerous observational studies (e. g. , Boss, 1996; Bonilla, 2015; Dyson, 1996; Ellis, 1989, 2006; Gao, 2005; Jansen, 2008; Liu, 2016; Pienemann, 1984, 1989, 1998, 2005; Wang, 2011; Zhang, 2001). They have generally provided support for the necessity of sequencing instructional input in accordance with the L2 staged development.

Furthermore, a number of classroom-based studies have offered evidence that the instructional input that sequences grammatical items based on the sequence of the learner's developmental readiness can enhance learning outcomes in L2 classrooms. In Mansouri & Duffy (2005), two groups of adult ESL learners of diverse L1 were respectively exposed to English syntactic structures in academic English programs of 10 to 40 weeks duration. The syntactic structures were taught either in the order as outlined and predicted in Processability Theory (PT), or in a different order. The comparison of results of oral and written tasks between pre-test and post-test showed that learners who were exposed to formal instruction in accordance with the developmental order produced the target structures with a higher level of grammatical accuracy. Mansouri & Duffy (2005, p. 97) concluded that grammatical input sequenced according to PT order contributed not only to the overall rate of acquisition but also to the durable improvement of L2 grammar.

Di Biase (2008) conducted a quasi-experimental classroom-based study on the development of Italian as a L2 in primary school students in Australia. His study was part of a larger longitudinal project over 8 years (see Di Biase, 2007). The data was collected from 18 students in the same primary school instructed by the same teacher over a period of 8 months. The students were evenly divided into an experimental group (nine students) and a control group (nine students). Both of the groups received 'developmentally guided instruction'—i. e. , instruction achieved through a variety of communicative-based games or tasks aimed at introducing target structures selected from the developmental schedule as stipulated in PT (Di Biase, 2008, p. 3). In addition, the experimental class consistently received focus-on-form feedback from the teacher that exclusively emphasized the developmentally learnable structures. In contrast, the control class merely obtained usual or random corrective feedback. The comparison between the pre-test and the postponed post-test revealed that 'developmentally guided instruction' generally sped up the progress of grammatical development of both groups. The experimental group, which received form-focused feedback, reached overall higher accuracy in the use of certain structures. It is suggested that the instructional input that sequences the target grammar in line with the path of L2 developmental readiness has beneficial effects on rate and accuracy of L2 learning and enhancement of teaching efficiency.

Inspired by the positive correlations between developmentally guided instruction and L2 grammatical development, Keßler, Liebner, & Mansouri (2011) and Keßler and Plesser (2011) propose that the developmentally moderated approach has great potential for formal intervention and provides an insight into the optimal way of presenting target grammar in instructional input to promote L2 development. The key point of 'sequencing' grammatical input is that learners should be provided input in terms of carefully chosen target structures in line with developmental stages in L2 acquisition in a single grammatical domain such as 'past tense' or 'negation' (Hulstijn, Ellis, & Eskildsen, 2015; Keßler et al., 2011).

2.5 Summary

This chapter grounds the research topic in SLA theory through the discussion of related key issues—input and sequence of grammatical structures. Input is a prerequisite for L2 acquisition to occur. In FL settings such as those that prevail in Mainland China, learners of L2 English have little opportunities for natural exposure to English and thus textbooks serve as the main source of L2 input in schools. Moreover, SLA research have attested that learners go through a universal developmental path in their L2 acquisition. It is therefore a sensible idea to conduct a SLA-based textbook evaluation to see whether the sequencing of grammatical structures in current textbooks is in line with the path of a staged L2 development. Within the context of English as a FL in Mainland China, the present study attempts to deal with the research question: whether or not the sequencing of key grammatical structures introduced as the teaching objectives in four English textbook series is compatible with the developmental sequence of L2 acquisition as hypothesized in Processability Theory (Pienemann, 1998, 2005).

Chapter 3

Review of Textbook Evaluation Research

This chapter reviews the literature on language textbook evaluation. The review focuses on four different methodologies. Firstly, predictive evaluation refers to predicting the potential effectiveness or value of textbooks before they are used. Secondly, retrospective evaluation focuses on measuring the actual effects of textbooks on users after they are used. Thirdly, Conversation Analysis-based evaluation aims to evaluate authenticity of dialogues or sufficiency of pragmatic information in the textbooks by adopting a conversation/discourse analytic approach. Fourthly, SLA-based evaluation involves conducting an assessment of whether the presentation of grammar in textbooks is consistent with the sequenced development of L2 acquisition as stipulated in Processability Theory.

The abundance of language textbooks available on the current educational market does not make it easy for teachers to select appropriate textbooks for the courses they teach. Textbook selection may have crucial effects on the language teaching and learning process, since teachers may utilize textbooks as guidelines for their classroom teaching (Harmer, 1991; McGrath, 2002) or plan and organize the whole language syllabus around them (Garinger, 2002; Harmer, 1991). The choice of textbooks may be associated with the achievement of teaching objectives. To choose the textbooks that best contribute to language teaching, it is paramount to carry out an assessment based on valid and reliable principles or approaches (Mukundan, Nimehchisalem, & Hajimohammadi, 2011).

3.1 Predictive evaluation

Predictive evaluation involves making predictions about the potential effectiveness or value of textbooks before they are used. The studies on predictive evaluation have proposed checklists of principles or questions serving as general guidelines in the textbook evaluation process. None of these studies have put the checklist to the test—none have applied the evaluation model they advocate to assess the actual value of a specific textbook.

For example, Breen and Candlin (1987) assembled a checklist of questions focusing on two phases of textbook evaluation. The first phase is to ask oneself preliminary questions regarding the usage of textbooks. The preliminary questions are designed around four issues in relation to learning materials, as shown below.

a) what the aims and content of the materials are
b) what they require learners to do
c) what they require you, as a teacher, to do
d) what function they have as a classroom resource

(Breen & Candlin, 1987, p. 13)

Following these four aspects, the evaluators (teachers) need to propose and answer a set of initial questions tailored to the learning materials. For example, for the first issue 'the aims and content of the materials', Breen and Candlin (1987) suggested that the evaluators could consider two related questions: 'when they finish their course, what should your learners know of and about the target language?' and 'what should they be able to do in and with the language?' (p. 14). The first phase requires the evaluators to provide their own understanding of the usage of the textbooks that are the target of the evaluation.

The second phase aims to assess the fitness of textbooks in particular teaching contexts. Breen and Candlin (1987) proposed that three aspects of learning materials need to be taken into account in this phase: 'learner needs and interests', 'learner approaches to language learning', and 'the teaching/learning process in your classroom' (p. 18). For instance, for the first aspect, three related questions were suggested by Breen and Candlin (1987).

19. How and to what extent do the materials fit your learners' long-term goals in learning the language and/or following your course?

20. How far do the materials directly call on what your learners already know of and about the language, and extend what they can already do with and in the language?

21. How far do the materials meet the immediate language learning needs of your learners as they perceive them? (Breen & Candlin, 1987, p. 19)

During this phase, the evaluators need to take on the perspective of the learners (or the users of the materials) they will be working with. The second phase requires the evaluators to think about the predetermined questions on behalf of the learners and to determine whether the materials meet the learning demands of the learners and are appropriate for the teaching process in their classrooms.

Breen and Candlin (1987) offered guidelines for language teachers to carry out their textbook evaluation at various levels and in various teaching contexts. The questions related to the two evaluation phases concerned the perspectives of language learning and teaching. The study highlighted the dominant role of teachers (evaluators) in the process of textbook evaluation and selection. However, Breen and Candlin (1987) attempted to look into all specific aspects of materials, and their proposed checklist of questions may well be too exhaustive to be easily applied in an actual evaluation.

Compared to Breen and Candlin (1987), Cunningsworth and Kusel (1991) simplified the pre-determined questions listed in the checklist to improve the operationality of the evaluation pattern. Cunningsworth and Kusel (1991) developed a checklist for global assessment that focuses on the underlying principles and detailed procedures of textbook evaluation. With regards to global assessment, Cunningsworth and Kusel (1991) provided an overview of general criteria for future teachers to evaluate the underlying approaches or assumptions in language materials.

> -What assumptions are made about the users' knowledge and experience of language teaching?
>
> -What assumptions are made about their knowledge of English?
>
> -What assumptions are made about their awareness of the cultural context portrayed in the course material?
>
> -How confident are the teachers assumed to be?
>
> (Cunningsworth & Kusel, 1991, p. 131)

Based on the answers to the general criteria above, the teachers (or evaluators) are expected to form a more specific checklist for further assessment of the information about language and language learning provided in materials (e. g. , what aspects of language are covered, what types of learning styles and strategies, the nature of learning activities) and the extent to which the materials develop teachers' general understanding of language teaching approaches or theories (e. g. , the rationale for teaching guidelines).

According to Cunningsworth and Kusel (1991), the following procedure is to carry out a detailed evaluation that aims to deal with the way in which the specific elements—such as objectives and teaching procedures—are presented in a textbook. It also takes into consideration how teachers can be actively involved in the evaluation process. The detailed assessment aims to look into a variety of key elements in textbooks. They include: the objectives and content (e. g. , pronunciation, functional units, topics covered, skills practiced), cultural awareness (e. g. , what cultural backgrounds or settings are given), procedural guidance (e. g. , whether materials provide specific guidance for teachers in the planning and preparation of lessons), testing and practices (e. g. , whether abundant tasks or exercises for testing students are provided), learner motivation (e. g. , whether the materials contribute to the sustainability of learner motivation), and presentation and use (cf. Cunningsworth & Kusel, 1991).

Unlike Breen and Candlin's (1987) proposal which attempted to look at every aspect of materials, Cunningsworth and Kusel (1991) further refined the aims of the evaluation phases with a view to making the evaluation a more targeted one. Within a 'global-detailed' appraisal framework, Cunningswork and Kusel (1991) perceived the textbook evaluation as a dynamic process which consisted of establishing criteria, employing the criteria to specific materials and acting on the outcome. In practical terms, the dominant role of teachers in the establishment and application of specific criteria may impact on the outcome of textbook assessment due to that teachers are actively engaged in classes and they may rely on their own intuitive judgment.

As with Cunningsworth and Kusel's (1991) dynamic process of textbook assessment, McDonough and Shaw (1993) generated a two-procedure evaluation model of English language teaching (ELT) teaching materials through the checklist method. They further extended the scope of textbook assessment by incorporating an external evaluation into their model. Their model includes two procedures. The first procedure is an external overview of how the textbooks have been organized as claimed by the writers or publishers through the cover, table of contents statements, and introduction. The main criteria to be considered in the external evaluation include: the intended audience (e. g. , young learners or mature adults), the proficiency level (e. g. , for beginners or advanced learners), the context in which the language materials are to be used (e. g. , teaching English for Academic Purposes or Business Purposes), the presentation of language and organization of lessons, the textbook writer's perceptions of language and methodology, and the layout. The second procedure is an internal evaluation aimed at seeing how far the textbooks live up to the claims stated by the writers with respect to different features. For the internal assessment, some relevant criteria to examine the consistency between the writers' claims and the internal content are: the presentation of language skills in the materials, authenticity of dialogues or exercises, suitability for different learning styles. Based on the two types of assessment above, the evaluators can conduct an overall assessment that generalizes the suitability of the materials for teachers and learners. McDonough and Shaw's (1993) evaluation paradigm contributes to assisting teachers to identify strengths and shortcomings in the materials within a given working context. Their paradigm distinguishes the purposes behind the procedural evaluation and appears to be more realistic for teachers to put it into practice. Again, similar to Cunningsworth and Kusel (1991), McDonough and Shaw (1993) also emphasizes the proactive engagement of teachers in the process of textbook evaluation through the systematic use of checklist of pertinent criteria.

Other studies on predictive evaluation also emphasize that textbook evaluation should involve an elaborate analysis of different components in textbooks. For instance, William (1983) created a checklist of items derived from four basic principles—up-to-date methodology, guidance for non-native teachers, needs of L2 learners and relevance to the socio-cultural environment. Dougill (1987) proposed an assessment checklist based on six aspects of textbooks: target group (e. g. , the age range and type of students, what kind of potential market), framework (e. g. , syllabus, progression of content, what aspects of language skills are catered for), the units (e. g. , length of the lesson, presentation of language, practices or exercises), subject-matter (e. g. , learners' interest, cultural backgrounds), format (e. g. , visual appeal, illustrations), and course supplementary materials (e. g. , cassette, teacher's manual, workbooks).

Some researchers further subdivided the general and specific features considered in textbook evaluation. Other than listing the features in parallel, they determined the general features that were suitable for any type of textbook and the specific features that were tailored to a certain kind of textbook. For example, Sheldon (1988) designed a checklist of common-core qualitative criteria, including rationale of textbooks (e. g. , the objectives and motivations of the materials), availability (e. g. , whether it is easy to access the copies of materials and the information of publishers for further enquiry), user definition (e. g. , the target age range of the users, cultural backgrounds, learning styles), layout or graphics, the authenticity of the content, cultural bias, and so on. Sheldon's (1988) guidelines provide an overview of general factors and constraints which may be operative in English language teaching (ELT) contexts worldwide and encourage reviewers to tailor the specific criteria that are emphatically local. Noteworthily, Sheldon (1988) also pointed out that while textbook evaluation through the cross-check of a checklist of criteria is inevitably subjective and intuitive, it is cost-effective and allows teachers to achieve the decision-making process within limited circumstances.

Stein, Stuen, Carnine, and Long (2001) suggested an integrated application of initial screening instruments and final evaluation instruments. The initial screening instruments include the textbook's instructional approach, and the relationship between the identified approach and the text. The final evaluation instruments consist of content organization, the presence of explicit and generalizable strategies, opportunities for scaffolded instruction, the strategic integration of skills and concepts, and judicious review. Tomlinson (2003) proposed a set of predetermined questions based on a distinction between general and local criteria. He suggested that evaluators should first brainstorm a list of general criteria that can be applied to any language textbooks anywhere for any learners, such as "Do the materials cater for different preferred learning styles?" (Tomlinson, 2003, p. 28). He also defined the local criteria as the pre-determined questions that are specific to particular learners in particular circumstances, as exemplified by the question "What is the amount of exposure to the target language outside the classroom?" (Tomlinson, 2003, p. 32). Mukundan, Hajimohammadi, and Nimehchisalem (2011) developed a tentative checklist to appraise general attributes of textbooks (such as relation to syllabus and curriculum, methodology, suitability to learners, physical and utilitarian attributes, and supplementary materials) and learning-teaching content (such as task quality, cultural sensitivity, vocabulary, pronunciation, and exercises).

As shown above, the use of checklists contributes to the systematicity of the evaluation, since almost all elements related to the textbook are considered in the assessment process, such as the layout, the underlying pedagogical method, and the tasks. The features of the textbook are recorded and grouped according to the categories in a checklist. Reviewers only need to perform a 'matching' activity to judge whether the features of the textbook are consistent with the description of the questions in the checklist. This is easily understood and cost effective for evaluators.

Although these two advantages lead to the prevailing use of checklist methods in textbook evaluation, this method also has a potential limitation. The descriptive nature of checklists means the evaluation is subjective both in its selection of criteria and in the judgements made by the reviewers. Most criteria are presented in the form of a set of questions, which means that the assessment depends on evaluators' responses to the questions. For example, in Cunningsworth and Kusel (1991), one of the questions listed in the checklist is "Is the advice given on teaching procedures explicit enough?" (p. 131). There is ambiguity regarding what kind of 'advice given on teaching procedures' could be considered 'explicit enough'. A similar problem is evident in the criteria developed by Tomlinson (2003, p. 28): "Are the instructions clear?". Evaluators may differ in their answers to the same question, because the answers rely upon their cognition and experience.

In addition, some researchers have carried out predictive evaluations through local analysis. For example, Hutchinson and Waters (1987) claimed that a close analysis of one or several extracts from a textbook is necessary in the evaluation process. Although their criteria are presented principally through a checklist (similar to the form of the checklist method), their evaluation focuses on some specific features instead of all elements of the textbooks. Hutchinson and Waters's (1987) evaluation focuses on the content of the textbook. Two questions are designed for assessing the linguistic input—one of the specific aspects of textbook content: "What type(s) of linguistic description is/are used in the materials?" and "What language points do the materials cover?" (Hutchinson & Waters, 1987, p. 100). In another study, Johnson (1986, as cited in McGrath, 2002) also advocated an investigation of several units of textbooks using a local analysis.

In contrast to the studies using the checklist method, the research using a local analysis (e.g., Hutchinson and Waters, 1987; Johnson, 1986) assessed whether textbooks are likely to achieve the claims being made for them regarding specific elements of the materials. However, the samples chosen for the analysis, such as some extracts, units, sections from the textbooks, may not be representative of the textbook as a whole. This results in the evaluation being limited in its scope. Such a textbook assessment can only provide a partial insight into certain features of the materials.

3.2 Retrospective evaluation

Unlike predictive evaluation research, studies on retrospective evaluation measure the actual effects of textbooks on users after they have been used. Compared to the studies on predictive evaluation that merely proposed evaluation models, the studies on retrospective evaluation applied the evaluation models or approaches to analysing a specific textbook. Such an evaluation provides language instructors with information, such as which textbooks enhance learning and which ones do not, so that language instructors can determine whether it is worthwhile using the textbooks again.

Some researchers employed the checklists developed by predictive evaluation research to test the validity of the evaluation models. For example, Guilani, Yasin, & Hua (2011) investigated the authenticity of three Iranian English textbooks at high school level, following Dougill's (1987) six-aspect checklist (as mentioned in Section 2. 1) including the textbook framework, units (or lessons), subject-matter and format. The evaluators were 30 experienced ESL teachers who had used the selected textbooks in their classes and 200 students who had studied the textbooks. Reliance on their own experiences and comments, those teachers cross-checked between the specific criteria listed in Dougill's (1987) checklist and the corresponding features of the textbooks. Next, the students reviewed and responded to some selected criteria of the evaluation checklist. Finally, the data collected from the teachers and the students were compared and discussed with regards to two aspects: the content and the presentation of textbooks. The results of evaluation showed inconsistency between the students' needs and the textbooks. Firstly, the content and presentation of the textbooks were lack of authenticity in comparison with naturally occurring English conversation. Secondly, the passages in the textbooks did not seem to be attractive and diverse for the users. Thirdly, the content in the textbooks was not presented from the simple to the complex and did not take into account much cultural backgrounds. While Guilani, Yasin, & Hua's (2011) textbook assessment followed the systematic framework developed in Dougil (1987) and combined the feedback from both teachers and students to ensure the authenticity and validity of the evaluation, its exclusive reliance on the teachers and students' comments and judgements on the checklist of criteria might be subjective and become a 'rule-of-thumb' activity.

Similarly, Fraidan (2012) assessed the suitability of two ESP (English for specific purposes) textbooks for ESP learners, using McDonough and Shaw's (1993) working model composed of external and internal evaluations (as mentioned in Section 2. 1). Fraidan (2012) selected two textbooks which were designed for Business English in an Arabic university. The first step was the external evaluation, namely, a quick glance at general features of the textbooks, including the textbook authors' claims, contents, and the introduction. The external evaluation revealed that: 1) one textbook did not contain the introduction but it introduced the objectives and tasks through the authors' claims and individual lessons instead, whilst the other one provided a brief introduction; 2) both of the textbooks included a range of vocabulary and terminology; 3) both were presented in a friendly and attractive way; 4) one textbook was intended for general business while the other one was designed for specialist business. The following step was to conduct a simplified version of McDonough and Shaw's (1993) internal evaluation of the textbooks regarding their language (e. g., presentation, organization), reading type, authenticity, appropriateness, and cultural awareness. Based on the two-procedure evaluation, Fraidan (2012) concluded that both of the textbooks were suitable to be used as core materials and incorporated into the course syllabus. Both were useful for all learners regardless of their preferences, but they needed some sort of adaption in relation to sufficiency of information and exemplification. As with Guilani, Yasin, & Hua (2011), Fraidan's (2012) evaluation appears to be cost-effective and time-saving in decision-making since it applies the checklist method. However, a common issue needs to be addressed here, namely, the subjective nature of checklist approach and its consequences on textbook selection and adaption. Fraiden (2012) also acknowledged this potential issue in his textbook appraisal.

Several studies on textbook assessment in China also advocated empirical research through the checklists, although the number of relevant scholarly publications is small. This empirical research in China was principally motivated by Breen and Candlin (1987), Cunningsworth and Kusel (1991), and McDonough and Shaw (1993). For instance, Shi and Ji (2011) analysed audio-visual teaching materials within the frameworks developed by McDonough and Shaw (1993) and Breen and Candlin (1987). Likewise, Lan and Meng (2009) applied the systematic model by Tomlinson (2003) to the evaluation of the *New College English* textbook.

Although these studies provide empirical evidence supporting the applicability of evaluation models in specific contexts, their assessment results are inevitably biased due to the limitations inherent in the methodology that they employed—i. e., the problem that also concerned the checklist approach: the evaluation was potentially subjective in both its criteria and the judgements made by evaluators.

Other studies on retrospective evaluation examined the effectiveness of textbooks on the basis of the feedback from informants, which contributes to reflective practice in teaching. For example, Tomlinson, Dat, Masuhara, and Rubdy (2001) provided an analysis of eight adult EFL coursebooks (*Clockwise*, *Cutting Edge*, *Inside Out*, *Language in Use*, *Landmark*, *Reward*, *True to Life*, *Wavelength*) for which four reviewers from different backgrounds were required to answer a list of 133 pre-determined questions. The 133 questions were previously developed from research into what teachers, students, and administrators needed from those coursebooks (Tomlinson et al., 2001, p. 80). Here is a sample of the questions used in the study; each question is measured on 10-point grading scale:

a) Would the course appeal to adult learners in any country?
b) Would the course be useful to adult learners in any country?
c) Does the course provide opportunities for learners to localize activities?
d) Does the course provide opportunity for teachers to localize activities?
e) Does the course facilitate a flexible approach?
f) Does the course provide opportunities for extensive reading?

(Tomlinson et al., 2001, p. 81)

Overall, the 133 pre-designed questions concerned a variety of components related to the textbooks, such as the claims made by publishers, flexibility of content for diverse contexts, course syllabus, language teaching approach, topic content, clarity and specificity in the instructions, textbook appearance and design, illustrations, and reading texts. The reviewers independently graded each question and then provided an overall average rating for each coursebook. The results of textbook evaluation indicated that: 1) four of the eight coursebooks, *Inside Out*, *Landmark*, *Language in Use*, and *Wavelength*, were highly rated since they had strong potential to motivate both teachers and students; 2) there was a positive trend towards the personalization of activities (i. e., to personalize the learning process by engaging students in related topics and texts) and the engagement of affect (i. e., to engage students in tasks and texts which inspired the expression of their feelings); 3) however, a common issue among those textbooks was lack of the provision of the language in use. Tomlinson et al. (2001) makes a positive attempt to conduct the checklist-based textbook assessment in a thorough and systematic manner, by means of the selection of reviewers from diverse backgrounds and the independent grading system. Nevertheless, to some extent, Tomlinson et al.'s (2001) evaluation results are still inevitably subjective in nature. As with the other studies based on checklist method, its selection of criteria and the judgements made by the reviewers are both subjective and lack of solid theoretical grounds.

A similar review was published in Campbell et al. (1998), who investigated five ELT serial textbooks for secondary school education based on the feedback from seven Estonian English teachers. Those teachers were provided with a list of pre-planned questions and reviewed them under the guidance of a British Council ELT Consultant. The list of questions generally concerned several aspects of the textbooks, including learner training, cross-cultural differences, cross-curricular developments, and mixed-ability teaching. During the assessment session, the teachers were required to discuss those questions based on their classroom-based teaching experiences and shared their reviews with each other. The final evaluation report was established on the basis of the teachers' common views on the selected textbooks. In order to enrich the understanding of the selected textbooks, Campbell et al. (1998) collected the feedback from a broader team of seven skilled English teachers, which contributed to gaining insights into their shared experience of the use of textbooks and their individual perspectives. However, the main disadvantage of Campbell et al.'s (1998) evaluation was that those teachers might prefer to offer their own perceptions and judge the textbooks according to different standards since their review in fact was a process of cross-checking and answering the question checklist.

A number of Chinese scholars also considered feedback from textbook users as a crucial part of their assessment of English textbooks. For instance, Deng, Duan, and Zhang (2002) assessed the level of difficulty of four serial college English textbooks according to the feedback of students, the readability of the texts and the amount of vocabulary. Dai (2008) and Yu, Fan, and Li (2008) both used questionnaires to obtain feedback from target students, in order to evaluate college English textbooks. Wang and Yang (2012) conducted a quantitative analysis of

New Practical English and *Practical English* based on two mathematics methods: the Delphi method and the analytic hierarchy process. The Delphi method (Dalkey, 1969) was designed to elicit and refine group judgements. The analytic hierarchy process (Saaty, 1980) is a way of measurement through pairwise comparisons and relies on the judgements of the experts to derive priority scales. Wang and Yang (2012) first applied the Delphi method to screen a series of criteria, and then used the analytic hierarchy process to establish a multi-level evaluation hierarchy that focuses on the feedback from textbook experts, teachers, and students. These studies contribute to extending the scope of research on textbook evaluation.

However, studies focusing on feedback may have some shortcomings due to the limitations of the questionnaires. First, the reliability and validity of questionnaires cannot be easily defined. A questionnaire is descriptive in nature, and informants might misunderstand certain questions, which could bias the outcome of textbook assessments. Second, the questionnaire is time-consuming to complete and assess. Researchers need to select appropriate participants, organize the investigation and analyse the feedback from respondents.

In conclusion, the studies pursuing the development of textbook evaluation have undertaken attempts to develop an effective method to judge the fitness of textbooks for particular teaching contexts and particular target users. The focus of these studies is either to predict the potential value of teaching materials, or to measure the actual effects of textbooks on the target users. Using the checklist approach, these studies have provided a systematic insight into almost all characteristics of materials. They also examined the underlying assumptions of materials through a local analysis of specific features, to assess whether the textbooks were likely to achieve the claims made by publishers or authors. In addition, an array of empirical studies offer evidence to determine the validity of the evaluation models and extend the scope of the research into textbook assessment. However, these studies are restricted due to subjectivity in their criteria and judgements made by reviewers.

3.3 Conversation analysis-based evaluation

Issues relating to authenticity of dialogues and pragmatic information in textbooks are complex and have been addressed by many researchers (Seedhouse, 2004, p. 228). A number of studies reveal that, for a variety of reasons, textbook writers prefer to invent dialogues or use artificial materials in the design of their textbooks. For example, Jaén and Basanta (2009, p. 287) pointed out that textbook conversations employ artificially scripted dialogues based on writers' intuitions about what people are likely to say, or in most cases drawn from written language. Schegloff, Koshik, Jacoby, and Olsher (2002, p. 17) stated that there is a common issue in the design of language materials—textbooks use invented dialogues based on intuitions of how certain language functions are achieved. Researchers in pragmatics also addressed the issue that some language teaching materials did not provide sufficient opportunities through a variety of activities to develop pragmatic competence (Vellenga, 2004). Pragmatic competence is defined as the ability to appropriately use and interpret the target language in a specific sociocultural context (Ishihara & Paller, 2016, p. 87). Pragmatic failure could possibly be attributed to miscommunication that can be perceived as an indication of impoliteness (Crandall & Basturkmen, 2004). Thus, textbooks are also expected to develop and facilitate pragmatic competence as a key component of the language instruction process.

To examine authenticity and issues of pragmatics in language materials, a number of researchers have applied knowledge derived from Conversation Analysis (or Discourse Analysis) to evaluate dialogues or activities in textbooks (Bernsten, 2002; Mori, 2005; Nguyen, 2011; Petraki & Bayes, 2013; Scotton & Bernsten, 1988; Wong, 2002, 2007).

Conversation Analysis (CA) is an interdisciplinary methodology for the analysis of naturally occurring talk-in-interaction. The first aim of CA is to portray the organization of the interaction, such as turn-taking, sequence, and repair of talk, and to examine the emic logic underlying this organization (Seedhouse, 2005). The second aim of CA is to investigate participants' experience of talk—how participants understand and respond to each other in their talk (Hutchby & Wooffitt, 1998). CA methodology can provide a detailed description of how people talk and interact with each other in reality. Therefore, CA is well positioned to depict the similarities and differences between artificial conversation and naturally occurring interaction (including ordinary conversation and institutional interaction) (Seedhouse, 2004, p. 228). CA is used as the theoretical approach by a number of studies on textbook evaluation.

Some CA-based studies on textbook evaluation focus on authenticity of dialogues in textbooks. Scotton and Bernsten (1988) compared dialogues in American ESL textbooks with natural conversations involving native speakers of American English in direction-giving. They found overwhelming uniformity between textbook dialogues and real talk-in-interaction with respect to the structure of direction-giving turns. On the other hand, Wong (2002) examined thirty telephone dialogues in eight English as a second language (ESL) textbooks published in the 1990s. She compared them with authentic telephone talk in CA research regarding four types of opening sequences—summons-answer, identification-recognition, greeting, 'how are you' (see Schegloff, 1986). Her analysis showed that there is a discrepancy between invented dialogues in textbooks and real telephone conversations. Sequences such as summons-answer, which are usually found in authentic telephone interactions, are missing, incomplete or problematic in the textbooks. In another study, Wong (2007) applied a similar approach to assess the telephone closings from 81 invented dialogues in 17 ESL textbooks, and found a mismatch between textbook dialogues and authentic telephone closings. Similarly, Bernsten (2002) used a CA-based approach to evaluate 68 dialogues from 22 ESL textbooks with regard to pre-sequences such as offers, requests, and invitations. Her study revealed a mismatch between textbook dialogues and naturally occurring conversations. The pre-sequences do not occur in textbook dialogues as frequently as in ordinary conversations. Furthermore, Mori (2005) analysed the use of the

Japanese question word *dooshite* 'why' in dialogues and exercises in two introductory and one intermediate level Japanese language textbooks. The study showed considerable differences between the way *dooshite* 'why' is presented in textbooks and the way that it is used in authentic talk-in-interaction. For example, in textbook exercises, *dooshite* 'why' was frequently used as a follow-up question word to request clarification. However, in real-life interaction, *dooshite* 'why' can be implying marker of challenge or disapproval (Mori, 2005, p. 268).

All of these studies reveal the potential problems of using invented materials in textbooks through depicting the mismatch between dialogues in textbooks and naturally occurring conversation. This mismatch may not benefit the learners when they attempt to transit from inside the language classroom to the world outside, because they may find the invented dialogues they learned from textbooks will not be useful to achieve real-life communication (Mori, 2005). This is why the use of transcriptions of naturally occurring conversation in the design of language teaching materials has been advocated by CA researchers (Sert & Seedhouse, 2011, p. 7). However, transcriptions of naturally occurring talk are not necessarily optimal materials for language teaching purposes. One possible consequence is that teaching objectives such as language functions and grammatical structures possibly cannot be well presented in textbook dialogues because transcriptions of naturally occurring talk may contain a lot of spontaneity, and may not focus on specific structures and functions that are required for classroom teaching (Sert & Seedhouse, 2011).

CA-based studies on textbook evaluation also pay attention to the adequacy of the pragmatic information included in textbooks. Nguyen (2011) evaluated the pragmatic content of three ESL textbooks intended for Vietnamese students aged 16 to 18, who have reached the upper-secondary level. The evaluation focused on three aspects: (1) the range and distribution of particular speech acts (such as requests, invitations, and disagreements); (2) the linguistic presentation of these speech acts; and (3) the type of contextual and meta-pragmatic information accompanying the presentations (p. 20). The study showed that textbooks do not include an accurate and adequate source of pragmatic information, especially intercultural differences between native-speaker communication and non-native-speaker communication. Petraki and Bayes (2013) also focused on assessing the pragmatic information in textbooks. The study evaluated types of requests in five intermediate-level ESL textbooks currently used in Australia. Their evaluation was conducted on the basis of five criteria derived from three main DA theories—speech act theory, politeness theory and CA. The criteria consist of whether, and the extent to which, the textbooks: (1) raise learners' cross-cultural awareness of requests; (2) expose learners to a variety of request forms; (3) adequately examine the contextual factors that affect the degree of politeness; (4) focus on preferred and dispreferred responses; and (5) explain pre-sequences and pre-requests (Petraki & Bayes, 2013, p. 504). The study showed that none of the textbooks meet all of the criteria. It revealed a gap between CA research in pragmatic information and ESL textbooks on the nature of requests.

In conclusion, CA-based studies on textbook evaluation assess whether or not textbook dialogues and exercises are adequate when compared to what is reported about naturally occurring talk in CA research. They not only analyse authenticity of invented dialogues (Bernsten, 2002; Mori, 2005; Wong, 2002, 2007), but also investigate appropriateness of pragmatic information included in textbooks (Nguyen, 2011; Petraki and Bayes, 2013). Research in CA-based textbook evaluation has highlighted the importance of using authentic examples and teaching pragmatic competence in textbooks.

Applied to language learning and teaching, CA-based textbook studies possibly have two significant pedagogical implications. First, the use of authentic conversations in textbook design could provide more opportunities for L2 learners to access input of target language and to improve their communicative skills. Second, considering pragmatic information in textbook design would be beneficial for L2 learners to improve their pragmatic and strategic competence (such as different request forms), as well as their awareness of cross-cultural differences between L1 and L2 (such as politeness).

However, the advocacy of using transcriptions of naturally occurring talk as textbook dialogues may not be practical for teaching purposes. Reliance on spontaneous conversations is probably not helpful to teach grammatical objectives and language functions.

3.4 SLA-based evaluation

Similar to CA-based studies, the fourth type of textbook evaluation is also driven by a theoretical framework. These studies (e. g. Lenzing, 2004, 2008; Zipser, 2012) apply Processability Theory (PT) (Pienemann, 1998), a psycholinguistically-based SLA theory focusing on the developmental sequence of L2 grammar. They aim to assess whether the grammar instruction in textbooks is sequenced in a way that is compatible with the L2 developmental path.

Grammar instruction plays an important role in L2 acquisition. It draws L2 learners' attention to specific grammatical structures so that learners either understand structures metalinguistically or process them in production, so that learners can internalize them in communication (Ellis, 2006, p. 84). Many current textbooks introduce grammar based on the traditional approach—i. e., graded from grammatically simple to grammatically complex (Keßler, 2011, p. 189). They do not consider how L2 learners learn grammatical structures, and ignore decisive insights from research in SLA, psycholinguistics and cognitive neuroscience (Keßler, 2011, p. 11). One SLA theory, namely PT, describes how L2 learners acquire grammatical structures in sequence and also specifies why, from a psycholinguistic point of view, some features are less complex than others. Lenzing's (2004, 2008[①]) and Zipser's (2012) studies on

① Lenzing (2008) is a summary of the main issues of Lenzing's unpublished Master degree's thesis in 2004, namely, Lenzing (2004).

textbook evaluation hence provide crucial insights into whether the grading of the grammatical structures that are presented in textbooks follow the developmental path of L2 acquisition. In the following, I will review only two studies involving a SLA-based textbook evaluation—Lenzing (2008) and Zipser (2012).

Lenzing (2008) reports on an analysis of two EFL coursebooks—*Playway* and *Ginger*—currently used in many German primary schools. Adopting PT (Pienemann, 1998), Lenzing addressed the question whether the learning objectives that are promoted in the textbooks are realistic, that is, whether the grading of learning objectives specified in the textbooks is consistent with the staged L2 development as stipulated in PT.

The first coursebook, *Playway*, consists of two volumes—*Playway* 3 for the first year of English education (Grade 3), and *Playway* 4 for the second year (Grade 4). The other coursebook, *Ginger* 1, is also intended for the first year of English education (Grade 3). The textbook analysis included two parts: (1) a comparison between the grading of grammatical structures that are presented in the textbooks and the developmental sequence of L2 acquisition as outlined in PT; and (2) a comparison between the linguistic input of the textbooks and their learning objectives.

In the actual textbook analysis, Lenzing (2008) analysed all the exercises that included the grammatical features that were introduced in the textbooks. She also analysed the learning objectives, namely, the focused structures that were required to be produced by the students. All the grammatical structures were then categorized according to a shorthand version of the original processability hierarchy (Pienemann, 1998)—*Rapid Profile*①. Lenzing (2008) determined the percentage of occurrence of the grammatical structures in the individual units of the textbooks. All the instances of the structures in the exercises and learning objectives were counted.

The results show that the presentation of the grammatical structures was rather random and not graded in line with the sequenced development of L2 acquisition. First, structures that are hypothesized by PT to be acquired at a low stage did not occur frequently or did not appear as learning objectives in the initial units of the textbook. For example, the Stage 2-structure '-ed' and 'poss -s (noun)' did not occur in *Playway* 3 (Lenzing, 2008, p. 228). In *Ginger* 1, the structures at Stage 2 are rarely introduced in the first unit.

Second, those structures that are only able to be acquired at an intermediate or high stage were introduced too frequently in the beginning units of the textbook. For instance, half of the morphological structures that are introduced as learning objectives in *Playway* 3 occur at Stage 4 or higher in the processability hierarchy. In *Playway* 3, the Stage 4-structures 'copula S' and

---

① *Rapid Profile* is a computer-assisted procedure developed by Manfred Pienemann (1990, 1992) to assess the language learners' level of morpho-syntactic development during ESL acquisition (Lenzing, 2014, p. 2). Compared to the original processability hierarchy (Pienemann, 1998), *Rapid Profile* includes revised labels for the structural outcomes that occur in the morpho-syntactic development of ESL learners.

'WH-copula S' questions account for 24% of the syntactic structures specified as learning objectives in the first unit. In the second unit, the only syntactic learning objective is the 'copula S' question. In *Ginger* 1, 70% of the morphological structures occur at Stage 4 or higher in the hierarchy.

In brief, the results reveal that the grammatical structures introduced as learning goals in the analysed textbooks are not presented in a way that is processable and learnable for the students.

Based on her results, Lenzing (2008) further pointed out that the unlearnability of the grammatical structures as introduced in the textbooks possibly affects the acquisition process in two ways (p. 237). First, the learners may use those structures that are beyond their processable stage as fixed formulae. Second, the learners may avoid using the structures they are not ready for and their acquisition process might be inhibited. Lenzing (2008) suggested that, to deal with the issue of premature teaching of grammar, the L2 acquisition sequence should be incorporated into the grading of the syllabus (p. 238). She advised it is of significance that early ELT teachers are informed about the underlying principles in the L2 acquisition process—i. e., about the processability hierarchy as stipulated in PT.

Lenzing's (2008) application of PT in the evaluation of grammar instruction in ESL textbooks breaks new ground. The author developed a methodology of conducting a SLA-based textbook evaluation. This type of evaluation aims to assess the presentation of the grammatical structures introduced as learning objectives in textbooks according to the underlying principles in the L2 acquisition process.

In practical terms, Lenzing (2008) has demonstrated the procedure of conducting a SLA-based textbook evaluation. Her study used a quantitative approach to calculate the percentage of occurrence of grammatical structures in the linguistic input of textbooks, and then determined whether the presentation of the structures is learnable for L2 learners according to two criteria: (1) the structures that are located at a low stage of the processability hierarchy should occur frequently in the initial units of the textbook; and (2) those structures that can only be processed at a higher stage should not be introduced too frequently in the beginning units of the textbook. Lenzing (2008) offers an explanatory basis for promoting more learnable grammatical introduction in L2 learning materials. She also provides an insight into the gap between SLA research and language pedagogy—crucial findings from SLA research about the developmental sequence have not been considered in the design of EFL textbooks. Lenzing (2008) goes a long way towards developing a learnable syllabus for ESL grammar instruction in language materials.

The other SLA-based textbook studies taking PT as the analytical paradigm is carried out by Zipser (2012). Zipser's (2012) empirical study aimed to cross-check how much the grammatical structures specified as learning objectives in an Italian textbook for beginners used in Austria agreed with the learning sequence that L2 learners of Italian actually went through (p. 55). Compared to Lenzing (2008) that exclusively focused on textbook analysis, Zipser (2012) not only looked into the grammatical structures and their progression in the textbook through following Lenzing's (2008) quantitative analytical method, but also conducted the oral speech analysis of those learners who had been using that textbook.

Firstly, Zipser (2012) selected *Buongiorno! Neu. Italienisch für Anfänger* (Brambilla, Crotti, and Von Albertini, 2003) as the target textbook. It consisted of 17 units in total. According to Zipser (2012, p. 57), this textbook was widely used for secondary schooling and adult education in Austria and highlighted L2 communicative needs within specific cultural contexts. The structures in the grammar section of the textbook appendix were analysed and grouped into the corresponding developmental stages, according to the morpho-syntactic categories contained in the five stages of acquisition for Italian as an L2 (see Di Biase and Bettoni, 2007). The following quantitative analysis looked into the total distribution of structures at the stages in individual units and the total percentages of the structures at individual stages in this whole textbook.

Secondly, Zipser (2012) carried out the oral production analysis of four adult Austrian learners of L2 Italian aged 19-35. The data was elicited by two picture stories developed in Mayer (1969) and an additional picture task depicting what an Italian woman did in her daily life (Zipser, 2012, pp. 62-63). The data elicitation was conducted through interview at the start of the third semester when the students had learned 10 units in class, namely, they had received 90 hours of formal instruction. As indicated in Zipser (2012, p. 63), the emergence criterion (the rate of rule application is 75%, see Di Biase, 1999) was applied to determining which acquisitional stages the informants had achieved in their development of L2 Italian.

With reference to the PT-based staged development of L2 Italian acquisition (see Di Biase and Bettoni, 2007), the results of the empirical study revealed a quite different situation between the selected textbook and the oral production of the informants. Firstly, the textbook analysis showed that the structures specified as learning objectives were not ordered in accordance with the PT-based learning sequence, and their distribution in individual units was fairly random. Specifically, all the other stages structures except for those requiring Stage 5 were found in the textbook, and in particular early-to-mid stages structures (Stages 1-3) occurred in every unit of the text (Zipser, 2012, pp. 61-62). Some structures at an early stage did not occur with a high percentage in the first units; instead, they were provided with a high percentage in a later unit. For example, the percentage of the structures at Stage 2 was very low in the initial units, whereas more than half of the structures in Unit 5, 10 and 14 were those requiring Stage 2 (Zipser, 2012, p. 62). Secondly, the learners' data analysis, by and large, confirmed the PT stage sequencing in the acquisition of Italian grammar. Except for structures requiring Stage 5, all the other stages structures (Stages 1-4) emerged in the learners' data. However, not all of the informants were able to produce all the required structures according to the emergence criterion (i. e., 75% rule application required). Two of the four informants seemed to fail to produce the Stages 2-3 structures (insufficient evidence of rule application), but they successfully produced those structures requiring Stage 4 (Zipser, 2012, p. 64). Nevertheless, Zipser (2012) argued that this issue could not be considered as contradictory evidence against the PT stage sequencing due to the limited data and the emergence criterion applied in the study.

Based on the findings of textbook analysis and learners' data analysis, Zipser (2012) concluded that it was rather difficult to distinguish between input, intake and learning objectives since the learners were required to produce an output similar to their input (p. 64). However, the learner was not capable of using the structures requiring a high stage if he or she was not developmentally ready at the beginning of L2 acquisition process. Therefore, language teachers and textbook writers should have a clear understanding of the staged development of L2 acquisition and also take the diversity of students' needs into account in L2 classes.

Focusing on L2 Italian acquisition, Zipser (2012) makes a further contribution to illuminating the relationship between teachability (as proposed by the textbook) and learnability (what the learner does actually learn given the textbook). Through a small analysis of learners' data, Zipser (2012) generally supported the PT stage sequencing. However, Zipser's (2012) speech analysis did not apply the pre- and post-test to compare the learners' performance, and thus it is still vague that how those students develop their interlanguage grammar over a period of time. Furthermore, how those learners who have been using the textbook progress in their L2 acquisition process.

To conclude, the established SLA-based studies on textbook evaluation were still limited in number and scope. They investigated into either L2 English textbooks used in Germany (cf. Lenzing, 2004, 2008) or L2 Italian textbooks used in Austria (cf. Zipser, 2012). However, no existing studies applied the SLA-based approach to the assessment of L2 textbooks used in China. As reviewed in Sections 2.1-2.3, those textbook studies which were based in China (e.g., Dai, 2008; Deng et al., 2002; Lan & Meng, 2009; Shi & Ji, 2011; Wang & Yang, 2012; Yu et al., 2008) usually employed the predictive or retrospective evaluation approach and none of them used the SLA-based approach. Therefore, my study is called for in order to provide an insight into the issue of learnability regarding grammatical sequencing in textbooks within the context of China and to add more empirical evidence to the SLA-based textbook studies. In addition, the literature review above shows that no previous studies looked into a complete coursebook series which included multiple and sequential volumes. Lenzing (2004, 2008) focused on three volumes from two English coursebooks designed for Grade 3 and Grade 4 at primary schools. Zipser (2012) selected a single Italian textbook that was used for beginners in Austrian secondary school as well as in adult education. Thus, a more comprehensive study investigating the whole textbook series is needed in order to take into account a broaden section of grammatical features and an integrated grammatical syllabus. Furthermore, an investigation of multiple and representative textbook series may reveal insights into the current situation of textbook compilation and account for the grammatical introduction presented in textbooks. In fact, this issue was not clearly addressed in the previous SLA-based textbook studies. Therefore, my study will fill these research gaps through a more extensive acquisition-based evaluation of four sets of

English textbooks that are widely used in China.

3.5 Summary

In the last thirty years, textbook evaluation has made progress, both as an academic field and as a practical undertaking. A literature review of textbook evaluation reveals that the focus of attention has been largely on identifying specific evaluation criteria for the key elements of textbooks. Approaches such as predictive evaluation and retrospective evaluation are generally organized in a manner that reflects "the decision-making process" (Ellis, 1997, p. 36). However, there is now an increasing consensus on incorporating features of theoretical frameworks of applied linguistics into the key principles of textbook evaluation. A number of researchers have been applying a conversation analytic approach to assessing authenticity of textbook dialogues or sufficiency of pragmatic information in textbooks. Crucial findings from SLA research on developmental sequences such as PT also have been considered to determine whether the grammar instruction in textbooks is learnable for L2 learners.

Although the research on predictive and retrospective evaluations provides a variety of checklists and guidelines for evaluators to carry out a systematic textbook evaluation, such an evaluation is fundamentally "a subjective, rule-of-thumb activity" (Sheldon, 1988, p. 245) due to the limitations of the criteria and the judgements made by reviewers. Motivated by a scientifically theoretical approach, the research in CA-based evaluation has highlighted the significance of teaching with authentic examples and supplying pragmatic information in language materials. Such studies contribute to drawing our attention to L2 learners' communicative skills, pragmatic competence and cross-cultural awareness in the development of language materials. However, some of them advocate reliance on transcriptions of naturally occurring talk in textbook dialogues. Using spontaneous conversations is probably not practical for teaching purposes (such as grammatical objectives and language functions).

Spearheaded by a psycholinguistically based SLA theory (PT), the research on SLA-based evaluation provides an insight into the sequencing of grammatical structures in L2 textbooks. Studies such as Lenzing (2008) have filled a gap that nearly no previous research ever paid attention to, even though it is a core issue for L2 learners: namely, how L2 learners acquire grammatical structures step-by-step. The research on SLA-based evaluation contributes to facilitating the application of SLA theory to language pedagogy.

My research will follow the line of research on SLA-based textbook evaluation in three respects. First, my research will apply the SLA-based methodology for textbook evaluation. My research focuses on the sequencing of the grammatical structures that are introduced as teaching objectives in textbooks. Second, my research will investigate a broader selection of textbooks—four English textbook series including 28 volumes that are widely used in schools in China. The investigation will provide an insight into the current teaching materials for early English education in that country. Third, my research will propose suggestions for developing an acquisition-based grammatical sequence that is suitable for Chinese ESL learners, to enrich our understanding of how the developmental path of L2 English acquisition can be considered in the design of grammatical syllabi and textbooks. The textbook evaluation I am about to undertake seeks to answer the question whether the grammatical items introduced as learning objectives (teaching objectives) in the textbooks are introduced in line with the L2 English acquisition sequence as stipulated in PT.

Through the achievement of abovementioned three aspects, my research will make two contributions. Firstly, the present study will be the first SLA-based evaluation of a broad selection of English textbooks used in mainland China. Secondly, it will have pedagogical implication for the development of quality ESL textbooks which will take learnability considerations.

The next chapter will provide an understanding of the theoretical approach (PT) employed in SLA-based textbook studies, including the current textbook evaluation. Early research on L2 acquisition sequences will be introduced first to pave the way for the discussion of the PT-based developmental sequence inherent in the L2 acquisition process.

Chapter 4

L2 Acquisitional Sequence and Processability Theory

This chapter discusses SLA research on developmental sequences, focusing on Processability Theory (PT) (Pienemann, 1998, 2005), in order to form the theoretical basis for the evaluation of the sequencing of morpho-syntactic structrues in the Chinese ESL textbooks selected for this study. It consists of four sections. The first section reviews early SLA research on the developmental orders or sequences of L2 acquisition, including the 'morpheme order studies', the ZISA study on German as a L2 word order language, and Clahsen's speech processing strategies. This preliminary review provides insights into the L2 learning sequence—how a learner acquires L2 grammar in a sequenced manner. It paves the way for the exposition of PT. The second section describes the tenets of PT. It provides a general understanding of how the L2 learning sequence is accounted for from a processability perspective. The third section discusses the learning sequence of L2 English stated in PT. The final section concludes the main ideas of this chapter.

4.1 SLA research on the sequence of L2 acquisition

Research on language acquisition addresses two core issues: (1) how is a language acquired? (2) how does language acquisition proceed? The first issue comes from the observation of the mismatch between the input that a child receives and the linguistic knowledge that he or she finally attains. The second issue was motivated by L1 research findings dating back to the 1970s (e.g., Brown, 1973) and relating to the existence of a natural order in the acquisition of a certain range of English morphemes. Scholars at the time attempted to examine whether and to what extent universal stages can be identified in the fixed order along which learners develop their knowledge of L2 grammatical structures over time (Hulstijn, Ellis, & Eskildsen, 2015).

4.1.1 Morpheme order studies

In the 1970s, a number of cross-sectional and longitudinal studies were conducted to investigate the acquisitional order of English grammatical morphemes by L2 learners of diverse L1s (Bailey, Madden, & Krashen, 1974; Dulay & Burt, 1973, 1974, 1975; Krashen, Madden, & Bailey, 1978; Rosansky, 1976). These studies are known as 'morpheme order studies'.

Dulay and Burt's (1973) study was the first SLA investigation into the order of acquisition of grammatical morphemes. Their study aimed to find out whether a natural order existed in the acquisition of English morphological structures by children in different L2 learning settings. Dulay and Burt carried out a cross-sectional study of oral productions of 155 L1 Spanish children aged 6-8 years. These children were divided into three groups. The authors used the Bilingual Syntax Measure to elicit oral spontaneous production from the children. Their study investigated the children's acquisition of eight English grammatical morphemes. The results showed that the acquisition order of those morphemes was strikingly similar across the three groups. Dulay and Burt (1973) pointed out that a universal order might exist in children's acquisition of L2 English morphemes. In 1974 and 1975, Dulay and Burt provided further evidence for the universality of the order of acquisition of English grammatical morphemes in L2 children of diverse L1 backgrounds and varying levels of L2 proficiency.

Dulay and Burt's (1973, 1974, 1975) investigations revealed that there was a natural route along which L2 children acquired a certain range of morphemes, irrespective of their L1 backgrounds, the learning environments, or the levels of their L2 proficiency. Subsequent researchers started to look at L2 acquisition by adults and mostly confirmed the existence of the natural sequence (cf. the 'natural order' for L2 acquisition in Krashen, 1977). For example, Bailey, Madden, and Krashen (1974) replicated the studies conducted by Dulay and Burt (1973, 1974) on 73 adults of English as L2. The subjects included 73 adults aged 17-55 from eight ESL classes. They came from Spanish-speaking and non-Spanish-speaking backgrounds. The results showed a high degree of consistency with the findings of Dulay and Burt (1973, 1974). The acquisition orders for these two groups were very similar.

Morpheme order studies provided a pioneering insight into the developmental dimension of L2 acquisition. They offered empirical evidence for the existence of a single order by which L2 learners acquired a certain range of grammatical morphemes. This natural order was highly similar among L2 learners of different L1. However, morpheme order studies were subject to several major problems: firstly, they were language-specific and therefore not amenable to cross-linguistic generalizations; and secondly, they suffered a lack of theoretical motivations and explanations of the observed order of L2 acquisition (Larsen-Freeman and Long, 1991).

4.1.2 The ZISA study on GSL word order

Later studies examined the acquisition of syntactic structures, such as negative structures in English as L2 (Butterworth & Hatch, 1978; Cazden, Cancino, Rosansky, & Schumann, 1975; Milon, 1974; Ravem, 1968; Wode, 1978, 1981), interrogatives in English as L2 (Cazden et al., 1975), and WH-questions in English as L2 (Ravem, 1970). These studies found that L2 learners from different L1 backgrounds tended to follow a similar path when acquiring certain syntactic structures. Secondly, there were marked similarities between L1 and L2 acquisition. Unlike morpheme order studies, researchers on syntactic structures focused on the systematic staged development of a number of interrelated structures rather than on isolated morphemes.

One of the most significant attempts to describe and explain the observed sequence of L2 acquisition of syntactic structures is the one by the Zweitspracherwerb Italienischer und Spanischer Arbeiter (ZISA) group in Germany in the early 1980s (Clahsen, 1980; Meisel, Clahsen, & Pienemann, 1981; Clahsen, Meisel, & Pienemann, 1983; Pienemann, 1980, 1981). The ZISA project investigated the acquisition of German word order rules in naturalistic L2 acquisition by Spanish, Italian, and Portuguese workers in Germany (Meisel et al., 1981, pp. 110-111). This project included a cross-sectional study of 45 learners through informal interviews and a two-year longitudinal study of 12 L2 learners.

One major finding of the ZISA project was a five-stage developmental sequence for German as a second language (GSL) word order rules (see Table 4.1). After an initial period during which learners (both children and adults) are only able to produce isolated words or formulae, they will follow a five-stage developmental sequence in their subsequent acquisition.

Table 4.1 Sequence of acquisition of GSL word order rules (Pienemann, 1998, p.45)

Stage	Word order rule	Example
x	Canonical order (SVO)	*die kinder spielen mim ball* 'the children play with the ball'
x+1	Adverb preposing (ADV)	*da kinder spielen* (Concetta) *'there children play'*
x+2	Verb separation (SEP)	*alle kinder muβ die pause machen* 'all children must the break have'
x+3	Inversion (INV)	*dann hat sie wieder die knoch gebringt* 'then has she again the bone bringed'
x+4	Verb final (V-END)	*er sagt, daβ er nach hause kommt* 'he said that he home comes'

The ZISA study provided a description of the five defined stages of L2 development (see Jansen, 1991; Meisel et al., 1981). As shown in Table 4.1, the first stage is a fixed order—'canonical word order' stage (subject-verb-object, or SVO). The second stage is 'adverb preposing', which requires learners to move an adverbial into sentence-initial position. The third stage is an obligatory word order rule in standard German—'verb separation'. At this stage, learners put non-finite verbal elements into clause-final position. The fourth stage is 'inversion'. For this stage, subject and inflected verb forms are required to be inverted after preposing of elements. The fifth stage, 'verb final', means that the finite verb in subordinate clauses is inserted in final position.

The five stages and relevant word order rules are intrinsically ranked: the presence of a rule at one stage implies the presence of a lower-stage rule, but it does not imply the presence of a higher-stage rule. For example, if a learner has acquired the word rule 'verb final', this means that he or she also has acquired the prior word order rules such as 'inversion' and 'verb separation'. But a learner who has acquired 'inversion' has not yet acquired the later rule 'verb final'.

To explain the developmental sequence of GSL word order rules, Clahsen (1984) developed three speech processing strategies (see below). These strategies were assumed to constrain the ordering and structuring of grammar in speech production. The strategies were hypothesized to be progressively abandoned in a sequenced manner in L2 development.

(1) The Canonical Order Strategy (COS)

This strategy does not allow permutation or reordering of constituents in a structure. The structure produced is organized in a 'flat' manner that reflects a direct mapping of meaning onto syntactic form.

(2) The Initialization-Finalization Strategy (IFS)

This strategy allows only the movement of an initial or final position of a sentence.

(3) The Subordinate Clause Strategy (SCS)

This strategy avoids permutations in subordinate clauses, but allows the movement to occur in a main clause.

At Stage 1, learners are only able to produce the canonical word order 'subject-verb-object' and their sentence processing is constrained by the strategies COS and SCS. Stage 2 allows the movement of elements from one salient position in a string to another salient position, such as initial or final position. However, learners are still constrained by the COS strategy, and are only capable of producing structures such as 'adverb preposing'. At Stage 3, strategies IFS and SCS are still maintained, but the COS strategy is abandoned. The canonical word order 'subject-verb-object' is disrupted. Learners are able to move the elements within a string to a salient position (such as initial or final position). For instance, learners can move non-finite verbal elements to clause-final position and produce the structure called 'verb separation'. At Stage 4, strategies COS and IFS are abandoned, but the SCS strategy is still adhered to. The learners are capable of reordering the canonical word order, and moving an internal element to another internal position. They can produce structures such as 'inversion'. At Stage 5, all the strategies are abandoned. The learners are able to move elements out of subordinate clauses to other positions, and to produce structures such as 'verb final'.

Clahsen's speech processing strategies were postulated to be universal and cross-linguistically falsifiable (Larsen-Freeman & Long, 1991). They can not only be applied to a larger range of German word order rules, but also to other second languages (e. g., Ellis, 1989; Jansen, 1991; Pienemann, 1984, 1998; Pienemann & Johnston, 1987; Yoshioka & Doi,

1988). The speech processing strategies were considered a contribution to SLA research on developmental sequences. Compared to the previous studies that merely described the sequence in L2 development, Clahsen's strategies provided an explanation of the observed sequence. However, two main limitations were identified in Pienemann (1998, pp. 49-53). One limitation was that since Clahsen's strategies applied the concepts of Transformational Grammar, which had no psychological plausibility to explain the acquisition of word order rules, these strategies could not be used to account for L2 acquisition from the perspective of language processing. The other limitation was that the descriptions for each of the stages did not include a set of explicit grammatical rules for the specification of linguistic forms. The strategies approach might not be valid when used to account for language-specific rules that were beyond the range of strategy description.

4.2 Processability Theory: Theoretical bases and tenets

Processability Theory (PT) (Pienemann, 1998, 2005) describes, explains and predicts the universal developmental sequence inherent in L2 acquisition from the perspective of language processing. The underlying logic of PT is that L2 learners at any level of development are able to produce only those grammatical structures which the current state of their language processor can process (Pienemann, 1998, pp. 4-5). The developmental sequence of L2 acquisition is determined by the order in which the necessary processing procedures are available to L2 learners.

4.2.1 Theoretical bases

PT perceives the learner's language acquisition as the acquisition of the procedural skills required for the processing of the formal properties of languages. PT relies on a number of L1 speech production models (e. g., Levelt, 1989; Kempen & Hoenkamp, 1987) to account for language processing, and Lexical-Functional Grammar (LFG) (Bresnan, 2001; Kaplan & Bresnan, 1982) to describe the target grammar in a formal manner.

Levelt's (1989) Model on speech production presents how the language is processed from intention to articulation in L1 speakers. The whole process of speech production proceeds in three levels: conceptualizing, formulating, and articulating (cf. Kempen & Hoenkamp, 1987). The first level is conceptualizing. The speaker goes from some sort of communicative intention to decide what kind of message to convey, namely, the preparation of lexical concepts. The second level is formulating, where linguistic structures and grammatical encoding occur. At this level, the speaker needs to convert the message into a linguistic form. Since the message contains one or multiple lexical concepts, the speaker must select the appropriate word, more specifically, a lemma (i. e., a specific meaning without sounds) from his or her mental lexicon based on the lexical concept to be expressed. Because the selection of a lemma makes available to access its syntactic information, thus the speaker can organize the words in the right order and add relevant grammatical elements (e. g. , tense or function). The third level is articulating, where the speaker must plan the syllabication and prosody of the words according to their morphological and phonological properties to deliver the message. This process is called 'phonological encoding'. After that, the speaker can make the articulatory gestures for the syllables, words and phrases in the utterance.

According to Kempen and Hoenkamp (1987), in order to achieve the high fluency of language production in real time, those three levels of information processing underlying speech production (conceptualizing, formulating, articulating) must run in parallel and are temporally aligned. In another word, the level of conceptualizing conveys the message to the level of formulating, irrespective of whether the lexical concepts have been completely prepared; once received the preverbal message, the level of formulating operates the process of grammatical encoding to convert the lexical concepts into linguistic form and then passes on the output to the level of articulating. While the process of formulating is still ongoing, the level of conceptualizing continues to generate another new fragment of concepts. As Levelt (1989) claimed, "…the next processor can start working on the incomplete output of the current processor…" (p. 24). Therefore, the process of sentence production is *incremental* and *piecemeal*, and its usefulness is closely associated with the efficiency of the processing capacities of working memory and other mechanisms contained in the levels of formulating and articulating (Kempen & Hoenkamp, 1987).

PT incorporates the level of formulating, where grammatical encoding takes place, to its theoretical framework to formulate the L2 processing procedures. A set of human psychological constraints such as the need for a very fast word retrieval and the limited capacity of human memory are imposed on the process of grammatical encoding. The incremental process of sentence construction calls for the use of storage facilities to deal with the non-linearity in the mapping of conceptual materials onto surface form (Pienemann, 1998). This is called the speaker's 'linearization problems' (Levelt, 1981, 1982, as cited in Levelt, 1983). One example of the non-linearity is found in the relationship between the natural order of events and the sequence of clauses (Levelt, 1983). For example, in the case of *He cleaned the kitchen after he finished lunch*, the event depicted in the second clause *he finished lunch* occurs before the event in the first clause *he cleaned the kitchen*. To deliver such a sentence, the speaker must deposit the propositional content in memory temporarily until the second event *he cleaned the kitchen* is produced. The other example involves the storage of grammatical information, which is of interest here. For instance, in English subject-verb agreement such as *He gets up at* 6 *o'clock*, the grammatical information in the subject *He* (person=3rd person; number=singular) must be temporarily stored in memory until the verb is selected and available to realize the information (person=3rd person; number=singular; tense=present); after that, the 3rd person singular morpheme -*s* is inserted.

According to Pienemann (1998, p. 60), since the capacity of human working memory is highly limited, thus it is not suitable to process great amounts of grammatical information at high speed. Therefore, grammatical information has to be deposited in grammatical memory store, which is highly task-specific and in which specialized grammatical processors can store information of a particular nature (Levelt, 1989; cf. Pienemann, 1998). Moreover, the grammatical memory buffer contains a series of specialized procedures which can process noun phrases, verb phrases, and so on (Kempen & Hoenkamp, 1987).

This set of psychological constraints operates in L2 acquisition as well. Based on the exchange and storage of grammatical information at different morpho-syntactic levels, these processing procedures are incrementally developed from psycholinguistically simpler ones to more complex ones (Pienemann, 1998). Therefore, this array of constraints constitutes a framework for the universal hierarchy of L2 processing procedures that underlies PT (see Section 4. 2. 3 for details).

To describe the interlanguage of learners in a formal way, PT relies on the Lexical-Functional Grammar (LFG). LFG was originally developed by Kaplan and Bresnan (1982) and further extended by Bresnan (2001). It is a lexically-driven and psychologically and typologically plausible theory of grammar, and it contributes to depicting and explaining the grammatical structures constrained by the processing procedures. PT incorporates two characteristics of LFG—feature unification (also termed as 'information exchange' in PT) and the correspondences between three parallel levels of structure (argument, functional and constituent structures), both of which account for a variety of morpho-syntactic structures related to different levels in the hierarchy of processing procedures.

The original version of PT (Pienemann, 1998) focuses on the transfer of grammatical information which is modelled using feature unification within word order (constituent structure). It is hypothesized that when the learner produces the linguistic structure, the corresponding grammatical information has to be held in memory. In order to produce grammatically acceptable structure, the values (such as '3rd' and 'singular') of the features (such as 'person' and 'number') need to be unified. Take the noun phrase 'a cat' for example. The lexical entries 'a' and 'cat' both have the feature 'number'. This feature has the value 'singular' in both cases. In order to produce the noun phrase that is grammatically correct, these two features must be unified. The syntactic level of information exchange such as from phrasal level to inter-phrasal level determines the processing complexity of structures particularly within the domain of morphology.

Based on the revised version of LFG (Bresnan, 2001), Pienemann, Di Biase, and Kawaguchi (2005) extends the PT framework through incorporating two elements: discourse functions (e. g. , TOP and FOC) which are represented in functional structure (f-structure), and the Lexical Mapping Theory which demonstrates the development of the process of mapping argument structure (a-structure) onto f-structure. While the original version of PT (Pienemann, 1998) relies on feature unification within constituent structure (c-structure) to capture one source of linguistic non-linearity, the incorporation of the two LFG elements above enables PT to portray the other two sources of linguistic non-linearity at the syntactic level, namely, the mappings of c-structure onto f-structure and a-structure onto f-structure. Also, these two non-linear mappings require processing resources, which can be included in the processability hierarchy (Pienemann et al. , 2005). Due to the limited scope of the present study, LFG and the mapping principles are not described in detail here.

Motivated by the correspondences among the LFG levels of structure, the extended version of PT (Pienemann et al. , 2005) expands its exposition of L2 syntactic development. Take L2 English development for example. At the beginning, L2 learners are unable to distinguish between the subject (SUBJ) and the topic (TOP). They can only produce utterances based on one-to-one correspondences between c-structure and f-structure—the canonical word order. At the following stage, L2 learners are aware that the initial position is not necessarily occupied by a subject, and that non-arguments such as the adjunct can also occur at the initial position to express prominent information. Learners can therefore produce syntactic structures that start with a WH-word but have the rest of the words in a canonical order. For L2 learners, this WH-word is only regarded as an additional XP in the beginning of a sentence. At the final stage, L2 learners can fully distinguish between the subject and the topic, and assign the arguments to the initial position of a sentence. This may result in subject-auxiliary inversion in the following word order (Dalrymple, 2001, p. 64, as cited in Pienemann et al. , 2005, p. 237).

To sum up, the interface between these two theoretical bases—Levelt's speech production model and LFG—strongly support PT's ability to make language-specific predictions about L2 grammatical development that can be tested empirically in typologically diverse languages. The hypotheses proposed by PT are psychologically and grammatically plausible.

4.2.2 The tenets of PT

Based on the two theoretical bases, PT describes, explains and predicts a universal developmental trajectory of L2 acquisition of morphology and syntax for typologically different L2s. This is achieved by focusing on the incremental development of the processing procedures required for the production of L2 grammatical structures. The tenets of PT are mainly discussed in Pienemann (1998), Pienemann, Di Biase, and Kawaguchi (2005), and Bettoni and Di Biase (2015). They are summarized below.

The first key concept of PT is the exchange of grammatical information. Grammatical information refers to diacritic features (such as person, number, or gender) and their values (such as third person, singular, or masculine) encoded in the lexicon. Acquiring a L2 is considered as the acquisition of L2 processing skills involving the activation of information exchange procedures. These skills are the same as those that mature L1 speakers develop when acquiring their native language. According to PT (Pienemann, 1998, p. 7), L2 processing skills are developed in a sequence that accords with the order of activation of processing resources in mature L1 speakers.

The sequenced activation of these processing procedures allows for the production of language structures (Bettoni & Di Biase, 2015, p. 52). Language structures that do not require any exchange of information among constituents are produced at the beginning, followed by those structures that ask for information exchange at the phrasal level. Structures that require exchange of information at the sentence and higher levels will not be produced until the end.

The second key notion of PT is implicational hierarchy. According to Pienemann (1998), the sequence of activation of L2 processing procedures is implicational in nature. A processing procedure can be activated and the corresponding structure can be produced only if all the previous processing skills have been developed (Bettoni & Di Biase, 2015). For example, if a L2 learner is able to apply processing procedure X, he or she will be able to produce grammatical structure (morphological or syntactic feature) Y through using procedure X. Next, if the learner can use processing procedure X+1 to produce structure Y+1, he or she has already been capable of using the preceding procedure X and producing the corresponding structure Y (cf. Bettoni & Di Biase, 2015). Accordingly, the process of acquiring L2 processing procedures and grammatical structures is accumulative.

The third key concept is that L2 acquisition is perceived as a sequentially gradual development from one stage to another (Pienemann, 1998). The sequenced activation of the processing procedures determines that L2 learners have to go through sequential progression, i. e. through a series of stages. PT accounts for the sequential progression of L2 morphology and syntax in interlanguage development. L2 morphological progression is actualized through feature unification, and measured by the different syntactic levels (such as phrase or sentence) at which exchange of grammatical information is required to achieve unification of diacritic features (Pienemann, 1998). L2 syntactic progression is operationalized on the basis of word order in c-structure the correspondences of a- (argument), f- (functional) and c- (constituent) structures (Pienemann et al., 2005). According to Lexical-Functional Grammar, these three levels of syntactic structure are motivated independently but mapped onto one another. Accordingly, Processability Theory measures L2 syntactic progression based on the mapping of c-structure onto f-structure and a-structure onto f-structure (Pienemann et al., 2005).

The fourth key notion is processing cost (Bettoni & Di Biase, 2015). During the sequential progression inherent in L2 acquisition, different stages indicate different levels of exchange of grammatical information. The exchange of grammatical information is cognitively costly, as the grammatical information contained in one constituent needs to be stored in our short-term memory until it can be checked against its correspondent constituents (Pienemann, 1998). However, our short-term memory is limited in its capability. The more grammatical information is required to be exchanged, the longer it needs to occupy space in short-term memory. Consequently, L2 learners need to pay more conscious attention, and a greater processing cost is involved. This set of psycholinguistic constraints determines that grammatical structures requiring greater processing cost are more difficult in L2 learning, and they will develop later in the interlanguage than those requiring less processing cost.

4.2.3 Hierarchy of L2 processing procedures

As discussed above in Section 4. 2. 1, a set of psychological constraints constitutes a framework for the universal hierarchy of L2 processing procedures that underlies PT. Following Levelt's (1989) Model of L1 speech production, Pienemann (1998, pp. 83-86) postulates a sequence of activation of L2 processing procedures.

Stage 1: Lemma access. At the very first beginning of L2 development, there is no any language-specific processing procedures involved. The learners have no syntactic information about the L2 lexical item. They are only able to map the underlying meaning onto single words (e. g. , *apple*) and formulaic structures (e. g. , *How are you?*). No grammatical information needs to be exchanged between constituents.

Stage 2: Category procedure. The category procedure enables the lexical items to be assigned a grammatical category such as nouns or verbs, and lexical morphemes can be produced without exchange of grammatical information. In the case of English, the simple past tense marker *-ed* (e. g. , *I cooked fish*) and the generic plural marker *-s* (e. g. , *They are monkeys*), are lexical morphemes. Take the simple past tense marker *-ed* for example. This verbal morpheme does not necessitate the temporal storage of grammatical information, since the verb lemma contains the features of the verb (e. g. , tense). Therefore, the insertion of *-ed* on verb can be achieved directly from conceptualization. Meanwhile, the learners cannot exchange grammatical information, and thus they are only able to map semantic roles (e. g. , agent, action, patient) onto surface forms directly and may produce strictly canonical word order such as SVO in English (e. g. , *They love food*).

Stage 3: Phrasal procedures. The phrasal procedures are developed, which enable the exchange of grammatical information within a phrase (e. g. , noun phrase or verbal phrase), namely, between the head and its modifiers. No grammatical information needs to be exchanged beyond the boundaries of phrases. Grammatical morphemes such as phrasal morphemes can be produced at this stage. For example, in the English phrase *three apples*, the storage is required for the grammatical information of the head noun (number = plural) until the phrasal morpheme—plural *-s*—is inserted on the noun (*apple*). In addition, within the domain of syntax, the strictly canonical word order is still maintained but the phrasal procedures make it available to add adjuncts (e. g. , time) to the initial and the final positions in a sentence, such as the English sentence *Today I have a class*. In this case, the adjunct *today* fills the sentence-initial positon while the rest part keeps in a canonical word order SVO.

Stage 4: Sentence procedure (S-procedure). At this stage, the S-procedure is activated. This allows grammatical information to be exchanged across phrasal boundaries within a sentence. Interphrasal morphemes can be produced. Take the subject-verb agreement in English for example. In *She plays football*, the grammatical information contained in the subject *she* (person=3rd person, number=singular) must be exchanged with that of the verb *plays* (number =singular, person = 3rd person, tense = present) to make sure that the 3rd person singular morpheme *-s* is inserted after the verb. In terms of syntax, the S-procedure allows for the assignment of grammatical functions (e. g. , the subject of a sentence) on individual phrases in a sentence, which enables the learners to produce language-specific word orders.

Stage 5: Subordinate clause procedure (S'-procedure). At the final stage, the subordinate clause procedure is activated. This allows for the occurrence of complex sentence structure such as subordinate clauses and embedded clauses. Interclausal information needs to be exchanged between the main clause and the dependent one. In some languages, some rules initially developed for the main clause need to be abandoned to produce a subordinate clause, such as the subject-verb inversion in English questions (Pienemann, 1998, p. 86).

As shown above, these processing procedures form a hierarchy, which is characterized by the exchange of grammatical information at different syntactic levels and the requirement for storage of information. This hierarchy follows an implicational pattern, in which the processing resources of each lower stage is a prerequisite for the functioning of the higher stage. The implicational hierarchy of L2 development as hypothesized in Processability Theory has been extensively supported by empirical studies against typologically diverse languages, such as English (Dyson, 2010; Di Biase, Kawaguchi, & Yamaguchi, 2015; Lenzing, 2013; Pienemann, 1998; Yamaguchi, 2008, 2009), Chinese (Zhang, 2001, 2005), German (Jansen, 2008; Pienemann, 1998), Japanese (Kawaguchi, 2005a, 2005b), Italian (Di Biase 2007; Di Biase, Bettoni, & Nuzzo, 2009), Arabic (Mansouri, 2005), Swedish (Hakansson & Norrby, 2010), and Turkish (Ozdemir, 2004).

4.3 The development of English as a second language

Within the universal hierarchy of L2 processing procedures stipulated in PT, the staged development of L2 English morpho-syntax can be accounted for from a processability perspective.

4.3.1 Morphological development

This subsection presents the universal hypothesis for morphological development applied to L2 English, with grammatical morphemes distributed implicationally and hierarchically, based on the exchange of grammatical information at phrasal and interphrasal levels. Processability Theory (Pienemann, 1998; Pienemann et al. , 2005) predicts five stages in ESL morphological development. Table 4. 2 gives an overview of how a range of English grammatical morphemes can be accounted for in the hypothesized processability hierarchy.

Table 4.2 Processability hierarchy: morphological development for L2 English (based on Pienemann, 1998; Pienemann et al., 2005)

Stage	Processing procedure	Morphology		Example
5	S-procedure	SV agreement (=3sg −*s*)		She plays football on Monday.
4	VP-procedure	tense agreement	be + V-ing	She is watching TV.
			have + V-*ed*	I have ordered a new book.
3	NP-procedure	NP agreement		I have ten bananas.
2	category procedure	plural -*s* (on nouns)		They're monkeys.
		possessive pronoun		It is your kite.
		simple past -*ed*		I cooked fish.
1	word/lemma	single words/formulas		Many thanks!

At the first stage, L2 lexical items are stored without any grammatical information, and no processing procedure is involved. L2 learners are only able to produce morphologically invariant forms (chunks or non-analysed material) such as single words (e.g., *here*) or formulaic expressions (e.g., *many thanks*).

At the second stage—the category procedure, L2 learners are able to identify the categories of lexical items such as ouns or verbs, but are unable to exchange grammatical information between each lexical item in the phrase or sentence structure. For L2 English, no less than three lexical morphemes are hypothesized to emerge at this stage. 'Plural -*s* on nouns' describes the lexical nominal plural marking -*s* on nouns. 'Simple past -*ed*' refers to the regular past tense marker -*ed*. 'Possessive pronoun' refers to possessive determiner for adjectives. 'Plural -*s* on nouns' requires identification of the noun category of lexical items, while 'simple past -*ed*' requires identification of the verb category. Take the acquisition of 'plural -*s* on nouns' for example. L2 learners need to determine whether the referent is one entity or more (*monkey* vs. *monkeys*) and then differentiate whether the referent is countable or not from the perspective of semantics (*monkeys* or *water*). Next, L2 learners need to learn that this -*s* ending marker is associated with generic countable entities, as in *They are monkeys*, but not with generic uncountable entities.

At the third stage, once the noun-phrasal procedure has been developed for the L2, diacritic features can be stored, exchanged and unified between the head of a noun phrase (NP) and its modifier. Grammatical information is therefore required to be exchanged within the NP to ensure that the diacritic features of words in the phrase are unified. PT hypothesizes the phrasal plural marking -s (to achieve 'NP agreement') to emerge at this stage. Take *ten bananas* for example. The plural feature appears in the head noun (the plural referent *bananas*) and its modifier (the numerical quantifier *ten*), and thus this information needs to be unified between two lexical items in this NP.

The fourth stage is the verb-phrasal procedure stage, which requires interphrasal agreement—exchanging grammatical information within a verb phrase (VP). The structure hypothesized to emerge at this stage of the interlanguage of L2 learners is the VP composed of the auxiliaries (AUX) and lexical verbs. To produce this structure, L2 learners need to learn to choose the AUX according to a range of temporal, aspectual or modal motivations (*be*, *have*, *modal*), and then unify these features with the corresponding ones in the lexical verbs (*V-ing*, *V-en*, *V*).

The next stage is the S-procedure stage. The activation of the S-procedure requires interphrasal agreement across different phrases—the subject (SUBJ) and the lexical verb (V)—within a sentence. As Processability Theory postulates, L2 English learners can produce the morphological structure known as the 3rd person singular marking -s in the simple present context, once they are capable of unifying the SUBJ feature information in the NP_{SUBJ} (PERSON $= 3^{rd}$; NUMBER = SINGULAR) with the associated V feature information (TENSE = PRESENT; SUBJ PERSON $= 3^{rd}$; SUBJ NUMBER = SINGULAR). The example of 3rd person singular marking -s is shown in Figure 4.1:

$[\text{She}]_{SUBJ}$ $[\text{plays}]_{V}$ football

PERSON=3
NUM=SINGULAR

TENSE=PRESENT
PERSON=3

Figure 4.1 Feature unification in 'she plays football'

4.3.2 Syntactic development

According to PT (Pienemann, 1998; Pienemann et al., 2005), six stages in the developmental process of syntax are predicted. Table 4.3 shows how a range of English syntactic structures are accounted for at each stage in the processability hierarchy.

Table 4.3 Processability hierarchy: syntactic development for L2 English (based on Pienemann, 1998; Pienemann et al., 2005)

Stage	Processing procedure	Syntax	Example
6	S'-procedure	Cancel inversion	They ask where you are.
5	S-procedure	Do-2nd	What do you do on Sundays?
		Aux-2nd	Why are you laughing?
4	VP-procedure	Yes/No inversion	Can you speak English?
		Copula inversion	Are you here?
3	NP-procedure	ADV-fronting	Later she could read.
		Do-fronting	Do you like meat?
2	category procedure	Canonical word order SV(O)	I like football.
1	word/lemma	single words/formulas	How are you?

At the first stage, L2 learners have not developed any language-specific procedures, and thus are unable to access any syntactic information. They can only produce single constituents that only require the activation of lemma access, such as *How are you*? or *No*.

At the second stage, L2 learners can activate the category procedure, and start to distinguish between verbal elements and nominal elements. Learners are able to organize their utterances based on the canonical order found in the input from the target language—English. For English syntax, the canonical word order is the subject-verb-object (SVO) structure. At this stage, L2 learners of English can map conceptual structures onto linguistic form (Pienemann et al., 2005, p. 26). Thus, canonical word order SVO is hypothesized to emerge at this stage of L2 syntactic development, as exemplified in 'I like football'.

Next, L2 learners can enter the third stage—the NP-procedure. At this stage, learners are able to place non-arguments (e. g., adjuncts) at the initial position of a canonical word sentence. The syntactic phenomenon known as 'ADV-fronting' is hypothesized to emerge by allowing adjuncts such as time or place circumstantial adverbials to appear in the initial position, as exemplified in *Later she could read*. L2 learners can also produce structures such as *Do you like meat*? by placing the auxiliary *do* in the initial position of the canonical order SVO (*you like meat*). This syntactic phenomenon is called 'Do-fronting'. However, the production of this structure does not indicate that learners have developed the knowledge of the lexical features of the auxiliary *do* or the verb (e. g., PERSON, TENSE, NUMBER) and can achieve the agreement of these features. For example, at this stage, learners are unable to produce interrogative sentences such as *Does she have lunch*?. This is because learners merely consider this *do* as an additional XP element in the first position of the canonical sequence.

At the fourth stage, L2 learners can activate the VP-procedure. They can produce syntactic phenomena such as 'Yes/No inversion' and 'Copula inversion' in non-canonical sequences, by assigning focal function to the auxiliary or copula verb to mark the whole sentence as a question. This results in the inversion between the subject and the auxiliary (or copula), as shown in the examples *Can you speak English*? and *Are you here*?.

At the fifth stage, L2 learners can activate the S-procedure and fully differentiate the topic from the subject. They are assumed to be able to implement the procedure of inversion, namely, placing the auxiliary or copula before the subject. After learning to assign a focal element (e. g., a WH-word) to the first position of a sentence, learners are hypothesized to become able to produce syntactic structures such as 'Do-2nd' and 'AUX-2nd', as exemplified in *What do you do on Sundays*? and *Why are you laughing*?. In the meantime, learners are also able to exchange the interphrasal information for agreement (see Stage 5 of L2 morphological development in Table 4.2). They can unify features (e. g., PERSON, NUMBER, TENSE) across constituent boundaries. Therefore, learners are hypothesized to become able to produce questions such as *What does she do*? or *What did she do*? by using the morphological form of *do* (e. g., *does*, *did*).

Once L2 learners have developed all the previous processing resources, they are able to get to the sixth stage. At the final stage, the learners activate the subordinate clause procedure (S'-procedure) to exchange information between the main clause and the dependent one. In the case of English syntax, such as the indirect question *They ask where you are*, the learners need to identify the main clause '*They ask*…' and the subclause '*where you are*' in order to abandon the rule—the subject-verb inversion in English questions (e. g., *where are you*?)—in the subclause. This syntactic phenomenon is called 'cancel inversion' in the processability hierarchy of L2 syntactic development.

4.3.3 Empirical support for the hypothesized ESL development

Since 1998, many empirical studies on SLA have been conducted within the theoretical framework of Processability Theory (PT) to investigate the process of ESL morpho-syntax (e. g., Dao, 2007; Dyson, 2004, 2008, 2010; Di Biase, Kawaguchi, & Yamaguchi, 2015[①]; Lenzing, 2013; Pienemann, 1998; Sakai, 2008; Yamaguchi, 2008, 2009[②], 2010; Zhang & Widyastuti, 2010). The plausibility of PT's hypotheses for L2 English morphology and syntax has been generally borne out in the majority of established studies with both cross-sectional and longitudinal data. In order to justify the application of PT-based processability hierarchy for ESL development to the following evaluation of primary-school textbooks, this subsection selectively reviews the empirical studies on PT's predictions for L2 English, focusing on three recent studies of ESL children or adolescents.

Yamaguchi (2010) reported a two-year longitudinal study of a L1 Japanese child at a primary-school level who learned English in Australia. This study aimed to investigate the acquisitional sequence of ESL morphology and syntax by a Japanese child within the framework of PT (Pienemann, 1998; Pienemann et al., 2005). The informant was a Japanese child named Kumi who had been learning English in a naturalistic setting since her first arrival in Australia at age 5. Kumi had extremely limited English competence, and thus she was assumed to be at Stage 1 in her interlanguage at the onset of the investigation. In addition to *semi-structured* interviews, a range of communicative tasks were used to elicit the informant's spontaneous oral production, including story-telling tasks, riddles, and 'spot-the-difference' tasks. The informant's production was audio-recorded regularly: Kumi was first recorded four weeks after her arrival; and the data collection sessions ran fortnightly for the initial two months, then every two months for the rest of the first year, and every three months in the second year (Yamaguchi, 2010, p.

① Di Biase, Kawaguchi, & Yamaguchi (2015) is based on Yamaguchi's (2010) empirical study of a Japanese primary-school child of L2 English.

② Yamaguchi's (2008, 2009) small-scale studies are incorporated into Yamaguchi's (2010) later PhD thesis. Therefore, Yamaguchi (2010) is reviewed here to understand her longitudinal study on the child's ESL acquisitional route.

90). The data analysis focused on the emergence of a range of grammatical structures included in PT-based processability hierarchy.

The results showed that although lexical morphemes (Stage 2) and noun phrasal morphology (Stage 3) were found to be acquired simultaneously, the subsequent morphological features were found to be acquired in an order that followed the staged L2 development as stipulated in PT (Yamaguchi, 2010, p. 193). With respect to the analysis of ESL syntax, the results revealed that the developmental stages for English word order rules found in the informant's ESL acquisition were generally consistent with the stages as hypothesized in PT, except that English declarative and interrogatives were found to be develop in rather independent manners (Yamaguchi, 2010, p. 190). Yamaguchi's (2010) empirical study generally supported for PT's hypothesized morpho-syntactic development in ESL acquisition. However, due to the limited data belonging to one single child learner, the study did not provide sufficient evidence for some syntactic features such as interrogatives and topicalization as well as the morphological structures hypothesized at the highest stage.

Another empirical support can be found in Dyson (2010) which reported on the longitudinal development of two adolescent ESL learners over a year. This study aimed to offer a comprehensive account of 'onset' of English grammar, namely, the first systematic use of a structure in the learners' interlanguage (Dyson, 2010, p. 30. 1). By applying the emergence analysis, Dyson (2010) investigated whether and when the grammatical structures in PT's hypothesized hierarchy have emerged in the learners' interlanguage, namely, when the learners have—in principle—grasped the use of the structures. Part of Dyson's (2010) research questions was to examine whether emergence analysis supported the ESL predictions as hypothesized in PT. The informants were two adolescent ESL learners, Amir (aged 11) and Samia (aged 12), who spoke Bosnian as L1 and German as L2. They had minimal English competence since they moved to Australia. Their oral production was elicited through communicative tasks such as story guessing, picture differences and interview on six different occasions (six samples), and audio-recorded for one hour each time.

Dyson's (2010) results showed that 1) Amir was processing at the interphrasal stage in the first sample, maintained this stage in the three following samples and then got into interclausal processing in the last two samples; and 2) Samia started at the phrasal stage and then progressed into the syntax and part of the morphology of stage 4. The findings confirmed that the emergence analysis did support for the ESL hypotheses as predicted in PT. The majority of the structures included in the PT's processability hierarchy were found to 'emerge' in the learners' interlanguage. Overall, the informants progressed in their ESL development in accordance with PT's predictions for morphology and syntax. The only exceptional finding was that there was no direct evidence of category procedure stage and verb-phrasal procedure stage and their patterns of emergence at the later stages (Dyson, 2010, p. 30. 18).

Lenzing (2013) examined the interlanguage grammatical development of early ESL learners in the primary-school setting with the provision of both cross-sectional and longitudinal data over two years. The informants were 24 German pupils including 13 boys and 11 girls from four primary schools in Germany. They had received the first year of formal instruction in English at the end of Grade 3 when the investigation began, namely, the informants were aged 8-10 years. Six different communicative tasks were utilized to elicit the production of specific morphological and syntactic structures in the informants' spontaneous oral speech, including two role-play games, a guessing-picture task, two 'spot-the-differences' tasks, and a picture-description task. All the informants were interviewed twice: the first data collection session occurred at the end of Grade 3 and then the second one happened at the end of Grade 4 (Lenzing, 2013, p. 149). Similar to the abovementioned studies Yamaguchi (2010) and Dyson (2010), Lenzing (2013) applied the emergence criterion to define the emergence of a specific structure in the learner's interlanguage, namely, when the structure has—in principle—been acquired by the learner.

The analysis showed that except for two learners almost all the informants progressed in their L2 development after two years of formal instruction in English (the end of Grade 4). At the onset of the first data collection session (the end of Grade 3), 20 of the 22 informants were at Stage 1 of the PT's hypothesized L2 acquisition process; the other two learners C04 and C11 were at Stage 2 (Lenzing, 2013, p. 208). When the second data collection session occurred, all other learners had reached Stage 2 or Stage 3 with the only exception of C17 who had remained at Stage 1 even after two years of formal instruction (Lenzing, 2013, p. 208). A comparison of the stages of L2 acquisition between the two data collection sessions revealed an overall implicational progression in the interlanguage development of the informants. No evidence showed that the 'stage-skipping' occurred during the acquisition process of those learners. Based on these findings, Lenzing (2013) concluded that 1) the interlanguage development of early ESL learners was highly implicational; and 2) all learners followed the identical sequence of ESL acquisition as predicted in PT (p. 252). The findings of Lenzing (2013) provide further evidence to secure the validity of PT's hypothesized ESL development within the context of children's acquisition.

To sum up, previous PT-based empirical studies have conducted observations on ESL development of children to test the L2 English predictions (e. g., Yamaguchi, 2010; Dyson, 2004, 2010; Lenzing, 2013). Overall, these studies have shown that children of different L1s (e. g., Japanese, Bosnian, German) progressed in their ESL development in line with the developmental sequence of ESL acquisition as hypothesized in PT. Although a few structures in the children's interlanguage remain questions, it could be argued that further research is needed due to the limited scope of previous studies (e. g., the number of informants). In general, PT's predictions on ESL development are tenable within the fields of children's L2 acquisition (e. g., Dyson, 2004, 2010; Ke? ler, 2006; Pienemann, Ke? ler, & Roos, 2006; Roos, 2007; Yamaguchi, 2008, 2009, 2010; Lenzing, 2013) and adult learners' L2 acquisition (e. g., Mansouri & Duffy, 2005; Sakai, 2008; Zhang & Widyastuti, 2010). The processability hierarchy for ESL development can serve as a reference for the cross-check of grammatical sequencing in primary-school English textbooks in the following textbook analysis.

4.4 Summary

This chapter has reviewed a range of SLA studies on the developmental sequences of L2 acquisition, focusing on a psycholinguistically based theory—PT (Pienemann, 1998, 2005). The research review has provided a general understanding of how L2 learners develop L2 grammar along a universal route through a cumulative and implicational process. In this context, PT was developed as an endeavour to account for how a learner's ability to process new linguistic rules develops. Based on language production models and LFG, PT describes, explain and predicts the development of morphological and syntactic structures for typologically diverse L2s. PT conceives L2 acquisition as a cumulative and sequential developmental process that involves the activation of information exchange procedures. The activation of implicationally ordered processing procedures drives L2 grammar learning through a hierarchy of acquisition stages. The stages of acquisition provide specific information on what L2 learners are able and unable to learn at different points in time.

PT and its hypotheses have been extensively supported by empirical studies on typologically different languages. The theory has the potential to contribute to pedagogical issues such as how L2 teaching should be organized to best fit the actual capacities and needs of L2 learners. In particular, the processability hierarchy of L2 English grammar proposed in PT provides an understanding of how an English learner develops L2 grammar from basic levels to intermediate and high levels. This understanding enables us to focus on the learner's level of ability and to optimize English teaching including textbook and syllabus design. To examine whether the sequence of grammatical structures introduced in English textbooks follows the hypothesized developmental sequence of L2 English acquisition, the following chapter will present a SLA-based textbook analysis of four English textbook series that are currently used in primary schools in China.

Chapter 5

Textbook Analysis: Methodology and Results

The present study aims to report on an acquisition-based evaluation of four English textbook series that are currently used in many primary schools in China. To achieve this objective, a textbook analysis is carried out to investigate the grading of grammatical items introduced in these textbook series. The investigation can provide an understanding of whether staged L2 development has been considered in the sequencing of grammar in current EFL textbooks in China.

The chapter starts with the research method including each of the following procedural steps: 1) identification and categorization of the grammatical structures in each lesson; 2) differentiation of variant and invariant forms; and 3) comparison between the sequencing of grammatical structures in the textbooks and their sequencing in the PT-based processability hierarchy. It is followed by a description of the four textbook series, including a presentation of their publishers and contents. The results of the analysis are presented last. The findings will serve as a basis for the discussion, in the following chapter, of current trends in English textbook design in China and enable us to come up with informed suggestions for the sequencing of grammar in EFL textbooks.

5.1 Method of textbook analysis

The textbook analysis is carried out in three steps①. The first step is to document the focal grammatical items that are introduced as the teaching objectives in the textbooks. As indicated in Section 5.2, overviews of the focal grammar are provided at the start of each textbook or at the start of individual units in a volume.

The second step is to analyse and define the specific grammatical structures contained in the listed focal items, using grammatical terminology (such as *morpheme*) and grammatical patterns (such as word order rules). As shown in Section 5.2, except for *New Standard English*, none

① Zhang (2005) used partially similar methods in her empirical study of L2 Chinese acquisition, namely, documenting the focal grammar from the textbooks and conducting grammatical description.

of the textbook series present the focal grammar in an explicit way. The majority of the focal items listed in *PEP English*, *Super Kids*, and *Join in* are exemplars of grammatical structures; there is no metalinguistic statement of the rules that are being taught. Thus, an explicit grammatical description is needed to provide a clear understanding of what specific grammatical structures are contained in the listed items. Two issues need to be taken into consideration.

The first issue is to differentiate formulaic structures from non-formulaic structures. The criterion used to make the distinction is to check whether the grammatical structure appears in different texts with or without variation. If the structure is provided without variation, it is considered to be an invariant form. Take *How are you?* as an example. This structure is listed as a teaching objective in Unit 3 of *PEP English*, Book 1 (see Table 5. 2). Since this structure appears in the texts and exercises without any variation, it is marked as a formulaic structure.

The second issue is to consider how to identify semi-formulaic expressions. Compared to fully formulaic expressions, semi-formulaic expressions show limited variation of internal constituents. According to Krashen and Scarcella (1978) and Towell (1987), expressions that are partly variable and partly fixed are regarded as semi-formulae. The criterion adopted to differentiate semi-formulae from non-formulaic structures in the current textbook analysis is to check whether the structure shows a high degree of formal invariance and is presented in highly limited contexts. For example, in *New Standard English*, Book 2, the sentence '*I have got a book*' is specified as the teaching objective. It seems that it is the structure 'have + got' that is expected to be produced by students. However, in the textbook, *have got* is presented in sentence frames with open slots, such as 'I have got ______ (a book / a sweater / a bike / a dress)'. The main constituents in these sentences are fixed, and only the NP_{obj} is variable. Thus, such a structure is considered to be a semi-formulaic expression.

It should be noted that although the present study applies Processability Theory (PT) as the theoretical approach to the textbook evaluation, the PT methodology 'emergence criterion' is not used here to determine what specific structures occur in the textbooks. As this study is not a SLA research, it is inappropriate to employ the acquisition research method 'emergence criterion'. According to Larsen-Freeman and Long (1991, p. 282), acquisition studies refer to measuring how far L2 learners were from the end of acquisition process (to achieve the target grammar) or investigating them as they crossed the finishing line. SLA research studies on the learner's interlanguage, which is a dynamic process of language development with variations. In line with this, the emergence criterion is designed to locate the onset of a linguistic structure in the learner's interlanguage grammar, namely, the first systematic and productive use of a structure by the learner (cf. Meisel et al., 1981; Pienemann, 1984). However, my study looks into the grammatical structures in the textbooks rather than the learner's interlanguage grammar. In contrast to interlanguage grammar which includes both target-like form and non-target form (*you are dancing* vs. *you dancing*), the textbook grammatical presentation solely contains the standard form of the target language (e. g., *you are dancing*). Therefore, it is not appropriate to adopt the emergence criterion in a textbook analysis. As discussed above, the key point to determine the presence of textbook grammatical structures is to distinguish formulaic (or semi-formulaic) expressions and non-formulaic structures.

The third step is to tag and group the focal grammatical structures introduced in the textbooks according to the morphological and syntactic categories outlined in the processability hierarchy for L2 English as stipulated in PT (see Table 4.1 and Table 4.2). For example, this study groups single words (*station*), chunks (*many thanks*), semi-formulaic structures (I have got ______ [a book / a sweater]) and fully formulaic expressions (*How are you*?) into Stage 1 of the processability hierarchy for L2 English.

The aim of the third step is to mark where in the textbooks the grammatical structures introduced as teaching objectives occur, and to compare their ordering with the sequence of the corresponding items in the processability hierarchy for L2 English. A distinction will be made between the initial occurrence of a structure defined as a teaching objective (a grammatical focus) and incidental later occurrences. According to PT (Pienemann, 1998, 2005), learning a second language is acquiring a set of L2 processing skills; a grammatical structure occurs in the learner's oral production when the underlying processing procedure becomes available. In the textbooks, the grammatical foci are those structures that are obligatory for pupils to learn and produce after a lesson. From a processing view of language development, learning a grammatical focus in fact is acquiring the underlying processing skills. For the present textbook evaluation, the initial occurrence of a grammatical focus aims to locate the point in time when the pupils are required to learn the relevant processing procedure for the first time in the textbook series. Thus, the ordering of the initial occurrence of grammatical foci can indicate the sequence of the underlying processing skill development required in the selected textbooks. This sequence will be compared with the sequenced development that L2 learners go through in acquiring English as stipulated in PT (Pienemann, 1998, 2005).

A specific grammatical structure can appear several times in a textbook series due to the communicative aspects of the textbooks or as the repetition of the structure. Apart from the initial occurrence, all the later reoccurrences of a structure are defined as incidental items in this study. As introduced in Section 5.2, the four textbook series are mainly designed on the basis of communicative syllabus, and thus the teaching objectives are systematized in functional terms (topics) such as 'describing daily activities'. The incidental items may appear as structural consequences of the primary teaching objective such as 'describing daily activities' in the corresponding lessons. In this case, the grammatical morpheme '3rd ps sg -s' may reoccur in the textbook in order to fulfil the required language function. In relation to L2 acquisition, this is defined as 'incidental acquisition', namely, L2 learners may 'pick up' specific grammatical structures from communicative input unintentionally while teaching is focused on other aspects of the L2 such as communicative needs (Shintani & Ellis, 2011, p. 608). A number of SLA research emphasize the importance of incidental acquisition and the high frequency of exposure to grammatical structures in communicative input (e. g. , Ellis, 2002; Krashen, 1985; Pica, 1994; Schmidt, 1994; Song & Sardegna, 2014; Shintani & Ellis, 2011). Since the present study is only concerned with the order of introduction (i. e. , the sequencing) of the structures that are teaching objectives, and not with the number of times the structures reoccur in the textbooks (incidental item), thus the initial occurrence of the structures that are grammatical foci in the whole textbook series will be my main preoccupation.

Based on the aforementioned three steps, the analysis seeks to determine whether the sequencing of grammatical structures introduced as teaching objectives is compatible with the developmental sequence of L2 English as stipulated in PT (Pienemann, 1998, 2005).

5.2 The textbooks

The four textbook series were selected on the basis of three criteria. First, all of them are officially approved by the Ministry of Education of China for the teaching of English in primary schools from Grade 3 to Grade 6. Second, they are published by two of the largest educational publishing companies in China—the People's Education Press, and the Foreign Language Teaching and Research Press—and used widely in schools throughout China. Third, they contain explicit syllabi of grammatical structures and vocabulary. As pointed out in the preface to each textbook series, while they focus on the communicative aspect of language and specific cultural contexts, they require mastery of certain grammatical structures and vocabulary to meet the communicative needs of students.

5.2.1 *New Standard English* (Chen & Ellis, 2012)

New Standard English is one of a series of English course books widely used in primary schools in China (see Figures 5. 1). It is co-published by Macmillan Publishers and the Foreign Language Teaching and Research Press. This course book uses both a drama- and a story-based approach that requires students to apply L2 English grammar in a variety of communicative situations. It contains a range of original songs, rhymes and chants to promote fluency and reinforce the use of the target language. Apart from textbooks, the course package includes cassettes, DVDs, CD-ROMs, supplementary readings, and activity books.

There are eight volumes in this primary school textbook series. Ranging from Grade 3 to Grade 6, they cover four levels. Each level consists of two volumes, corresponding to each of the two semesters in a school year. There are ten learning modules in each volume, a review module, four vocabulary lists, a supplementary reading passage, and an additional project (e. g. , making a poster together with other students).

The learning modules in the textbooks introduce the target language by means of various activities such as 'listen and say', 'point and say', 'memory game', and so on. Each learning module comprises two units. The first unit includes three dialogues (or stories) followed by

Figure 5. 1: The cover of *New Standard English*, Book 1

speaking practice. The second unit contains two dialogues (or stories), a listening activity, a song (or rhyme), and two role-play activities.

The review module provides a variety of exercises for students to practise the aspects of the target language in the learning modules. The vocabulary list presents all the words that students are expected to memorize. The supplementary reading passage gives an additional opportunity for students to engage in reading practice after class. The additional project includes two hands-on activities that require group or whole class work, such as making posters or drawing pictures.

The teaching objectives of each module are specified in the table of contents of each volume. Table 5. 1 is an extract of the table of contents of the first volume, namely, Book 1, which has been selected to serve as an example. The grammatical items introduced as teaching objectives of the volume appear in the fourth column. They are listed according to the order in which they are presented in individual modules.

Table 5. 1 Table of contents of *New Standard English*, Book 1

Module	Theme	Function	Grammar
1	Greetings	Greetings and saying farewell; introducing oneself	Words/formulas: *Hello/Hi, I'm…* *Goodbye/Bye-bye* *Good morning. How are you? I'm fine. Thank you.*
2	Introduction	Greeting; introducing oneself	Words/formulas: *Good afternoon. What's your name? I'm …*
3	Classroom	Responding to instructions; identifying classroom objects	Imperative sentences: *Sit down, please. Please stand up. Point to…*

Table 5.1 Table of contents of *New Standard English*, Book 1 (continued)

Module	Theme	Function	Grammar
4	Animals	Describing the specific animals; stating your pet	SVO sentences: *It is a cat. It's a black dog. I have a panda.*
5	Numbers 1-12	Recognising and counting numbers 1-12	Words/formulas: Numbers 1-12; *How many?*
6	Birthday	Talking about age	Formulas: *Happy birthday. Here's… Thank you. How old are you? I'm…*
7	School	Identifying objects; asking about objects	Formulas: *What's this? This is a…*
8	Friends	Asking about objects; talking about location	Semi-formulas: *Where's…? It's in…* Yes-or-no question: *Is it a…? Are they…? Are you in…? Yes, it is. /No, it isn't.*
9	Family	Talking about family members; talking about jobs	Possessive determiners: *This is my mother. This is her brother. This is our grandpa.* SVO sentences: *He's a (n)… She's a (n)… They're…*
10	Body	Describing body parts	Possessive determiners: *This is his…/her…/your…* Imperative sentence: *Point to…*

Of the other columns in Table 5.1, the first refers to the modules in Book 1. The second presents the themes of individual modules. For example, the theme of Module 1 is 'Greetings'. The third column lists the specific language functions related to the themes of the modules, i.e., the communicative purposes for which learners use the language. For instance, the function addressed in Module 1 is 'Greeting and saying farewell'. As mentioned before, the fourth column lists the grammatical items that are taught in each module. They include the focal grammar 'words/formulas' and the target language such as *Hello/Hi/Goodbye/Bye-bye*.

5.2.2 *People's Education Press English* (Wu, 2012)

People's Education Press (PEP) English is the most commonly used English textbook series in primary schools in China (see Figures 5.2). It was co-developed and is co-published by the People Education Press and Canada's Lingo Media. This textbook series includes eight volumes, eight activity books, eight sets of wall charts, 16 cassette tapes (two for each book), eight sets of flashcards, 100 slides, and eight VCDs.

Figure 5.2 The cover of *People's Education Press English*, Book 1

The eight volumes cover eight semesters (Grade 3 to Grade 6 of primary school). Each volume is used for one semester. Except for Book 8, each volume consists of six reading units, two review units, and three appendices. In Book 8, there are four reading units and two review units. The three appendices contain a list of words in each unit, a list of key vocabulary for the whole volume, and a list of useful expressions.

Each reading unit consists of three sections. In each section, new target language is provided in dialogues, stories, rhymes, and chants. A variety of activities are incorporated in the units, such as singing, playing, drawing, acting, chanting, story time, pair work, group work and so on. The focal grammar is listed at the beginning of each unit. Table 5.2 is a summary of the focal grammar introduced in each of the units of Book 1.

Table 5.2 Focal grammar in each unit of *PEP English*, Book 1

Unit	Focal grammar
1	Greetings: hello / hi Farewells: goodbye/bye Self-introduction: I'm … Asking and giving names: What's your name? My name is…
2	Greetings: Good morning! Good afternoon! Nice to meet you. This is …
3	Greetings. How are you? I'm fine, thank you. / Very well, thanks. Using *let* to make a proposal: Let's go to school. Let me make a puppet. Using *this is* to describe: This is the Great Wall. This is my arm.

R1	Review of Units 1-3

Table 5.2 Focal grammar in each unit of *PEP English*, Book 1 (continued)

Unit	Focal grammar
4	What's this? What's that? It's a duck. It's a cat. Compliment: cool. I like it.
5	Have some water. I'd like some water. Here you are. Can I have some water, please? Here you are. You're welcome.
6	How many? Five cards / three cats / six chairs… How old are you? I'm … years old.
R2	Review of Units 4-6

In Table 5.2, the first column refers to the units of Book 1 ('R' in front of a number indicates a review unit), while the second column presents the grammatical items that are the teaching objectives in individual units. Since the focal grammatical items are not explicitly presented using grammatical terminology, I need to provide a description of what specific grammatical structures (such as grammatical morphemes or syntactic structures) are involved in the listed items. For example, in Unit 1, '*hello*', '*hi*, '*goodbye* and '*bye*' are considered as single words. The item *I'm*… is considered to be semi-formulaic structure, because it is presented in sentence structures with open slots (e.g., 'I'm ___________ [Amy/David/Xiaoli]'). The main constituents, i.e., the subject and the copula verb, are fixed. Similarly, *What's your name*? is described as a formulaic structure and *My name is*… is considered to be a semi-formulaic structure. An explicit description of the grammatical structures in each unit of Book 1 is presented in Table 5.3.

Table 5.3 Analysed version of focal grammatical structures in *PEP English*, Book 1

Unit	Focal grammatical structures
1	single words: hello / hi / goodbye / bye semi-formulaic structures: I'm … / My name is … formulaic structure: What's your name?
2	chunks: good morning / good afternoon / nice to meet you. semi-formulaic structure: This is …
3	formulaic structures: How are you? I'm fine. chunks: very well, thanks. lexical phrases: Let's go to school / Let me make a puppet. semi-formulaic structures: This is the Great Wall / This is my arm.
R1	Review of Units 1-3
4	semi-formulaic structures: What's this? /What's that? /It's a duck/It's a cat. single word: cool formulaic structure: I like it.

Table 5.3 Analysed version of focal grammatical structures in *PEP English*, Book 1 (continued)

Unit	Focal grammatical structures
5	formulaic structures: Have some water. / I'd like some water. / Here you are. / Can I have some water, please? / You're welcome.
6	chunk: how many? phrasal plural marking -s (NP agreement): five cards / three cats / six chairs… formulaic structure: How old are you? semi-formulaic structure: I'm … years old.
R2	Review of Units 4-6

5.2.3 *Super Kids* (Liu et al., 2012)

Jointly compiled and published by the People Education Press in China and the Pearson Longman Publishing Group in the United States, *Super Kids* is a four-level course book for primary school students in China (see Figures 5.3). This course book focuses on presenting and teaching the target language through functional dialogues and classroom activities, while at the same time developing key vocabulary, grammar skills in context, and writing skills. Each level of *Super Kids* comes complete with textbooks, activity books, supplementary cassettes, and flashcards.

Figure 5.3 The cover of *Super Kids*, Book 1

The textbooks contain four volumes, starting from Grade 3. Each volume is designed for an entire school year. For example, Book 1 is used for the first year of English education (Grade 3). Book 2 is intended for the second year of English education (Grade 4). The structure of each book is as follows. There are nine reading units that introduce the new target grammatical structures through an entire story. Three review units reinforce and expand on previously taught language. Four culture appendices develop international awareness through cultural supplements.

In each reading unit, there are seven sections presenting the target grammatical structures in different contexts such as dialogues, stories, chants, and so on. For example, the first section, 'Talk about it', introduces new target language in the form of dialogues. This section provides students with a general understanding of English grammar. The second and third sections are 'Build it 1' and 'Build it 2'. Learners are required to practise the key grammatical items. The fourth section, 'Review it 1', redeploys the key grammatical items in a variety of contexts such as listening and writing, and pair-work conversation. In the fifth section, 'Read it', learners are required to listen to and spell the key words. The next section is 'Match it'. Learners need to listen to a chant that contains four pieces of information, and then match the four pictures given in this section with the corresponding information. The last section, 'Review it 2', redeploys the focal grammatical items through stories and chants.

The focal grammatical items that are the teaching objectives are presented at the beginning of each volume, on a separate page following the table of contents, under the title 'Syllabus'. Table 5.4 is an excerpt of the syllabus for Book 1. The focal grammatical items are shown in the last column of the table. The first column refers to the units in Book 1. 'R' in front of a number refers to a review unit. The second column lists the specific functions and the required grammatical items of individual units. For example, in Unit 1, the functions are 'greetings', 'farewell', 'introducing and asking for name', and 'asking for information', which are followed by a range of target language containing key grammar.

Table 5.4 Focal grammar in unit of *Super Kids*, Book 1

Unit	Focal grammar
1	Greetings and farewell: Hello/Hi. Goodbye/Bye-bye. See you later. Introducing and asking for name: What's your name? I'm Jack/David… Asking for information: What's this? It's a mouse/book/pen.
2	Asking and introducing family: Is he your brother? Is she Helen's sister? Yes, he is. /No, he isn't. /Yes, she is. /No, she isn't.
3	Is it little/big. It's big/little. They're huge/small.
R1	Review of Units 1-3
4	Do you have a pen? Do they have…? Discussing likes or dislikes: I like candy. I don't like chicken. Here you are.
5	Sports: Can you skate? Could you try it? Yes, I can. / No, I can't. I can swim. I can't skate.
6	What are you doing? What are they playing? I'm watching TV. We're playing football.
R2	Review of Units 4-6

Table 5.4 Focal grammar in unit of *Super Kids*, Book 1 (continued)

Unit	Focal grammar
7	Possessions: I have a notebook. I don't have a pencil. Do you have a book? Yes, I do. Do you own this book? No, I don't.
8	What's he doing? What's she playing? He's riding a bike. She's playing soccer. He's throwing the ball. She's hitting the ball.
9	prepositions: in/on/under… Asking the location of things: Where's the paintbrush? Where's the pencil box? The pen/pencil/book/ it is in/on/under the book.
R3	Review of Units 7-9

As Table 5.4 shows, the focal grammar is presented in sentence structures, and thus an explicit grammatical description needs to be conducted to provide a clear picture of what specific grammatical structures are contained in the listed items. Take Unit 1 for example. '*Hello/Hi/Goodbye/Bye-bye/See you later*' are considered as single words or chunks to express greetings or farewell. '*What's your name?*' and '*What's this?*' are identified as formulaic structures because all the constituents in these two questions are not variable. Similarly, the sentences 'I'm ________[Jack/David]' and 'It's a ______[mouse/book/pen]' are regarded as semi-formulaic structures, since the main constituents—the subject and the verb—are fixed. Table 5.5 presents the analysed version of the specific grammatical structures contained in individual units in Book 1.

Table 5.5 Analysed version of focal grammatical structures in *Super Kids*, Book 1

Unit	Grammatical structures		
1	single words	semi-formulaic structure	formulaic structure
2	possessive determiner	copula verb + S(X)	
3	semi-formulaic structure	SVO	
R1	Review of Units 1-3		
4	formulaic structure	Do-fronting	SVO
5	SVO	AUX + SVO	
6	present continuous tense V-ing	SVO	*Wh*-word + AUX +SVO
R2	Review of Units 4-6		
7	Do-fronting	SVO	
8	present continuous tense V-ing	SVO	*Wh*-word + AUX + SVO
9	prepositions	SVO	copula verb + S(X)
R3	Review of Units 7-9		

5.2.4 *Join in* (Zhang, 2014)

Join in is a four-level course book for English education in primary schools in China (see Figures 5.4). The four levels are designed for Grades 3 to 6. This course book was co-developed and is co-published by the Foreign Language Teaching and Research Press and Cambridge University Press. *Join in* features a number of songs and stories to provide students with a motivating and enjoyable way to learn English. Apart from the textbooks, optional extras, such as videos, flashcards, holiday packs, and CD-ROMs, provide supplementary practice. The optional CD-ROMs are full of games and activities. The holiday packs offer a large number of puzzles and games for students to do at home or during the holidays (including colour activity books and audio cassettes).

Figure 5.4 The cover of *Join in*, Book 1

The major part of this four-level course book is the textbooks. There are eight volumes. Each level consists of two volumes. For example, Book 1 and Book 2 are used for Level 1 (Grade 3). Each volume contains a starter unit, six reading units, two review units, and three appendices. The starter unit includes eight 'Warm-up' activities that provide a general understanding of the topics in the volume. The reading units introduce the target language in different texts such as stories, dialogues, songs, and chants. The review units recycle the target grammar that has been taught in the reading units through a variety of exercises. The three appendices contain a word list, a list of key vocabulary, and a 'Grammar focus' section.

The reading unit is the main part of the textbook. Each reading unit consists of a culture section, writing activities, and a 'Look' section. The 'Look' section highlights focal grammatical items that are subsequently summarized in the 'Grammar focus' section at the end of the textbook. Table 5.6 is an extract of the 'Grammar focus' section in Book 1. The focal grammatical items are listed in the second column of the table.

Table 5.6 Grammar foci in *Join in*, Book 1

Unit	Target grammar
Starter	N/A
1	What's your name? How old are you? I'm seven / six / eight. hello / hi. bye-bye / goodbye. Thank you.
2	What's it? It is … How many? Number: one, two, three…
3	What colour is it? Here you are. Good morning. / Good night. Colours: yellow, black, red…
R1	Review of units 1-3
4	What's this? It's my book /his pen / her coat / your gift… What colour is it? It's purple / black… The pen is black / The hat is yellow… See you tomorrow. How many? Two pens / three books / five hats…
5	Happy birthday. Today is my birthday. Have an apple / a pear / a cake… Thank you. Can I have an ice cream / an apple / a cake…? Yes. Here you are.
6	What's in your classroom / room / home / kitchen? Two windows. Three doors. A blackboard. Desks and chairs. Plates / cups / chopsticks
R2	Review of Units 4-6

As shown in Table 5.6, the focal grammar is not explicitly presented using grammatical terminology. An explicit grammatical description is needed to provide a clear picture of what specific grammatical structures are contained in the listed items. For instance, in Unit 1, the focal grammatical items are 'What's your name?', 'How old are you?', 'I'm ________ (seven/six/eight…)', 'hello / hi', 'bye bye / goodbye', and 'Thank you'. Since the main constituents in these items are fixed and allow little or no variation, they can be described as formulaic structures, semi-formulaic structures ('I'm ______'), and single words ('hello'). Table 5.7 shows the analysed version of the specific grammatical structures taught in individual units of Book 1.

Table 5.7 Analysed version of focal grammatical structures in *Join in*, Book 1

Unit	Grammatical structures
1	single words semi-formulaic structures formulaic structures
2	formulaic structure semi-formulaic structure single words
3	formulaic structure single words
R1	Review of Unit 1-3
4	formulaic structure semi-formulaic structure possessive determiner SVO phrasal plural -*s*
5	formulaic structure semi-formulaic structure
6	semi-formulaic structure phrasal plural -*s* lexical plural -*s*
R2	Review of Unit 4-6

This concludes the second section of chapter 5. General information has been provided for the four textbook series selected for this study, including publishers, contents, and structure of the lessons. In each case, there is a syllabus of focal grammatical items that need to be taught to L2 English students. In addition to the abovementioned tables of focal grammatical items for Book 1 of these four textbook series, all the key grammatical morphemes and sentence structures including target language listed in individual volumes for the four sets of textbooks are tabulated and attached in the appendices (Appendices A-X). Appendices A-G are designed for Books 2-8 of the *New Standard English* series. Appendices H-N are used for Books 2-8 of the *PEP English* series. Appendices O-Q are intended for Books 2-4 of the *Super Kids* series. Appendices R-X are designed for Books 2-8 of the *Join in* series. The following section will present the results of the actual textbook analysis in the current study.

5.3 Results of the textbook analysis

The previous sections have described the method of analysis and the textbooks. This section presents the results, focusing on the occurrences and the ordering of morphemes and syntactic structures in the textbooks. The results will answer the research question: i. e., whether the sequencing of grammatical structures that are teaching objectives in the four textbook series follows the learning sequence for L2 English as stated in PT. Section 5.3.1 presents the results of the sequencing of grammatical morphemes. Section 5.3.2 presents the results of the sequencing of syntactic structures. Section 5.3.3 compares and summarizes the results of the analysis of the four textbook series in both areas of morphology and syntax.

5.3.1 Grading of morphological items

The first part of the analysis looks into eight items in the morphological development of L2 English outlined in the processability hierarchy (Pienemann, 1998, 2005). They are: words/formulas, simple past tense *-ed*, possessive determiner, lexical plural *-s*, phrasal plural *-s*, progressive V-*ing* (VP form), perfective V-*en* (VP form), and 3rd person singular *-s*. L2 learners are hypothesized to go through five stages in their acquisition of English morphology (Pienemann, 1998).

Stage 1—lemma access: words/formulas

Stage 2—category procedure: simple past *-ed*, possessive determiner, lexical plural *-s*

Stage 3—NP procedure: phrasal plural *-s*

Stage 4—VP procedure: *be* + V-*ing*, *have* + V-*en*

Stage 5—S-procedure: 3rd ps sg *-s*

In the following, the findings for each textbook series are provided and discussed separately.

5.3.1.1 Results—*New Standard English*

General findings of the textbook series. Table 5.8 shows all occurrences of the morphological items that are teaching objectives in the eight volumes of *New Standard English*. The utmost left column lists the volumes in the series. The top row lists the developmental stages of L2 English acquisition as hypothesized in PT (Pienemann, 1998, 2005) The second row lists the morphological items that can be acquired at a given stage. The symbol '?' indicates where the item is initially taught as a grammatical focus (teaching objective) in the textbook. The symbol 'x' represents any incidental occurrences of the item (incidental item). Where a specific item is not introduced, the corresponding cell is left blank.

Table 5.8 Occurrences of PT-morphological items in *New Standard English*

Stage	1	2			3	4		5
Morphology	words/ formulas	past-ed	possessive determiner	lexical plural -s	phrasal plural -s	V-ing (VP)	V-en (VP)	3rd ps sg-s
Book 1	Δ		Δ					
Book 2	x		x					Δ
Book 3					Δ	Δ		
Book 4		Δ						
Book 5					x			x
Book 6		x		Δ		x		
Book 7			x	x	x			x
Book 8		x				x		

Table 5.8 shows that all the developmental stages hypothesized in PT (Pienemann, 1998, 2005) are included in *New Standard English*, according to the criterion (stipulated in Section 5.1) that at least one structure at each stage is introduced as a teaching objective in the textbook series. All morphological items, bar one (the morpheme 'V-*en*'), appear as teaching objectives in this textbook series, including 'words/formulas', 'simple past *-ed*', 'possessive determiner', 'lexical plural *-s*', 'phrasal plural -s', 'V-ing', and '3rd ps sg -s'.

Focusing on the initial occurrence of the morphological items as teaching objectives (marked as '?'), Table 5.8 reveals: in Book 1, the teaching objectives are 'words/formulas'; in Book 2, the only teaching objective is '3rd ps sg *-s*'; in Book 3, two morphemes 'phrasal plural *-s*' and 'V -ing' are specified as the teaching objectives; in Book 4, 'past *-ed*' is the only teaching objective; in Book 5, no teaching objectives exist; in Book 6, 'lexical plural -s' is the teaching objective; in Book 7, no morphemes are introduced as the teaching objective; in Book 8, no morphemes are instructed as the teaching objectives.

Considering their sequencing as hypothesized in PT's progression (Pienemann, 1998, 2005), the initial occurrence of these teaching objectives suggests that: 1) 'words/formulas' starts at the first volume of this textbook series, namely, Book 1; 2) 'past -ed' and 'lexical plural -s' are taught after the preceding-stage item 'words/formulas' as stipulated in the PT's hypotheses (Pienemann, 1998); 3) 'phrasal plural -s' is taught after 'possessive determiner' but earlier than the instruction of 'past -ed' and 'lexical plural -s'; 4) '3rd ps sg -s' is introduced prior to 'V -ing' in the textbook series. The pedagogical teaching sequence of these two morphemes does not follow their ordering in PT's predictions (Pienemann, 2005), namely, 'V-ing' should precede '3rd ps sg -s' since the underlying VP procedure is the necessary prerequisite for the following S-procedure; and 5) two morphemes both occur at the same volume with their preceding-stage structures, namely, 'possessive determiner' and 'V -ing'. This appears to violate the PT's predictions that a processing procedure can be activated and the corresponding structure can be produced only if all the previous processing skills have been developed (Bettoni & Di Biase, 2015; Pienemann, 1998). 'Possessive determiner' and 'V-ing' cannot be acquired simultaneously with their preceding-stage structures, since their underlying processing procedures are developed in an accumulative manner. However, the general analysis of the whole series (see Table 5.8) does not provide enough evidence that 'possessive determiner' and 'V-ing' are taught with their previous-stage structures in the same lessons. Therefore, a closer analysis of Book 1 and Book 3 where 'possessive determiner' and 'V-ing' occur is needed in order to investigate their pedagogical teaching sequence in the lessons. The local analyses of individual volumes are provided as follows, in order to examine the abovementioned issues.

Local analysis of Book 1. A study of initial occurrences of structures reveals that *New Standard English* Book 1 starts with the introduction of 'words/formulas' as a teaching objective of Module 1. The other teaching objective 'possessive determiner' is initially taught in Module 9. As far as order of occurrence as teaching objectives in Book 1 is concerned, 'words/formulas' precedes 'possessive determiner'. Their sequencing in *New Standard English* follows the learning sequence as outlined in the PT-based processability hierarchy.

It should be noted that, in all modules of Book 1, students are required to learn and memorize a range of single words and semi- or fully formulaic expressions such as *hello / hi*, *I'm …*, *thank you*, and *good morning*. The lexical morpheme 'possessive determiner', exemplified in (5) and (6) below, is the grammatical focus of Module 9, where students need to learn how to introduce their or each other's family members.

(5) This is my mother.
(6) This is his/her father.

The morpheme 'possessive determiner' recurs in Module 10, where it is used with body parts, as in (7) and (8).

(7) This is his nose.
(8) This is her mouth.

Local analysis of Book 2. *New Standard English*, Book 2 recycles the use of 'words/formulas' and 'possessive determiner' as incidental items through a broader selection of exemplars such as (9) and (10). In these examples, the teaching focus is either on the adjectives that are used to describe someone's appearance or on the use of the morpheme '3rd ps sg -s' to talk about the grammatical subject's routines.

(9) This man is ________ (short / fat / small / thin / big).

(10) Tom plays with his friends.

The morpheme '3rd ps sg -s' is the only teaching objective in Book 2. As a morpheme that cannot be acquired until late in the L2 English acquisition process, '3rd ps sg -s' should appear after the instruction of the Stage 4 morphemes. However, it is a grammatical focus very early on in *New Standard English*. A closer look at '3rd ps sg -s' in Book 2 reveals that this morpheme is the teaching focus of Module 5 and recurs in Module 8. Students are required to learn how to describe their daily activities (or those of others) by using third-person singular present statements, such as (11) and (12).

(11) Amy goes to school on Mondays.

(12) Daming files a kite in the park.

However, none of the structures pertaining to Stages 3 and 4, including 'phrasal plural -s', 'V-ing (VP form)' and 'V-en (VP form)', are taught in Book 2. Without having mastered the earlier stages, students are unable to learn the high-stage morpheme '3rd ps sg -s' at this point. Although '3rd ps sg -s' is the teaching focus of Book 2, students may at best memorize this structure as a formulaic expression and reproduce it only in limited contexts. The instruction of '3rd ps sg -s' in Book 2 comes too early for students and is not consistent with the learning sequence as stated in PT (Pienemann, 1998).

Local analysis of Book 3. In Book 3, 'phrasal plural -s' and 'V-ing (VP form)', are specified as grammatical foci. As far as their ordering in this volume is concerned, the Stage 4 morpheme 'V-ing' precedes the Stage 3 morpheme 'phrasal plural -*s*'.

'V-ing' is the grammatical focus of Module 3. Students need to describe their present continuous activities (or those of others), as exemplified in (13) and (14).

(13) She is watching TV.

(14) He is making lunch.

'Phrasal plural -s' is the grammatical focus of Module 8. It is illustrated in (15) and (16).

(15) I can run the 100 metres.

(16) I can jump the 40 inches.

'Phrasal plural -s', which should be acquired earlier in L2 English development, appears to occur later in Book 3 than 'V-ing'. This may be related to the choice of topic for Module 8: planning your Sports Day. Students are required to talk about their plans for Sports Day and estimate their prospective achievements in specific sports. Thus, the morpheme 'phrasal plural -s' is the grammatical focus of Module 8. However, the sequencing of 'phrasal plural -s' and 'V-ing' is apparently not consistent with their sequencing in the PT-based processability hierarchy (Pienemann, 2005).

Local analysis of Book 4. The lexical morpheme 'simple past *-ed*' is the only teaching objective in Book 4. It is taught as the grammatical focus of Module 9. In Module 9, students need to describe activities that happened in the past such as what they did at school or home during the previous weekend. Exemplars are shown in (17) and (18).

(17) I helped Mum.

(18) I played basketball yesterday.

Local analysis of Book 5. In this volume, only two morphemes, 'phrasal plural *-s*' and '3rd ps sg *-s*', recur as incidental items. In other words, no new grammatical foci are added here. 'Phrasal plural -s' is repeatedly presented as an incidental item in Modules 2 and 5, while '3rd ps sg -s' recurs in Module 8. The repetition of these two morphemes merely provides an opportunity for students to practice the use of 'there are' or the expression of specific times, as shown in the following exemplars.

(19) There are ten pencils.

(20) There are five pens.

(21) The school starts at nine o'clock.

Local analysis of Book 6. In this volume, the only teaching focus added to the list is the lexical morpheme 'lexical plural -s'. The other morphemes, 'possessive determiner' and 'V-ing', are incidental items.

'Lexical plural -s' occurs as the grammatical focus in Module 4. Students need to come up with generalizations. To refer to a whole category, both the generic plural form of the noun, with no article, and the construction '*the* + plural noun' are used. The following are exemplars taken from Module 4.

(22) Computers are very interesting.

(23) The books in the library are useful.

The morphemes 'simple past *-ed*' and 'V-*ing*' both recur as incidental items in Module 2.

One of the teaching foci is the irregular form of the past tense of some specific verbs such as *build* and *buy*. Students need to look at the difference between 'simple past tense *-ed*' and the irregular past tense form and then produce the correct form of certain verbs that cannot be simply suffixed by *-ed* to mark the past tense. Examples are presented in (24) and (25).

(24) He built a house.

(25) She bought a new scarf.

The other teaching focus in Module 2 is on students comparing their grandparents' experience learning foreign languages in the past and the present. In this case, students are required to learn the names of different languages (e. g., *English*, *Russian*, *French*) and communicate with each other by means of sentences such as (26) and (27). The use of 'V-ing' merely provides a context for the production of language names; it is not the teaching focus.

(26) He is learning English now.

(27) He learnt Russian before.

Local analysis of Book 7. There are no new grammatical foci, while four morphemes recur as incidental items: 'possessive determiner', 'lexical plural *-s*', 'phrasal plural *-s*', and '3rd ps sg *-s*'.

The morphemes 'lexical plural -s', 'possessive determiner' and phrasal plural -s' appear as incidental items in Module 3. Students are required to introduce and discuss their hobbies or favourite stuff, as in (28) and (29). These three morphemes are not teaching foci but recur in the texts to help fulfil other necessary language functions.

(28) I have lots of stamps. This stamp is from China.

(29) My favourite sports are soccer and basketball.

Similarly, '3rd ps sg -s' recurs as an incidental item to fulfil the focal function in Module 7, namely, describing and inquiring about animal facts or behaviours, as in (30).

(30) The panda loves bamboo.

Local analysis of Book 8. A similar result is found in the analysis of Book 8. Two morphemes, 'simple past -ed' and 'V-ing', recur as incidental items. No new grammatical focus is added.

In Module 4, students need to learn how to proactively offer assistance to someone else or reject a request for assistance. The incidental occurrence of 'V-*ing*' is used to fulfil the focal functions, as shown in (31) and (32).

(31) Who can help me? Sorry, I can't. I'm making the birthday card.
(32) Who can help me? I can.

The other morpheme 'simple past *-ed*' is present as an incidental item in Module 7. The teaching focus is the use of the irregular past tense form of some specific verbs. 'Simple past -*ed*' is only used as a basis for comparison with the irregular past tense form. Based on the differences between the two kinds of tense forms, students are required to acquire the correct tense form for specific verbs such as *spend* and *fly*. Exemplars are shown in (33) and (34).

(33) Shenzhou V flew into space with Yang Liwei.
(34) Yang Liwei spent about twenty-one days in space.

Given that 'simple past -ed' and 'V-ing' are presented as incidental items, their sequencing in Book 8 is not a matter of concern in this study. Their presence is required only for the reinforcement of language use and the fulfilment of necessary language functions.

Summary of the findings. The results of the analysis of the *New Standard English* series show that the sequencing of the morphological items is partially consistent with their sequencing as outlined in the PT-based processability hierarchy (Pienemann, 1998, 2005). The structures belonging to the initial three stages, including 'words/formulas', 'simple past -ed', 'possessive determiner', 'lexical plural -s', and 'phrasal plural -s' are generally presented as teaching objectives in accordance with the learning sequence as stated in PT (Pienemann, 1998, 2005). According to PT (Pienemann, 1998, 2005), 'simple past -ed', 'possessive determiner' and 'lexical plural -s' are located at the same level—the category procedure (Stage 2). The abovementioned analysis reveals that the three grammatical morphemes are taught as instructional foci in different books (see Table 5. 8). Based on the analytic methods defined in Section 5. 1, the earliest point in time when the category procedure (Stage 2) is required in the whole series is at Module 9 of Book 1 where 'possessive determiner' is introduced as a teaching objective. Thus, the skill development of the lemma access (Stage 1), the category procedure (Stage 2), and the NP procedure (Stage 3) required in this textbook series is consistent with the PT's hypotheses (Pienemann, 1998, 2005).

However, the sequencing of structures at Stages 4 and 5 does not follow the PT-based learning sequence. For example, 'V-ing' (Stage 4) and 'phrasal plural -s' (Stage 3) are both grammatical foci in Book 3, but the instruction of 'V-ing' precedes that of 'phrasal plural -s'. This implies that the pupils are expected to develop the VP procedural skills (Stage 4) before the NP procedural skills (Stage 3) in the textbook series. Such a skill development violates the PT's predictions of ESL development that the NP procedure is the prerequisite for the VP procedure

(Pienemann, 1998, 2005). Similarly, the Stage 5 morpheme '3rd ps sg -s' appears as a grammatical focus earlier than the Stage 4 morpheme 'V-ing'. '3rd ps sg -s' is the focus of Book 2, and comes before the instruction of 'V-ing' in Book 3. The S-procedural skills (Stage 5) are obligatory for the students to develop earlier than the previous VP procedural skills (Stage 4) in this textbook series. This is opposite to the sequenced development of ESL acquisition as stipulated in PT (Pienemann, 1998, 2005), namely, the S-procedure becomes available only when the learner has developed all the VP procedural skills.

Based on specific analyses of individual volumes, there appears to be a connection between the focal introduction of those structures and the topics (context) in the corresponding lessons (modules). In terms of 'words/formulas', its focal instruction occurs in Module 1 of Book 1 where students are expected to learn 'Greetings' such as *hello/hi* and *how are you*?. Similarly, the instruction of 'possessive determiner' as a teaching objective in Module 9 of Book 1 is called for in the related context of 'Family' which requires students to introduce their or each other's relatives, as exemplified in one of the key sentences *This is my mother*. The next grammatical focus is '3rd ps sg -s' which appears in Module 5 of Book 2; in the lesson students need to describe their (or others') daily activities. Given this context, the third-person singular statement is called for when students discuss about each other's routines such as *Amy goes to school on Monday*. The following teaching objectives 'phrasal plural -s' and 'V-ing' are provided in Book 3 to fulfil the necessary functions in relation to specific topics; by the provision of 'V-ing' in Module 3, students can describe their (or others') present continuous activities such as *She is watching TV*; similarly, the instruction of 'phrasal plural -s' in Module 8 serves to exchange their ideas about planning activities on 'Sports Day', when students need to estimate their prospective achievements in specific sports such as the long jump (*I can jump the* 40 *inches*). The next grammatical focus 'simple past -ed' is used to talk about their activities in the past (*I helped Mum*) in Module 9 of Book 4. The following focal structure 'lexical plural -s' is introduced in Book 6, where students need to make a general description of the stuff in the library (*The books in the library are useful*).

As shown above, those grammatical foci are not ordered in a way that follows the PT-based hypothesized sequencing of grammar. Their organization in *New Standard English* textbook series is more associated with a range of topics that are very closely related to the primary-school children's daily life. Those topics such as 'Greetings' and 'Family' are more likely to be of interest for the pupils in naturally-occurring conversation and thus they are presented in the initial lessons. Given such topics, some words/formulaic expressions such as *hello/hi* or *how are you* and the lexical morpheme such as 'possessive determiner' which may be necessary for relationship introduction are used as target language very early in the textbooks. In addition, some topics appear more than once, such as 'Activities' (routines, present continuous or past activities). The frequent topics can cover a variety of grammatical items such as tense markers (e.g., 3rd ps sg -s, V-ing, simple past -ed). Considering the characteristics of this textbook series (as mentioned in Section 5.2.1), it could be argued that communicative aspects of language use have impacts on the organization and sequencing of the grammatical foci.

5.3.1.2 Results—*People's Education Press English*

General findings of the textbook series. Table 5.9 presents all the occurrences of morphological items that are teaching objectives in the eight volumes of *People's Education Press (PEP) English*. The utmost left column shows the volumes of this textbook set. The top row lists the developmental stages of L2 English acquisition as predicted in PT (Pienemann, 1998, 2005). The second row presents the morphological items that can be acquired at a given stage. The first occurrence of a morphological item as a grammatical focus in the textbook is marked by means of the symbol '?'. 'x' refers to the later, incidental, presence of an item. A blank cell means that no morphological item is introduced at that particular point.

Table 5.9 Occurrences of PT-morphological items in *PEP English*

Stage	1	2			3	4		5
Morphology	words/ formulas	past-ed	possessive determiner	lexical plural -s	phrasal plural -s	V-ing (VP)	V-en (VP)	3rd ps sg-s
Book 1	Δ				Δ			
Book 2	x		Δ	Δ	x			
Book 3	x		x	x	x			Δ
Book 4	x		x	x	x	Δ		
Book 5			x	x	x			
Book 6			x	x	x	x		x
Book 7	x		x	x		x		x
Book 8	x	Δ	x	x		x		x

First of all, since at least one structure at every stage is introduced as a learning objective in the textbook series, as shown in Table 5.9, we can conclude that all the developmental stages predicted in PT are included in *PEP English*. Almost all morphological items, with the exception of 'V-en', occur in this set of textbooks. They are: 'words/formulas', 'simple past -ed', 'possessive determiner', 'lexical plural -s', 'phrasal plural -s', 'V-ing (VP form)', and '3rd ps sg -s'.

Secondly, a closer look at the initial occurrence of the structures (marked as '?') shows that: *PEP English* begins with the introduction of 'words/formulas' and 'phrasal plural -s' as the teaching objectives of Book 1; in Book 2, the other two morphemes 'possessive determiner' and 'lexical plural -s' are specified as the teaching objectives; in Book 3, the only teaching focus is '3rd ps sg -s'; Book 4 merely has single one teaching objective 'V -ing'; the following volume Book 5 does not provide any new teaching foci; similarly, there is no new grammatical focus taught in Book 6; in Book 7, no structures are instructed as the teaching objectives; Book 8 includes one teaching focus 'past -ed'.

As can be seen from the first occurrence of those structures, we can conclude three general findings regarding their sequencing in *PEP English*. 1) The introduction of 'words/formulas' (Stage 1) as a teaching focus in the first volume is consistent with PT predictions. 2) Four morphemes appear as the teaching objectives after the focal instruction of their preceding-stage structures in line with the ESL hypotheses as proposed in PT (Pienemann, 1998, 2005). They are 'past -ed', 'possessive determiner', 'lexical plural -s', and V -ing'. 3) However, 'phrasal plural -s' and '3rd ps sg -s' are taught as a grammatical focus too early in this textbook series. The initial occurrence of these two morphemes precedes their previous-stage morphemes, which is apparently contradictory to PT predictions. The following part will provide a further analysis of these structures in each volume.

Local analysis of Book 1. The Stage 1's item 'words/formulas' appears in all units of Book 1. This means that students need to memorize and reproduce a certain range of single words and semi- or fully formulaic expressions such as *many thanks*, *hello / hi*, *goodbye / bye*, and *station*. The only productive use of a morpheme that is a grammatical focus occurs in Unit 6, and concerns the phrasal plural marking -s. Exemplars are shown in (35) and (36).

(35) How many plates? Six plates.

(36) Two cakes. Three candles.

In Unit 6, students are expected to learn how to count with numbers and produce the nominal plural marker -s with countable nouns, particularly in the context of someone's birthday party. The topic of 'birthday party' is a popular one with students and can contextualize the use of focal grammar such as 'phrasal plural -s'.

In terms of grammatical sequencing, the instruction of 'phrasal plural -s' in Book 1 appears to be premature. According to the PT-based processability hierarchy (Pienemann, 1998), this morpheme is not able to be acquired before the mastery of the stage 2 structures 'simple past -ed', 'possessive determiner', or 'lexical plural -s'. However, no Stage 2 structures are introduced as grammatical foci in Book 1. 'Phrasal plural -s' occurs simultaneously with the single words and formulas in Book 1. Its instruction in the first volume goes apparently against the learning sequence as stated in PT.

Local analysis of Book 2. 'Words/formulas' such as *Good morning* and *Hi* repeatedly appear as incidental items in the units of Book 2. Students only need to memorize these expressions as rote-learned items. Similarly, 'phrasal plural -s' recurs as an incidental item in Unit 6, as exemplified in (37) and (38).

(37) Would you like some apples?

(38) Do you want some cakes?

In Unit 6, the teaching focus is the use of 'would you like…' or 'do you want…' as polite ways of offering something to someone. The morpheme 'phrasal plural -s' is not the teaching focus, but it recurs as an incidental component to make up the focal sentences and to fulfil the necessary functions.

The lexical morphemes 'possessive determiner' and 'lexical plural -s' are the grammatical foci which are initially presented in Book 2. 'Possessive determiner' occurs in Unit 2, where students are required to introduce others by using possessive determiners (or adjectives) such as *my* or *our*. Exemplars are presented in (39) and (40).

(39) Who's she? She's my mother.

(40) Who's she? She's our teacher.

The other morpheme, 'lexical plural -s', is introduced as the teaching focus of Unit 5. Students need to differentiate the singular form and the plural form, and produce noun phrases comprising a quantifier (or numeral) and the plural form of a countable noun. For example, in the 'guess game', the teacher will put different kinds of fruits in a box, and the students need to guess what is in the box, as in (41) and (42).

(41) What's in the box? Bananas?

(42) An apple? Mandarins? Oranges?

With respect to the sequencing of 'possessive determiner' and 'lexical plural -s', their occurrences and ordering in Book 2 are consistent with the PT-based processability hierarchy, because they are taught later than the 'words/formulas' in Book 1. Therefore, their sequencing in the *PEP English* series follows the learning sequence as hypothesized in PT (Pienemann, 1998).

Local analysis of Book 3. The morpheme '3rd ps sg -s' is the grammatical focus of Unit 3 and recurs in Unit 6. Students need to describe what their friends or classmates usually do in daily life by using a third-person present statement. '3rd ps sg -s' is thus specified as the teaching focus of Unit 3, as per (43) and (44).

(43) My friend goes to school on Monday.

(44) David plays soccer in the afternoon.

However, the instruction of '3rd ps sg -s' in Book 3 seems premature. Table 5.9 has revealed that Stage 4 morphemes such as 'V-ing' are not provided in the first three volumes of the *PEP English* series. According to the processability hierarchy for L2 English development

(Pienemann, 1998, 2005), the Stage 5 morpheme '3rd ps sg -s' is not able to be acquired without the emergence of the structures at the previous stage (Stage 4). Therefore, the fact that '3rd ps sg -s' is a grammatical focus as early as in Book 3 is not in accordance with the learning sequence as stated in PT.

Other morphemes such as 'possessive determiner', 'lexical plural -s', and 'phrasal plural -s' are not considered to be grammatical foci; however, they are repeatedly present as incidental items to provide more opportunities for students to understand and practice the teaching foci. For example, in Unit 3, 'possessive determiner' serves as an incidental component to assist students with the contextualization of the use of the teaching focus '3rd ps sg -s', as exemplified in (43). In this case, students need to understand the basic rule for when to use the third-person singular present statement, namely when the subject is a third person such as *she*, *he*, *David*, *my friend*. The lexical morpheme 'possessive determiner' is thus a given in this context.

Local analysis of Book 4. The VP morpheme 'V-ing' is the grammatical focus of Unit 4. The topic of this unit is the 'weather'. Students need to respond to what the weather is like today and describe their feeling about it. In this context, students are expected to produce the present progressive tense marking 'V-ing'. (45) and (46) are exemplars from the text.

(45) What's the weather like today? It's hot today. I am wearing a T-shirt.

(46) What's the weather like today? It's rainy today. That man is holding an umbrella.

The instruction of 'V-ing' in Book 4 is in line with the learning sequence as stipulated in PT. As Table 5.9 shows, the Stage 3 morpheme 'phrasal plural -s' has been presented as a grammatical focus in Book 1. The presence of the Stage 4 morpheme 'V-ing' in Book 4 occurs after the instruction of 'phrasal plural -s' in this textbook series. Thus, the sequencing of 'V-ing' and 'phrasal plural -s' is consistent with the sequence outlined in the PT-based processability hierarchy (Pienemann, 2005).

In addition, other morphemes such as 'possessive determiner', 'lexical plural -s', and 'phrasal plural -s' are not the grammatical foci, but they recur as incidental items to contextualize the production of focal grammar or fulfil necessary functions related to specific topics. For instance, the lexical morpheme 'possessive determiner' appears as an incidental item in Unit 3, where students are required to learn how to make a request or issue an order through the use of imperative sentences, such as (47) and (48).

(47) Put on your T-shirt.

(48) Hang up my skirt.

'Possessive determiner' is mainly used here to form the target sentences. It is part of a specific context for students to reinforce their language use.

Local analysis of Book 5. 'Possessive determiner', 'lexical plural -s', and 'phrasal plural -s' are repeatedly used as incidental items in Book 5. For example, in Unit 2, the teaching focus is the use of WH-questions to request specific information, relating for instance to regular activities or classes on weekdays. Exemplars are shown in (49), (50), and (51).

(49) What do we have on Mondays? Maths, Chinese, English…
(50) We have Moral Education on Tuesdays.
(51) My English class is on Wednesday.

In these three examples, 'lexical plural -s' and 'possessive determiner' are included as incidental items, but they are not the teaching foci. They are used to construct complete target sentences and provide an opportunity for students to practice in a variety of contexts.

Local analyses of Book 6 and Book 7. Similar results are also found in the analyses of Books 6 and 7. Tables 5.9 has indicated that no new grammatical foci are taught in these two volumes. The morphological items that appear in the two volumes are incidental items. They recur for repeated language practice, and also to help with the fulfilment of the specific functions related to the topics. For example, in Unit 1, students need to learn and produce WH-questions to request information about someone's timetable, as exemplified in (52).

(52) When do you do morning exercises?

In this case, the presence of 'lexical plural -s' is incidental, since the teaching focus is the use of WH-questions. But this morpheme acts as a component of the target sentences in order to contextualize the practice of the focal grammar.

Local analysis of Book 8. In Book 8, the lexical morpheme 'simple past -ed' is the grammatical focus of Unit 2. Students are required to talk about their activities of the previous weekend, such as what they did on Saturday. The teaching focus is the production of the past tense form of verbs, including the regular past -ed and irregular past tense forms. (53), (54) and (55) are exemplars from the text.

(53) I played football.
(54) I visited grandma.
(55) I went to the park.

Since 'simple past -ed' is the grammatical focus of Book 8, its instruction occurs after the instruction of 'words/formulas' in Book 1. The sequencing of 'simple past -ed' (Stage 2) and 'words/formulas' (Stage 1) is apparently consistent with the sequence stipulated in the PT-based processability hierarchy (Pienemann, 1998).

Summary of the findings. In summary, the findings of our investigation into the *PEP English* series reveal that the sequencing of the morphological items partially follows the sequence stipulated in the PT-based processability hierarchy (Pienemann, 1998, 2005). Structures belonging to Stages 1, 2, and 4, such as 'words/formulas', 'simple past -ed', 'possessive determiner', 'lexical plural -s', and 'V-ing (VP)', are taught as grammatical foci in line with the PT-based learning sequence (Pienemann, 1998, 2005). Three grammatical morphemes, 'simple past -ed', 'possessive determiner', and 'lexical plural -s', are all located at the category procedure stage (Stage 2). The earliest point when the category procedural skills are expected to be learned in this series is in Unit 2 of Book 2 where 'possessive determiner' is taught. Thus, the skill development of the lemma access and the category procedure in this set of textbooks agrees with the PT's hypotheses (Pienemann, 1998). Similarly, the VP morpheme 'V-ing' is taught after the NP morpheme 'phrasal plural -s'; this is consistent with the PT's prediction that the learner has to develop all the NP procedural skills before he or she moves to the next level—the VP procedure stage (Pienemann, 1998).

However, the instruction of structures that belong to Stages 3 and 5 is not consist with the L2 learning sequence as hypothesized in PT (Pienemann, 1998, 2005). For instance, the Stage 3 morpheme 'phrasal plural -s' is provided as a grammatical focus in Book 1, simultaneously with the instruction of 'words/formulas'. 'Phrasal plural -s' is supposedly to appear later than the Stage 2 morphemes, but it precedes Stage 2 morphemes such as 'possessive determiner' and 'lexical plural -s' in this set of textbooks. According to PT (Pienemann, 1998), the learner is not able to 'skip' the category procedure stage (Stage 2) to acquire the NP procedural skills (Stage 3), since the necessary precondition of the NP procedure is the category procedure. Thus, the simultaneous instruction of invariant forms and 'phrasal plural -s' is not learnable for the pupils. Similarly, the Stage 5 morpheme '3rd ps sg -s' is the grammatical focus of Book 3, preceding the instruction of the Stage 4 morpheme 'V-ing' in Book 4. The learners are not able to acquire '3rd ps sg -s' in Book 3 due to that they have not developed the VP procedural skills yet.

From a processability perspective, the sequencing of the grammatical structures in *PEP* English shows that the instruction of structures at the first two stages and one of VP morphemes ('V-ing') at Stage 4 are processable and learnable for the primary-school students, while the Stage 3's 'phrasal plural -s' and '3rd ps sg -s' at Stage 5 are not taught in a learnable manner.

Apart from that, the local analyses of individual books show that the ordering of those structures may be closely related to the functions required for the topics in the lessons. The focal instruction of 'words/formulas' in the beginning of the textbook series is called for in the topic of Unit 1 of Book 1 where students need to learn basic greetings and farewells such as *hello/hi* and *goodbye/bye*. The following grammatical objective is 'phrasal plural -s' in Unit 6 of Book 1, whereby students can express the number of relevant things such as *cakes* or *candles* within the given topic 'Birthday Party' (*Two cakes. Three candles*). Two lexical morphemes 'possessive determiner' and 'lexical plural -s' are produced as structural consequences of the important topics; the former is used for the introduction of students' acquaintance such as *She's our teacher*, while the latter is produced in the context where students need to guess specific things in 'Guess Game' (*What's in the box? Bananas*). The next teaching objective '3rd ps sg -s' occurs in Unit 3 of Book 3 to fulfil the language function specified in this lesson, namely, describing the routines of students' friends or schoolmates (*David plays soccer in the afternoon*). The last grammatical focus 'V-ing' taught in Unit 4 of Book 4 is used in the context where students are required to express their feeling about the current weather (*It's hot today. I am wearing a T-shirt*).

The arrangement of grammatical items in *PEP English* series reveals evidence that the topics and necessary functions may play more important role in the organization of textbook content. The topics of lessons provide a variety of communicative contexts for students to master the related language functions through the explicit presentation of useful grammatical forms. All the topics are highly relevant to the elementary-school students' personal life, such as 'Greetings', 'Introduction', 'Birthday Party', and 'Weather'.

5.3.1.3 Results—*Super Kids*

General findings of the textbook series. Table 5.10 represents all occurrences of morphological items that are teaching objectives in the four volumes of the *Super Kids* textbook series. The top row shows the five developmental stages hypothesized in PT (Pienemann, 1998, 2005) for the eight targeted morphological items, which are listed in the second row. The utmost left column lists the volumes in this textbook set. The triangle sign '?' indicates the structure is among the grammatical foci of the corresponding volume. The symbol 'x' means there is an incidental presence of the structure. Empty cells indicate the structure does not occur.

Table 5.10 Occurrences of PT-morphological items in *Super Kids*

Stage	1	2			3	4		5
Morphology	words/ formulas	past-ed	possessive determiner	lexical plural -s	phrasal plural -s	V-ing (VP)	V-en (VP)	3rd ps sg-s
Book 1	Δ		Δ			Δ		
Book 2	x	Δ		Δ	Δ			Δ
Book 3	x	x	x		x	x		x
Book 4	x			x	x	x		x

Table 5.10 reveals that all the hypothesized developmental stages are included in *Super Kids*. Except for the VP morpheme 'V-en', all targeted morphological items are provided as learning objectives in this set of textbooks. The morphological items shown in this series include

'words/formulas', the lexical morphemes 'simple past -ed', 'possessive determiner', lexical plural -s', the NP morpheme 'phrasal plural -s', the VP morpheme 'V-ing', and '3rd ps sg -s'.

Focusing on the nature of the structures that are teaching foci (marked as '?'), we find that: 1) Book 1 introduces three structures as teaching objectives, including 'words/formulas', 'possessive determiner', and 'V -ing'; 2) Book 2 provides four English morphemes as teaching foci—'past -ed', 'lexical plural -s', 'phrasal plural -s', and '3rd ps sg -s'; 3) in Book 3, there is no new grammatical focus added to the list of teaching objectives; 4) similarly, Book 4 has no teaching objective.

In general, several findings related to the ordering of the structures can be concluded. 1) *Super Kids* begins with the provision of single words or formulaic expressions as the teaching objective in Book 1. Such an instruction of Stage 1's structure apparently follows PT predictions. 2) Two of the three morphemes at Stage 2, 'past -ed' and 'lexical plural -s', are taught as grammatical foci after the instruction of 'words/formulas' (Stage 1). This appears to be consistent with their sequencing as hypothesized in PT (Pienemann, 1998). Similarly, '3rd ps sg -s' is instructed as the teaching focus after its previous-stage morpheme 'V -ing' (Stage 4). The instruction of '3rd ps sg -s' seems to follow PT predictions. 3) However, the first occurrence of 'V -ing' as a teaching objective precedes that of Stage 3's morpheme 'phrasal plural -s', which differs from the ordering of 'V -ing' predicted in the PT-based processability hierarchy (Pienemann, 2005). 4) The ordering of 'possessive determiner' and 'phrasal plural -s' remains cloudy. Since these two morphemes are taught as grammatical foci in the same volumes with their preceding-stage structures, thus a further analysis of the corresponding volumes is needed in order to confirm whether they are ordered in line with PT's hypothesized sequence (Pienemann, 1998, 2005).

Local analysis of Book 1. 'Words/formulas' is initially presented as the grammatical focus of Unit 1 and recurs as an incidental item in Units 3, 4, 5, and 7. Students need to learn single words such as *mouse* formulaic expressions such as *How are you* and *Many thanks*. The lexical morpheme 'possessive determiner' is considered as the grammatical focus of Unit 2, as exemplified in (56) and (57).

(56) He's my brother.
(57) She's our teacher.

In Unit 2, students are required to productively use 'possessive determiner' to introduce their family, teachers or schoolmates and also to identify their relationship to others. Since the lexical morpheme 'possessive determiner' is taught in Unit 2 after the instruction of 'words/formulas' in Unit 1, their sequencing in *Super Kids* agrees with the learning sequence as stated in PT (Pienemann, 1998).

The VP morpheme 'V-ing' is taught as the grammatical focus in Unit 6 and recurs in Unit 8. Students are required to talk about the present activities, such as 'She is eating lunch' and 'The elephant is sleeping'. According to PT (Pienemann, 2005), the instruction of 'V-ing' necessitates the emergence of the Stage 3-morpheme such as 'phrasal plural -s' as the precondition. However, 'phrasal plural -s' does not appear in Book 1. Thus, the instruction of 'V-ing' in Book 1 is not consistent with the PT-based learning sequence (Pienemann, 2005).

Local analysis of Book 2. The Stage 2 morpheme 'simple past -ed' is the grammatical focus of Unit 5. Students are expected to discuss their activities or those of others in the past through the use of the regular past tense form of verbs. The sentences in (58) and (59) are exemplars from the text.

(58) I played soccer yesterday.
(59) I cooked dinner.

As far as the instruction of 'simple past -ed' is concerned, its presence as a grammatical focus occurs in Book 2, after the instruction of 'words/formulas' in Book 1. Thus, the sequencing of 'simple past -ed' and 'words/formulas' follows their sequencing as outlined in the PT-based processability hierarchy (Pienemann, 1998).

The other lexical morpheme, 'lexical plural -s', is introduced as the grammatical focus of Unit 6 and recurs in Unit 7. Students are required to differentiate between the singular and plural forms of nouns and produce the lexical plural marking -s on countable nouns. Exemplars are shown in (60) and (61).

(60) I like puppets.
(61) I like model cars.

Since 'lexical plural -s' appears as a grammatical focus in Book 2, after the instruction of 'words/formulas' in Book 1, the sequencing of these two items is consistent with their sequencing as depicted in the PT-based processability hierarchy (Pienemann, 1998).

The NP morpheme 'phrasal plural -s' is the grammatical focus of Unit 7 and recurs in Unit 9. A closer look at the content of the lessons reveals that students need to learn to order or request food by specifying, in a given context such as a restaurant or a shops, the name of the food item and the quantity they want. 'Phrasal plural -s', exemplified in (62) and (63), is thus specified as the teaching focus if this unit.

(62) We want some noodles.
(63) I want two bananas.

The occurrence of 'phrasal plural -s' as a grammatical focus appears to follow that of lexical morphemes such as 'simple past -ed' and 'lexical plural -s'. According to the processability hierarchy for L2 English (Pienemann, 1998), 'phrasal plural -s', located at Stage 3, is acquired later than Stage 2 morphemes such as 'simple past -ed' and 'lexical plural -s'. Accordingly, in this volume, 'phrasal plural -s' appears after the Stage 2 morphemes. Their sequencing is generally consistent with the learning sequence as stipulated in PT (Pienemann, 1998).

The Stage 5 morpheme '3rd ps sg -s' occurs for the first time in Book 2. The local analysis of Book 2 indicates that this morpheme is introduced as a grammatical focus in Unit 8. Students are expected to ask and answer questions about someone's hobbies or dislikes. The targeted grammar is represented in dialogue (64).

(64) A: Does she like snakes?
B: No, she doesn't. She likes lizards.

According to the PT-based processability hierarchy (Pienemann, 2005), the acquisition of the morpheme '3rd ps sg -s' necessitates mastery of the morphemes located at the previous stage (Stage 4). Because the Stage 4 morpheme 'V-ing' was introduced as a grammatical focus in Book 1, the ordering of '3rd ps sg -s' is consistent with the sequencing in the processability hierarchy (Pienemann, 2005).

Local analysis of Book 3. 'Simple past -ed', 'possessive determiner', 'phrasal plural -s', 'V-ing', and '3rd ps sg -s' are repeatedly presented as incidental items in Book 3. These morphemes are not the teaching foci of this volume, but their repetition can provide an opportunity for students to practice the target language in different contexts. For instance, the lexical morpheme 'possessive determiner' recurs in Units 5 and 6. Students are required to talk about their body parts and the months of the year. 'Possessive determiner' thus appears as an incidental item and is used to construct target sentences, such as (65) and (66). Since 'possessive determiner' and other incidental items were the grammatical foci of previous volumes, their occurrence in Book 3 is considered as a reinforcement of the focal grammar and serves towards the fulfilment of other topics.

(65) This is my face.
(66) Our school fair is in October.

Local analysis of Book 4. Similar to Book 3, Book 4 does not introduce any new grammatical foci. The morphological items that recur in this volume are incidental items. They are: 'word or formulas', 'lexical plural -s', 'phrasal plural -s', 'V-ing', and '3rd ps sg -s'.

The recurrence of these morphemes in Book 4 goes towards the contextualization of focal grammar that was taught in previous volumes. Although they are not considered to be the teaching foci of Book 4, they still provide a variety of contexts for students to reinforce what they have learned. For example, in Unit 7, the teaching focus is the use of the gerunds, especially after the verb *go*, as exemplified in (67) and (68).

(67) She wants to go swimming.

(68) I like to go shopping.

In a case such as (67), the teaching focus is the production of '*go* + gerund'. The provision of '3rd ps sg -s' serves as a component of the target sentence where the use of 'go + gerund' is contextualized. Apart from that, students may 'pick' grammatical structures they have already learned in previous volumes, such as '3rd ps sg -s', and reinforce the practice of this structure in a different context.

Summary of the findings. To sum up, the analysis of the *Super Kids* textbook series reveals that the sequencing of the targeted morphological items is mostly consistent with their sequencing as hypothesized in PT (Pienemann, 1998, 2005). The structures that belong to the first three stages, including 'words/formulas', 'simple past -ed', 'possessive determiner', 'lexical plural -s', and 'phrasal plural -s', as well as the Stage 5 morpheme '3rd ps sg -s', are generally presented as grammatical foci in line with the learning sequence as stated in PT (Pienemann, 1998, 2005). The grammatical morphemes 'simple past -ed', 'possessive determiner', and 'lexical plural -s' are all situated at the category procedure stage (Stage 2). Since 'possessive determiner' is initially taught in Unit 2 of Book 1, thus the earliest point in time when the pupils have to learn the category procedural skills is located at Unit 2 of Book 1. The pedagogical teaching sequence of the lemma, the category procedural skills, and the NP procedural skills follows the sequenced development that the learners go through in acquiring English as an L2 as stipulated in PT (Pienemann, 1998, 2005). Similarly, '3rd ps sg -s' is taught after the instruction of 'V-ing'; this agrees with the PT's hypothesis that the learners can acquire the S-procedural skills only when they have developed all the previous VP procedural skills.

However, the Stage 4 morpheme 'V-ing' is conversely taught prior to the instruction of 'phrasal plural -s'. According to the processability hierarchy for L2 English (Pienemann, 2005), the VP procedural skills cannot be acquired without mastery of the previous NP procedural skills. Thus, the instruction of 'V-ing' in the *Super Kids* series is premature.

Overall, the majority of the key morphological items with the only exception of 'V-ing' are taught in a way that is processable and learnable for the primary-school children according to the learning sequence as stipulated in PT (Pienemann, 1998, 2005). In addition, the local analyses of individual books demonstrate that the introduction of those grammatical foci probably follows the arrangement of certain topics and related language functions. The first lesson starts with 'word/formulas' since the topic focuses on basic expression of greetings and gratitude such as

How are you and *Many thanks*. The second teaching objective 'possessive determiner' is used to introduce the pupils' family, teachers or classmates in Unit 2 of Book 1, such as *He's my brother*. The next grammatical focus is 'V-ing' in Unit 6 of Book 1 where students are required to talk about the present activities, as exemplified in the target language *She is eating lunch*. Given the lesson ('Weekend') of Unit 5 of Book 2, the lexical morpheme 'simple past -ed' is utilized by students to depict their activities or those of others last weekend (*I played soccer yesterday*). The following morphological item 'lexical plural -s' is called for in Unit 6 of Book 2, since the lesson topic is related to 'Likes' and students are expected to distinguish between the singular and plural forms of nouns (*I like puppets*). The focal instruction of 'phrasal plural -s' in Unit 7 arises from the required functions that students need to learn how to order food in restaurants or shops (*I want two bananas*). The morpheme '3rd ps sg -s' appears in Unit 8 of Book 2 where pupils need to ask and answer questions about someone's likes or dislikes (*She likes lizards*).

The instruction of key morphological items and the related content in the textbooks showed a consistency between the ordering of those structures and the arrangement of the corresponding lesson topics. The need for the communicative use of target language takes more effects in the organization of grammatical items. A range of different topics such as 'Greetings', 'Food', and 'Likes' are highly relevant to the school kids' daily life or interests. The fact that most of morphological items are ordered in line with the L2 learning sequence also implies that the authors of *Super Kids*, to a certain extent, manage to balance the learnability of grammar and the communicative need in language teaching.

5.3.1.4 Results—*Join in*

General findings of the textbook series. Table 5.11 displays all occurrences of targeted morphological items in the eight volumes of the *Join in* textbook series. The top row lists the five developmental stages as hypothesized in PT (Pienemann, 1998, 2005). The second row presents the eight targeted morphological items. The utmost left column identifies the individual volumes of this textbook series. The symbol '?' indicates the occurrence of a structure as a grammatical focus. The symbol 'x' is used for incidental occurrences of a structure. An empty cell means none of the targeted structures are present in the corresponding textbooks.

Table 5.11 Occurrences of PT-morphological items in *Join in*

Stage	1	2			3	4		5
Morphology	words/ formulas	past-ed	possessive determiner	lexical plural -s	phrasal plural -s	V-ing (VP)	V-en (VP)	3rd ps sg-s
Book 1	Δ	Δ	Δ	Δ	Δ			
Book 2	x		x	x	x	Δ	Δ	Δ
Book 3	x		x	x	x		x	x
Book 4	x		x	x	x	x	x	x

Table 5.11 Occurrences of PT-morphological items in *Join in* (continued)

Stage	1	2			3	4		5
Morphology	words/ formulas	past-ed	possessive determiner	lexical plural -s	phrasal plural -s	V-ing (VP)	V-en (VP)	3rd ps sg-s
Book 5	x		x	x	x	x		
Book 6	x		x	x	x	x		x
Book 7			x	x	x			x
Book 8			x	x	x		x	x

First, Table 5.11 shows that all developmental stages postulated in PT (Pienemann, 1998, 2005) are included in *Join in*, according to the criterion specified in Section 5.1 that at least one structure at each stage must be introduced as a learning objective in the textbook series. All eight targeted morphological items appear as learning objectives in the *Join in* series. They are: 'words/formulas', 'simple past -ed', 'possessive determiner', 'lexical plural -s', 'phrasal plural -s', the VP morphemes 'V-ing' and 'V-en', and '3rd ps sg -s'.

Second, Table 5.11 offers an understand of the initial occurrence of the structures as a teaching objective in each volume (highlighted as '△'). 1) Book 1 includes five teaching objectives, namely, 'words/formulas', 'simple past -ed', 'possessive determiner', 'lexical plural -s', and 'phrasal plural -s'. 2) In Book 2, three morphemes are provided as teaching foci, including 'V -ing', 'V -en', and '3rd ps sg -s'. 3) Books 3-8 do not introduce any new teaching objectives.

Based on the abovementioned observations, we can make a preliminary generalization about the ordering of those structures in *Join in*. 1) Similar to the previous three sets of textbooks, *Join in* also starts with the introduction of 'words/formulas' as one of the teaching foci in Book 1. This is obviously consistent with PT hypotheses (Pienemann, 1998). 2) Two morphemes, 'V -ing', and 'V -en', are taught as grammatical foci after their previous-stage structures. This finding suggests that these two morphemes are ordered in accordance with PT predictions (Pienemann, 2005). 3) However, it should be noted that the ordering of 'simple past -ed', 'possessive determiner', 'lexical plural -s', 'phrasal plural -s', and '3rd ps sg -s' seems to be unclear, due to that they appear as teaching foci in the same volumes with their preceding-stage structures. Therefore, a closer analysis of those morphemes in the corresponding volumes is required in order to clarify their ordering in *Join in* series.

Local analysis of Book 1. 'Words/formulas' is the grammatical focus of Unit 1 and recurs in all other units except for Unit 6. Students need to memorize and use some single words or formulaic structures such as 'here', 'goodbye', 'hello', or 'many thanks'. The lexical morpheme 'possessive determiner' is introduced as a grammatical focus in Unit 4 and recurs in Unit 6. A closer look at Unit 4 shows that the topics of this unit are about 'school things'.

Students are required to identify specific possessions and answer the question 'what's this?' In this case, 'possessive determiner' is specified as the teaching focus. The sentences in (69) and (70) are extracted from Unit 4.

(69) It's my book.

(70) It's her pen.

Since 'possessive determiner' is taught as a grammatical focus in Unit 4, after the instruction of 'words/formulas' in Unit 1, their sequencing in *Join in* is found to agree with the learning sequence as outlined in the PT-based processability hierarchy (Pienemann, 1998).

The other lexical morpheme, 'lexical plural -s', also occurs as a grammatical focus in Unit 4 and recurs in the last two units. In Unit 4, students need to differentiate between the singular and the plural forms of nouns, and produce the lexical plural marking -s on countable nouns. Exemplars are shown in (71) and (72).

(71) Open your schoolbags.

(72) Put in your books.

Similar to 'possessive determiner', the instruction of 'lexical plural -s' also follows the learning sequence as stated in PT (Pienemann, 1998), because it is taught as a grammatical focus in Unit 4, and its instruction occurs after the teaching of 'words/formulas'. Thus, the sequencing of 'lexical plural -s' and 'words/formulas' follows their ordering in the PT-based processability hierarchy (Pienemann, 1998).

'Simple past -ed' appears as another teaching focus of Unit 4 and recurs in Unit 5. Students need to describe activities or actions in the past through the use of the regular or irregular form of verbs. A few exemplars are reproduced in (73) and (74).

(73) He broke his right arm.

(74) They called the school office.

As discussed before, 'words/formulas' (Stage 1) was one of the grammatical foci of Book 1. The lexical morpheme 'simple past -ed' can be acquired at Stage 2. Thus, the sequencing of 'simple past -ed' and 'words/formulas' agrees with the learning sequence as stipulated in PT (Pienemann, 1998).

'Phrasal plural -s' is the final grammatical focus of Unit 4 and that it recurs in Unit 6. Students are expected to answer questions starting off with the words *how many*, followed by the plural form of a countable noun, such as 'How many pens?' They also need to describe their classrooms or bedrooms by using NPs consisting of a quantifier (or, optionally, a numeral) and a countable noun. An example is provided in dialogue (75).

(75) A: What's in your classroom?
B: Two windows. A blackboard. Desks and chairs.

'Phrasal plural -s', which is acquired at Stage 3, is one of the grammatical foci of Unit 4 of Book 1, simultaneously with Stage 2 morphemes such as 'possessive determiner', 'lexical plural -s' and 'simple past -ed'. According to the staged L2 development as stipulated in PT (Pienemann, 1998), the acquisition of 'phrasal plural -s' requires the mastery of the Stage 2 morphemes. Thus, the instruction of 'phrasal plural -s' in Unit 4 appears to come a little early for L2 students.

Local analysis of Book 2. As Table 5.11 shows, the morphological items situated at Stages 1 to 3 are recycled in individual units of Book 2. They are not presented as teaching foci but still offer an opportunity for students to practice what they have acquired in prior lessons. They also serve as a component to constitute target sentences. Take the occurrence of 'possessive determiner' in Unit 3 as an example. The teaching focus in Unit 3 is on the VP morpheme 'V-ing'. Exemplars are shown in (76).

(74) My favourite colour is red. I am wearing a red T-shirt.

In cases such as (76), the possessive determiner '*my*' is presented as an incidental item to construct a target sentence that contains the grammatical focus 'V-ing'. Students also get the chance to reproduce 'possessive determiner', which was taught in the previous book. The repetition of such morphemes in the textbooks can provide a variety of contexts enabling students to practice their language skills.

The Stage 4 morpheme 'V-ing' is taught in Unit 3 and recurs in Unit 4. Students need to describe someone's outfit or appearance by using the present progressive marker *-ing*. (77) and (78) are exemplars from Unit 3.

(77) Sophie is wearing a pink cap.
(78) Anna is using makeup.

Since the previous stage morpheme 'phrasal plural -s' was taught as one of the grammatical foci in Book 1, the instruction of 'V-ing' in Book 2 is in agreement with the learning sequence as hypothesized in PT (Pienemann, 2005).

The other Stage 4 morpheme, 'V-en', is introduced as the grammatical focus of Unit 4 and recurs in Unit 6. Students are expected to discuss an action that was completed at some point in the past or that extends to the current moment. 'V-en' is shown in exemplars (79) and (80).

(79) I've walked three miles.

(80) I have finished my homework.

Similar to 'V-ing', the instruction of 'V-en' in Book 2 occurs later than that of the Stage 3 morpheme 'phrasal plural -s' in Book 1. That is to say, the sequencing of 'V-en' and 'phrasal plural -s' is consistent with their sequencing as outlined in the PT-based processability hierarchy (Pienemann, 2005).

The Stage 5 morpheme '3rd ps sg -s' is presented as the grammatical focus of Unit 2 and recurs in Unit 4. Students are asked to describe regular activities of their friends or classmates through the use of a third-person present statement, such as in (81) and (82).

(81) Emma paints a red bridge on Monday.

(82) He plays basketball on Tuesday.

However, having '3rd ps sg -s' as the grammatical focus of Unit 2 is problematic. According to PT, this morpheme cannot be acquired before Stage 5 in L2 English development and its acquisition necessitates the mastery of Stage 4 structures. However, '3rd ps sg -s' is taught in Unit 2, earlier than the instruction of 'V-ing' and 'V-en'. The instruction of '3rd ps sg -s' in the *Join in* series is premature, as it is not consistent with the PT-based learning sequence (Pienemann, 2005).

Local analyses of Books 3-8. In none of the following volumes (Books 3-8), there are any new grammatical foci. Almost all the morphological items that have been taught before recur as incidental items. This means that students are provided with opportunities to reinforce language practice and may reproduce what they have learned in a variety of contexts. Thus, no further discussion concerning the ordering of structures is needed here.

Summary of the findings. In summary, the analysis of the *Join in* series reveals that the sequencing of the targeted morphological items is mostly consistent with their sequencing as hypothesized in the PT-based processability hierarchy (Pienemann, 1998, 2005). 'Words/formulas', 'simple past -ed', 'possessive determiner', and 'lexical plural -s' (all of which belong to Stages 1 and 2) as well as 'V-ing' and 'V-en' (Stage 4) are generally introduced as grammatical foci in accordance with the learning sequence as stated in PT (Pienemann, 1998, 2005). The lexical morphemes 'simple past -ed', 'possessive determiner', and 'lexical plural -s' are taught as the grammatical foci in Unit 4 of Book 2. This also locates the point when the category procedure becomes obligatory for the pupils for the first time in the whole series. Thus, the pedagogical teaching order of the lemma and the category procedural skills in this series is presented in a learnable way, namely, the learner can only map the conceptual structures onto single words or formulae before he or she develops the category procedural skills and produce lexical morphemes (cf. Pienemann, 1998, p. 83).

However, the instruction of structures at Stage 3 and Stage 5 does not agree with the PT-based learning sequence (Pienemann, 1998, 2005). For instance, 'phrasal plural -s' (Stage 3) is introduced as a grammatical focus simultaneously with the instruction of 'possessive determiner' and 'lexical plural -s' in Unit 4 of Book 1. The lexical morphemes and the NP morpheme should not be instructed at the same time, since the learner is able to acquire the NP procedure only when the previous category procedural skills have been developed. The Stage 5 morpheme '3rd ps sg -s' is a grammatical focus earlier than the Stage 4 morphemes 'V-ing' and 'V-en'. This also goes against the sequenced development of L2 processing skills, namely, the learners have to develop the VP procedural skills before they progress to the S-procedure stage.

From a processability perspective, most of focal morphological items in *Join in* series are processable and learnable for the primary-school English learners. In addition, the specific investigation of each book provides more insights into the arrangement of those morphological foci in the whole textbook series. Since the very first lesson exclusively focuses on 'Greetings', thus students only need to memorize and use single words or formulaic structures such as *hello* or *many thanks*. The following teaching focus is 'possessive determiner' in Unit 4 of Book 1; the lesson topic concerns 'School Things' and thus students are required to identify specific possessions, such as *It's her pen*. In the same lesson, students also need to differentiate between the singular and the plural forms of nouns, and thus 'lexical plural -s' is provided to fulfil the language use (*Open your schoolbags*). The next teaching focus 'simple past -ed' is also produced in relation to another function required in Unit 4 of Book 7—to talk about the past activities or actions in schools, such as *They called the school office*. Again, within the same topic of Unit 4 of Book 1, 'phrasal plural -s' is also called for in the context that students are expected to describe their classrooms including specific facilities, such as *Two windows*. Next, the provision of '3rd ps sg -s' is associated with the lesson topic and related context, namely, to describe regular activities of friends or schoolmates (*Emma paints a red bridge on Monday*). The following grammatical focus 'V-ing' is introduced in Unit 3 of Book 2, where students need to depict someone's current outfit or appearance (*Sophie is wearing a pink cap*). The final teaching focus 'V-en' occurs in Unit 4 of Book 2, as students need to discuss an action or activity that was completed at some point in the past (*I have finished my homework*).

The organization of focal morphological items in *Join in* appears to be highly influenced by the corresponding lesson topics especially by those that appear more than once. One is 'Activities'. This topic seems to be very closely related to the school children's daily life, since it can cover a range of communicative situations such as activities (actions) in the present or the past. Thus, the tense markers such as 'simple past -ed', 'V-ing', 'V-en', and '3rd ps sg -s' are more likely to be provided in such contexts. While the learnable instruction of most of the morphological foci implies that textbook writers may take into account the actual learning difficulty, the arrangement of textbook content and the premature teaching of 'phrasal plural -s' and '3rd ps sg -s' suggest that the primary concern of textbook compilation is the communicative aspects of language use, more specifically, language functions in a given situation.

In the following, the sequencing of syntactic structures in the four series will be presented and discussed.

5.3.2 Grading of syntactic structures

This part of the analysis looks into nine items in the syntactic development of L2 English as stipulated in the processability hierarchy (Pienemann, 1998, 2005). They are: words/formulas, canonical word order SV(O), ADV-fronting, *do*-fronting, yes/no inversion, copula inversion, *do*-2nd, AUX-2nd, and cancel inversion. According to Processability Theory (Pienemann, 1998), L2 learners are hypothesized to go through six stages in their acquisition of English syntax.

Stage 1—lemma access: words/formulas
Stage 2—category procedure: canonical word order SV(O)
Stage 3—NP procedure: ADV-fronting, do-fronting
Stage 4—VP procedure: yes/no inversion, copula inversion
Stage 5—S-procedure: do-2nd, AUX-2nd
Stage 6—S'-procedure: cancel inversion

As before, the sequences implemented in each textbook series are discussed separately.

5.3.2.1 Results—*New Standard English*

General findings of the textbook series. Table 5.12 tabulates all occurrences of the nine syntactic items that are teaching objectives in the eight volumes of *New Standard English*. The layout of this table is similar to that adopted in the analysis of morphological items. The top two rows indicate the six developmental stages hypothesized in PT (Pienemann, 1998, 2005) and the corresponding syntactic structures of L2 English. The occurrence of a targeted structure as a grammatical focus is marked by means of the triangle sign '?'. The symbol 'x' means that a given structure recurs as an incidental item. A blank cell indicates that no specific structures are introduced.

Table 5.12 Occurrences of PT-based syntactic structures in *New Standard English*

Stage	1	2	3		4		5		6
Syntax	words/formulas	SV(O)	ADV-fronting	do-fronting	yes/no inversion	copula inversion	do-2nd	AUX-2nd	cancel inversion
Book 1	Δ	Δ				Δ			
Book 2	x	x		Δ	Δ	x	Δ		
Book 3		x		x	x			Δ	
Book 4		x			x				

Table 5.12 Occurrences of PT-based syntactic structures in *New Standard English* (continued)

Stage	1	2	3		4		5		6
Syntax	words/ formulas	SV(O)	ADV-fronting	do-fronting	yes/no inversion	copula inversion	do-2nd	AUX-2nd	cancel inversion
Book 5		x		x	x		x		
Book 6		x				x	x	x	
Book 7					x				
Book 8						x	x	x	

As illustrated in Table 5.12, all developmental stages as hypothesized in PT (Pienemann, 1998, 2005) are included in the *New Standard English* series, with the exception of Stage 6. Apart from 'ADV-fronting' and 'cancel inversion', all other seven syntactic items appear as learning objectives in this set of textbooks. They are: 'words/formulas', 'canonical order word SV(O)', 'do-fronting', 'yes/no inversion', 'copula inversion', 'do-2nd', and 'AUX-2nd'.

A closer look at the initial occurrence of the structures as a teaching objective (marked as '?') indicates that: 1) three structures are taught as grammatical foci of Book 1, including 'words/formulas', 'canonical word order SV(O)', and 'copula inversion'. 2) In Book 2, three word orders are presented as teaching foci—'do-fronting', 'yes/no inversion', and 'do-2nd'. 3) In Book 3, the only new grammatical focus is the Stage 5 word order 'AUX-2nd'. 4) There are no new teaching objectives in Books 4 to 8.

Based on these observations, several preliminary findings can be summed up in relation to the ordering of the target syntactic features in *New Standard English*. 1) This textbook series starts with the introduction of formulaic sequence (Stage 1) as one of the teaching foci in Book 1, which follows the PT prediction that 'words/formulas' can be acquired at the very first beginning of L2 acquisition process. 2) Two word order rules, 'do-fronting' and 'AUX-2nd', appear as a teaching objective later than the provision of their previous-stage structures. This means that these two syntactic structures are ordered in line with the hypothesized L2 learning sequence as stipulated in PT (Pienemann, 1998, 2005). 3) However, 'copula inversion' (Stage 4) precedes 'do-fronting' (Stage 3) in this textbook series, which goes against their sequencing as hypothesized in PT (Pienemann, 2005). The instruction of 'copula inversion' appears to be premature. 4) Noteworthily, the ordering of three word order rules still seems to be vague. 'Canonical word order SV(O)' and 'yes/no inversion' are taught as a grammatical focus at the same volumes with their preceding-stage structures. 'Do-2nd' (Stage 5) occurs as a teaching objective after one of the Stage 4's structures—'copula inversion' but in the same volume with the other word order at Stage 4—'yes/no inversion'. Therefore, we need to look into the corresponding volumes to examine whether these features are ordered in accordance with PT predictions (Pienemann, 1998, 2005).

Local analysis of Book 1. In the majority of modules in Book 1, students need to learn and memorize some formulaic expressions such as 'How are you?', 'I'm fine', and 'What's your name?' The canonical word order SV(O) is considered as the grammatical focus of Module 4. The theme of this module is 'We love animals'. Students are required to produce simple SVO sentences to talk about animals. Some exemplars are shown in (83) and (84).

(83) I have a panda.
(84) It is a cat.

According to PT, 'words/formulas' and 'canonical word order SV(O)' are acquired at the first two stages of L2 English syntactic development. In Book 1, the Stage 2 structure 'canonical word order SV(O)' is found to occur as a grammatical focus after 'words/formulas' at Stage 1. Their sequencing is consistent with the learning sequence as stipulated in PT (Pienemann, 1998).

The Stage 4 word order 'copula inversion' is the grammatical focus of Unit 8 in Book 1. Students need to ask yes-or-no questions by putting the subject after the copula verb, to confirm what exactly the referred entity is, as represented in dialogue (85).

(85) A: What's that?
B: I don't know.
A: Is it a kite?
C: Yes, it is.

The investigation of the texts and exercises also reveals that the instruction of 'copula inversion' is possibly based on the topics of the previous lesson. In Module 7, themes include the discussion of things that are not nearby, such as 'What's that?' and 'That is our house'. However, such structures are only provided in the texts and exercises, not being specified as teaching foci for the lesson. The following lesson (Module 8) continues to talk about entities that are not nearby and does so through the use of the 'copula inversion' structure. However, 'copula inversion' becomes a grammatical focus without the instruction of the Stage 3 structures 'ADV-fronting' and 'Do-fronting'. As can be seen from Table 5.14, 'ADV-fronting' and 'Do-fronting' do not appear in Book 1. Thus, according to the PT-based learning sequence (Pienemann, 2005), the instruction of 'copula inversion' in *New Standard English* is premature.

Local analysis of Book 2. The Stage 2 word order 'canonical word order SV(O)' is recycled as an incidental item in almost all modules with the only exception of Module 4. Students thus get more opportunities to reproduce this structure, taught as the focal grammar in the previous volume, in a broader range of contexts, as exemplified in (86) and (87).

(86) We have a new friend today.

(87) I'm from Canada.

The Stage 3 word order 'do-fronting' is the grammatical focus of Module 4. Students are required to talk about their favourite foods or dislikes by producing *yes-or-no* questions in which the auxiliary *do* is placed in the initial position. Sentences (88) and (89) are exemplars from Module 4.

(88) Do you like meat?

(89) Do you eat fish?

Since the Stage 2 word order SVO was one of the grammatical foci of Book 1, the instruction of 'do fronting' in Book 2 is consistent with the learning sequence as stated in PT (Pienemann, 1998).

The Stage 4 word order 'yes/no inversion' is the grammatical focus of Module 5 and then recurs in Module 9. In Module 5, students need to produce *yes-or-no* questions in which the auxiliary is located first. For example, in a game in which students are asked to find some missing stuff, they use the kind of question exemplified in (90).

(90) Can you find the toy box?

According to PT, 'yes/no inversion' is acquired at Stage 4 of the L2 English acquisition process. Its acquisition requires the mastery of Stage 3 structures such as 'do-fronting'. As discussed above, 'do-fronting' was the grammatical focus of Module 4. This means that 'do-fronting' precedes 'yes/no inversion'. Their sequencing is therefore consistent with the PT-based learning sequence (Pienemann, 2005).

The Stage 5 word order 'do-2nd' appears as the grammatical focus of Unit 6. Students are expected to request specific information in regards to the daily activities of their friends or schoolmates through the use of WH-questions. Some exemplars are presented in (91) and (92).

(91) What do you do on Sundays?

(92) What does Lingling have at school?

Since the Stage 4 structure 'yes/no inversion' was the grammatical focus of Module 5 in Book 2 and 'copula inversion' was taught in Book 1, the instruction of 'do-2nd' in Module 6 of Book 2 is consistent with the hypothesized learning sequence for L2 English (Pienemann, 2005).

Local analysis of Book **3**. The syntactic structure 'canonical word order SV(O)' is recycled in the majority of modules in Book 3. As discussed before, the repeated presence of structures in different texts can offer opportunities for students to reinforce the use of grammar taught in previous lessons. Examples (93) and (94) are extracted from Module 1.

(93) We have a new classroom.
(94) I have a dog.

Similarly, 'do-fronting' occurs as an incidental item in Module 5, while 'yes/no inversion' recurs in Modules 6 and 9, as exemplified in (95) and (96).

(95) Do you have rice?
(96) Can I have some soup?

The only new grammatical focus, 'AUX-2nd', occurs in Module 4 and recurs in Module 8. Students are expected to request some specific information through the use of WH-questions. For instance, they need to ask others to describe items present in a particular location or current activities, as exemplified in (97) and (98).

(97) What can you see in my room?
I can see a window, a door, a chair, a desk, and a bed.
(98) What are they doing?
They are rowing a dragon boat.

The analysis of Book 2 reveals that the Stage 4 structures 'copula inversion' and 'yes/no inversion' are first instructed in Books 1 and 2, respectively. That is to say, the instruction of the Stage 4 structures precedes that of 'AUX-2nd'. The sequencing of 'AUX-2nd' and the Stage 4 structures 'copula inversion' and 'yes/no inversion' agrees with their sequencing in the PT-based processability hierarchy for L2 English development (Pienemann, 2005).

Local analyses of Books 4-8. No new teaching objectives are provided in Books 4 to 8. The word order rules taught as grammatical foci in previous volumes occur repeatedly as incidental items, including 'canonical word order SV(O)', 'do-fronting', 'yes/no inversion', 'copula inversion', 'do-2nd', and 'AUX-2nd'.

The recycling of the syntactic structures in Books 4 to 8 gives students more chances to reinforce the use of target grammar. For example, sentences (99) and (100) involving 'canonical word order SV(O)' are extracted from the texts of Book 4. The teaching focus is the use of specific adjectives such as *nice*, *shy*, and *big*. Through the presentation of simple sentences of the SV(O) type, students can contextualize the use of these adjectives.

(99) She's very nice. But she's a bit shy.

(100) London is the capital of England. And it's very big.

Summary of the findings. In summary, the analysis of the *New Standard English* series indicates that the sequencing of the syntactic items that are grammatical foci shows a high degree of consistency with their sequencing as stipulated in the PT-based processability hierarchy for L2 English development (Pienemann, 1998, 2005). The syntactic items belonging to the first three stages ('words/formulas', 'canonical word order SV(O)', and 'do-fronting') are sequenced in keeping with the learning sequence as hypothesized in PT (Pienemann, 1998, 2005). Their pedagogical teaching sequence indicates that, in this textbook series, the students are required to start with the formulaic structures (e. g., *how are you*?) and then to develop the category procedural skills (e. g., the SVO structure). Based on all the previous processing skills, the students are able to go up to the next stage—the NP procedure (e. g., 'do-fronting') while studying Book 2. For the word order rules at Stage 4, 'copula inversion' is firstly taught in Book 1. This also locates the earliest point in time when the VP procedure is required in the whole series. However, according to PT (Pienemann, 1998, 2005), the VP procedural skills cannot be acquired without the mastery of the NP procedural skills. Thus, the instruction of 'copula inversion' is premature for the pupils in this set of textbooks. The earliest point when the students are expected to acquire the S-procedural skills (Stage 5) for the first time is in Book 2 where 'do-2nd' is taught as a grammatical focus. This indicates that the pupils are required to acquire the S-procedural skills after they have developed the previous VP procedural skills. Thus, the instruction of the Stage 5 syntactic structures in this series is learnable for the pupils. Another interesting finding is that the Stage 6 word order 'cancel inversion' is missing in this textbook series.

As indicated above, except for 'copula inversion', the majority of the key syntactic items are taught in a learnable way according to PT-based developmental path of L2 English acquisition (Pienemann, 1998, 2005). It can be argued that the grammatical learnability has been fairly considered in the ordering of the sentence structures specified as the teaching objectives in *New Standard English* series. Nevertheless, the specific analyses of individual books reveal evidence that the learnability of grammar may not be the dominant factor in the textbook compilation, and the organization of those syntactic items may be highly associated with the arrangement of lesson topics and required language functions.

In the first lesson ('Greetings'), students only need to learn very basic expressions to start simple conversation, and thus some formulaic structures such as *How are you*? and *What's your name*? are taught as the teaching objectives. The following syntactic item 'canonical word order SV(O)' is obligatorily provided based on the topic-related context ('We Love Animals'), namely, students need to talk about animals through declarative statements such as *It is a cat*. The focal instruction of 'copula inversion' is closely related to the lesson of Module 8 of Book 1 where students are required to discuss entities that are not nearby (*Is it a kite?*). The next syntactic focus 'do-fronting' is called for in Module 4 of Book 2 where learners are expected to talk about their favourite foods or dislikes (*Do you like fish?*). The following teaching objective 'yes/no inversion' is taught in Module 5 of Book 2, according to the lesson context of requesting information about missing stuff (*Can you find the toy box?*). Next, 'do-2nd' is obligatorily used in Module 6 of Book 2 to ask specific information in regards to daily activities (*What do you do on Sundays?*). The provision of 'AUX-2nd' in Module 4 of Book 3 arises from the given context of requesting specific information about someone's current activities (*What are they doing?*).

The connection between the lesson topics and the obligatory syntactic items shows that the design of the *New Standard English* series concerns more about the selection of topics in relation to children's experiences or interests, such as 'Greetings', 'Animals', 'Activities' or 'Likes'. Given a specific topic, a range of key sentence structures are chosen as structural consequences to fulfil the relevant language functions within various communicative situations. Thus, whether the sentence structure is psycholinguistically processable and learnable does not seem to be a primary concern in this textbook series.

5.3.2.2 Results—*People's Education Press English*

General findings of the textbook series. Table 5.13 shows all occurrences of the targeted syntactic structures that appear as teaching objectives in the eight volumes of *People's Education Press (PEP) English.* The top row lists the hypothesized six developmental stages for L2 English syntax (Pienemann, 1998, 2005). The second row maps onto these the syntactic items acquired at each of these stages. The presence of a structure that is given grammatical focus is shown by means of the symbol '?'. 'x' refers to incidental occurrences of a structure. Empty cells indicate that no relevant structures occur at all.

Table 5.13 Occurrences of PT-syntactic items in *PEP English*

Stage	1	2	3	4			5		6
Syntax	words/ formulas	SV(O)	ADV-fronting	do-fronting	yes/no inversion	copula inversion	do-2nd	AUX-2nd	cancel inversion
Book 1	Δ	Δ							
Book 2	x	x		Δ		Δ			
Book 3	x	x	Δ		Δ	x	Δ	Δ	
Book 4	x					x	x	x	
Book 5		x			x	x	x	x	
Book 6		x			x	x	x	x	
Book 7	x	x	x		x	x	x	x	
Book 8	x	x			x		x		

Table 5.13 shows that, except for Stage 6, all other developmental stages predicted in PT

(Pienemann, 1998, 2005) are included in *PEP English*. All eight syntactic items, with the sole exception of 'cancel inversion', are introduced as learning objectives in this set of textbooks. They are: 'words/formulas', 'canonical word order SV(O)', 'ADV-fronting', 'do-fronting', 'yes/no inversion', 'copula inversion', 'do-2nd', and 'AUX-2nd'.

Focusing on the initial occurrence of structures as a teaching objective (highlighted by '?' in Table 5.13), we can find that: 1) Book 1 includes two teaching foci, namely, 'words/formulas' and 'canonical word order SV(O)'. 2) In Book 2, two new word order rules ('do-fronting' and 'copula inversion') are introduced as grammatical foci. 3) In Book 3, there are four new teaching foci: 'ADV-fronting', yes/no inversion', 'do-2nd' and 'AUX-2nd'. 4) In Book 4, no new grammatical focus is introduced. 5) For all of Books 5-8, there are no new grammatical foci added into the list of teaching objectives.

In regards to the ordering of the abovementioned syntactic items in *PEP English*, several preliminary findings can be concluded here. 1) The focal instruction of 'words/formulas' in Book 1 apparently follows the PT hypotheses (Pienemann, 1998). 2) Two word order rules at Stage 3, 'ADV-fronting' and 'do-fronting', are both introduced as a teaching objective after the focal instruction of Stage 2 structure 'canonical word order SV(O)'. Such an ordering is consistent with the hypothesized sequence in PT-based processability hierarchy (Pienemann, 1998). 3) However, the sequencing of five word order rules in this set of textbooks remains issues. 'Canonical word order SV(O)' is introduced as a grammatical focus in the same volume (Book 1) with its previous-stage feature 'words/formulas'. A closer look at the occurrence of SV(O) in Book 1 is needed in order to confirm whether it is introduced prior to formulaic sequence according to PT predictions. Similarly, 'copula inversion' is specified as a teaching objective at the same volume with one of its previous-stage word order rules—'do-fronting' but earlier than the other one feature—'ADV-fronting'. 'Yes/no inversion', 'do-2nd' and 'AUX-2nd' all appear after one of their preceding structures but at the same volume with the other one. Therefore, the following analyses will look into the corresponding volumes.

Local analysis of Book 1. 'Words/formulas' is the grammatical focus of Unit 1 and is recycled in all the following units of Book 1. Students need to memorize a range of formulaic expressions such as 'How are you?' and 'What's your name?' The canonical word order SV(O) occurs as the grammatical focus of Unit 5. In this unit, students are required to describe their favourite foods or offer food to someone by using a simple SVO sentence. Examples (101) and (102) are extracted from Unit 5.

(101) I like chicken.
(102) You can have some orange juice.

According to PT hypotheses (Pienemann, 1998), 'words/formulas' and 'canonical word order SV(O)' are able to be acquired at the beginning of the L2 English acquisition process. The individual analysis of Book 1 also shows that the Stage 2 word order 'canonical word order SV (O)' is taught after 'words/formulas' of Stage 1. Thus, the sequencing of these two structures follows their sequencing in the PT-based processability hierarchy (Pienemann, 1998).

Local analysis of Book 2. 'Words/formulas' is repeatedly present in Units 1, 2, 4, and 5. The Stage 2 word order SVO, exemplified in (103) and (104), recurs as an incidental item in all units.

(103) She's my mother.
(104) I like hamburgers.

The Stage 3 word order 'do-fronting' is the grammatical focus of Unit 5. Students are expected to talk about their favourite fruits and request relevant information from others by producing yes-or-no questions in which the auxiliary *do* appears in first position. Exemplars are shown in (105) and (106).

(105) Do you want pears?
(106) Do you like bananas?

Since the Stage 2 word order SVO was a grammatical focus of Book 1, the instruction of the Stage 3 word order 'do-fronting' in Book 2 is consistent with the learning sequence as stipulated in PT (Pienemann, 1998).

The other word order, 'copula inversion', occurs as the grammatical focus of Unit 2 and is recycled in Unit 4. In Unit 2, students need to ask about and introduce their family members by means of pictures, entities or contexts, as exemplified in (107).

(107) A: Is he your father?
B: Yes, he is.

In Unit 4, students are expected to ask questions in relation to the location of specific entities, as in (108).

(108) A: Is my cap under the desk?
B: No, it isn't.

Based on their communicative needs, students need to acquire and produce the structure 'copula inversion' to talk about their daily lives, including family and personal stuff.

With respect to the sequencing of grammatical foci in Book 2, it can be seen that the instruction of 'copula inversion' precedes that of the Stage 3 word order 'do-fronting'.

According to the PT-based processability hierarchy (Pienemann, 2005), 'copula inversion' is acquired at Stage 4, and the prerequisite of its acquisition is the mastery of Stage 3-structures such as 'do-fronting'. Therefore, the ordering of 'copula inversion' is apparently against the learning sequence as hypothesized in PT (Pienemann, 2005).

Local analysis of Book 3. In this volume, the word order rule 'ADV-fronting' is the grammatical focus of Unit 1. Students need to produce the sentence structure SVO with a fronted adverb or adverbial that refers to time. In the process, they learn how to use this structure to emphasize the focal constituent. Exemplars are provided in (109) and (110).

(109) Sometimes I go hiking.
(110) On Sunday I go shopping.

Since the Stage 2 structure 'canonical word order SV(O)' was a grammatical focus in Book 1, the instruction of the Stage 3 structure 'ADV-fronting' in Book 3 is consistent with the learning sequence as stated in PT (Pienemann, 1998).

The other grammatical focus, 'yes/no inversion', is provided in Unit 4. Students are required to produce yes-or-no questions in which the auxiliary is placed in initial position to confirm specific information, as exemplified in (111) and (112).

(111) Can I wear my new T-shirt?
(112) Is he wearing a black cap?

According to the processability hierarchy hypothesized in PT (Pienemann, 2005), the word order 'yes/no inversion' is acquired at Stage 4, and the acquisition of this word order needs the Stage 3 structures as a prerequisite. The previous analysis has found that one of Stage 3's word order rules—'do-fronting' was a grammatical focus in Book 2. Moreover, the other structure at Stage 3 'ADV-fronting' is taught in Unit 1 of Book 3. Therefore, the ordering of 'yes/no inversion' follows the sequencing as outlined in PT-based processability hierarchy (Pienemann, 2005).

In addition, the Stage 5 word order 'do-2nd' appears as the grammatical focus of Unit 6. Its instruction is associated with the theme of the lesson, which is related to students' daily life. In Unit 6, students are required to ask WH-questions in regards to their possessions or in regards to quantities, as in (113).

(113) How many pencils do you have?

Since the Stage 4 structures 'copula inversion' has been taught in Book 2 and 'yes/no inversion' appears as a grammatical focus in Unit 4 of Book 3, thus the teaching of 'do-2nd' in

Unit 6 of Book 3 follows the hypothesized sequence as stated in PT (Pienemann, 2005).

'AUX-2nd' is the grammatical focus of Unit 5. Students are asked to produce and answer WH-questions related to their daily meals. Sentences (114) and (115) are extracted from the texts of Unit 5.

(114) What would you like for dinner?

(115) What will you eat for lunch?

In the PT-based processability hierarchy for L2 English (Pienemann, 2005), the word order 'AUX-2nd' is acquired at Stage 5, and requires the mastery of Stage 4 structures such as 'copula inversion'. The previous analysis has indicated that 'copula inversion' is one of the grammatical foci of Book 2. Also, 'yes/no inversion' is taught in Unit 4 of Book 3. Thus, the ordering of 'AUX-2nd' is consistent with the sequencing as outlined in the processability hierarchy for L2 English development (Pienemann, 2005).

Local analysis of Book 4. 'Words/formulas' is recycled in Unit 2. The Stage 4 word order 'copula inversion' is repeatedly present in the last three units. The Stage 5 structure 'do-2nd' recurs in Unit 6, while 'AUX-2nd' is recycled in Unit 4. The repetition of these incidental items in the volume provides further contextualization for the teaching focus, which is thus not presented as an isolated item to be acquired in isolation. For example, in Unit 4, one teaching focus is the use of key adjectives that describe the weather. Since students have learned 'copula inversion' as a focal grammar item in Book 2, they can reproduce this structure to contextualize the use of adjectives such as *warm*, *cold*, *hot*, and *cool*. Dialogue (116) is excerpted from the texts of Unit 4.

(116) A: Is it cold in Kunming?
B: No, it's warm.

Local analyses of Books 5-8. As shown in Table 5.13, none of the following volumes have any new grammatical foci. Syntactic items taught in previous volumes recur as incidental items in Books 5-8. Thus, no further insights into these volumes are needed since the primary concern of this study is about the sequencing of teaching objectives rather than incidental items.

Summary of the findings. In conclusion, the analysis of the *PEP English* series shows that the sequencing of the targeted syntactic items mostly agrees with their sequencing as outlined in the PT-based processability hierarchy (Pienemann, 1998, 2005). The syntactic items at the initial three stages are taught in a learnable manner. The pedagogical teaching sequence reveals that: at first, the pupils only need to learn some formulaic structures ('words/formulas'); subsequently, they are required to develop the category procedural skills ('canonical word order SV(O)'); after developing all the processing resources, the pupils are expected to acquire the NP procedural skills ('ADV-fronting' and 'do-fronting'). However, the instruction of 'copula inversion' is premature for the students. As analysed above, this structure is the grammatical focus of Unit 2 of Book 2, preceding the instruction of 'do-fronting' (Stage 3) in Unit 5 of Book 2. The initial occurrences of 'do-fronting' and 'copula inversion' also locate the points in time when the NP procedure (Stage 3) and the VP procedure (Stage 4) are required for the first time in this textbook series. The teaching order that the VP procedural skills are developed before the NP procedural skills apparently violates the PT-based learning sequence (Pienemann, 1998, 2005). In terms of the Stage 5 syntactic features 'do-2nd' and 'AUX-2nd', they are taught after the VP procedural skill becomes the instructional focus ('copula inversion'). This means that the students need to acquire the S-procedural skills after they have developed the VP procedural skills. Therefore, the instruction of 'do-2nd' and 'AUX-2nd' is considered learnable in *PEP* English series.

The local analyses of individual volumes offer more insights into the organization of those syntactic foci in the whole textbook series. There is evidence that the provision of the syntactic items is possibly determined by their usefulness in fulfilment of language functions within a given topic. The first lesson only concerns basic expression including greetings and self-introduction, therefore the obligatory items are formulaic strings such as *How are you*? and *What's your name*?. The second syntactic focus 'canonical word order SV(O)' is provided in Unit 5 of Book 1, where students need to describe their favourite foods such as *I like chicken*. The instruction of the following teaching objective is 'copula inversion' in Unit 2 of Book 2; in this lesson, students are expected to ask information about specific matters such as family or possessions (*Is he your father*?). The next focal word order 'do-fronting' appears in Unit 5 of Book 2, since the required function in the given lesson is to question about someone's favourite fruits (*Do you want pears*?). The subsequent teaching focus 'ADV-fronting' is called for in Unit 1 of Book 3, where learners need to describe their activities at a specific time such as *On Sunday I go shopping*. Next, the word order 'yes/no inversion' is obligatorily used in Unit 4 of Book 3, since this lesson requires students to confirm specific information about outfit or appearance (*Can I wear my new T-shirt*?). The following syntactic focus 'AUX-2nd' is taught in Unit 5 of Book 3, as the lesson requires students to ask/answer information about their daily meals (*What would you like for dinner*?). The focal instruction of 'do-2nd' in Unit 6 of Book 3 arises from the topic-related context where learners need to request specific information about the quantities of possessions (*How many pencils do you have*?).

As shown above, a range of general topics such as 'Self-introduction', 'Favourite Food', 'Activities', and 'Daily Meals' are designed on the basis of students' daily life or personal experiences. They can provide a variety of contexts for students to achieve the communicative use of target language by means of related sentence structures. For example, two types of English questions such as the *yes-or-no* questions and WH-questions are frequently provided as the syntactic foci in the textbooks, since they are very useful for students to request or confirm specific information in different communicative situations. Thus, the organization of the syntactic items is highly related to the arrangement of topics and necessary functions.

5.3.2.3 Results—*Super Kids*

General findings of the textbook series. Table 5.14 tabulates all occurrences of the targeted syntactic items that are teaching objectives in the four volumes of *Super Kids*. The top row shows the hypothesized six developmental stages for the nine targeted structures (Pienemann, 1998, 2005), which are listed in the second row. The occurrences of a structure that is a grammatical focus is marked by means of the triangle symbol '?'. Incidental occurrences of the structures are marked with 'x'. Where no specific structure is used, the cell is left empty.

Table 5.14 Occurrences of PT-syntactic items in *Super Kids*

Stage	1	2	3		4		5		6
Syntax	words/ formulas	SV(O)	ADV-fronting	do-fronting	yes/no inversion	copula inversion	do-2nd	AUX-2nd	cancel inversion
Book 1	Δ	Δ		Δ	Δ	Δ		Δ	
Book 2	x	x			x	x	Δ		
Book 3	x	x		x	x	x	x	x	
Book 4	x	x			x	x	x	x	

As shown in Table 5.14, all developmental stages hypothesized in PT (Pienemann, 1998, 2005) are included in the *Super Kids* textbook series, with the only exception of Stage 6. Apart from 'ADV-fronting' and 'cancel inversion', all other syntactic items appear as learning objectives in this textbook series. They are: 'words/formulas', 'canonical word order SV(O)', 'do-fronting', 'yes/no inversion', 'copula inversion', 'do-2nd', and 'AUX-2nd'.

The initial occurrence of the structures (marked as '?') indicates that: 1) Book 1 includes six teaching objectives—'words/formulas', 'canonical word order SV(O)', 'do-fronting', 'yes/no inversion', 'copula inversion', and 'AUX-2nd. 2) In Book 2, the only teaching focus is 'do-2nd'. 3) For both of the last two volumes, there are no new grammatical foci added into the list of teaching objectives.

Based on the observations of Table 5.14, we can conclude three general findings regarding the sequencing of the target structures in *Super Kids*. 1) The instruction of Stage 1 feature 'words/formulas' as a teaching focus in the first volume shows agreement with PT predictions (Pienemann, 1998). 2) 'Do-2nd' (Stage 5) is taught as a grammatical focus later than the word order rules at Stage 4 such as 'yes/no inversion' and 'copula inversion', which is consistent with the PT-based processability hierarchy (Pienemann, 2005). 3) Noteworthily, the ordering of five syntactic features seems to be unclear. To be specific, 'canonical word order SV(O)', 'do-fronting', 'yes/no inversion', 'copula inversion', and 'AUX-2nd' appear as the teaching objectives in the same volume—Book 1. Therefore, we need to conduct further investigation into the individual volumes particularly Book 1 to confirm their sequencing in this textbook series.

Local analysis of Book 1. 'Words/formulas' is the grammatical focus of Unit 1 and is recycled in the majority of units in Book 1. Incidental occurrences of 'canonical word order SV (O)' appear in all units that follow the one where it is the grammatical focus (Unit 3). For 'words/formulas', students need to use a certain range of formulaic expressions as rote-learned items, such as 'I'm ________ (Miss Williams/John/Alice)' and 'What's your name?' For 'canonical word order SV(O)', students are expected to express their favourite colours through the use of simple SVO sentences. Exemplars (117) and (118) are excerpted from Unit 3.

(117) I like red.
(118) I love green.

According to the processability hierarchy for L2 English development (Pienemann, 1998), 'words/formulas' is acquired at Stage 1 and 'canonical word order SV(O)' is acquired at Stage 2. Since 'canonical word order SV(O)' is the grammatical focus after the instruction of 'words/formulas' in Book 1, their sequencing is found to be in agreement with the learning sequence as stated in PT (Pienemann, 1998).

Another word order, 'do-fronting', illustrated in example (119), is introduced as the grammatical focus of Unit 4 and is recycled in Unit 7.

(119) A: Do you like water?
B: Yes, I do.

Students are required to ask yes-or-no questions (with *do* as the auxiliary verb) with respect to their favourite things, hobbies, or possessions. The structure 'do-fronting' is thus specified as the focal grammar of the lessons. Since the Stage 2 word order SVO was the grammatical focus of Unit 3, the instruction of 'do-fronting' in Unit 4 is consistent with the PT-based processability hierarchy (Pienemann, 1998).

The Stage 4 structure 'yes/no inversion' is the grammatical focus of Unit 5. Students need to request or confirm specific information by using yes-or-no questions. As one type of yes-or-no questions, the word order 'yes/no inversion', in which the auxiliary is fronted, is provided as the focal grammar in this unit, as exemplified in dialogue (120).

(120) A: Can you skate?
B: Yes, I can.

The previous analysis has indicated that the Stage 3 structure 'do-fronting' was the grammatical focus of Unit 4. The teaching of the Stage 4 structure 'yes/no inversion' in Unit 5 occurs after that of 'do-fronting'. Thus, the sequencing of these two word order rules follows their sequencing as outlined in the PT-based processability hierarchy (Pienemann, 2005).

However, 'copula inversion', the other word order also acquired at Stage 4, appears as a teaching focus too early in Book 1. It is the grammatical focus of Unit 2, preceding the instruction of the Stage 3 structure 'do-fronting' in Unit 4. The occurrence of 'copula inversion' as a grammatical focus is premature for L2 students in *Super Kids*. A closer look at 'copula inversion' in the texts and exercises reveals that its instruction as the focal grammar may be attributed to the communicative emphasis of Book 1, which largely focuses on the use of yes-or-no questions in requesting specific information. As one kind of yes-or-no questions, 'copula inversion' thus occurs as the teaching focus very early in Book 1. Dialogue (121) is extracted from Unit 2.

(121) A: Is he your brother?
B: Yes, he is.

The word order 'AUX-2nd' is the grammatical focus of Unit 6 and recurs in Unit 8. Students need to produce WH-questions in which the auxiliary is placed in second position to request specific information such as the number of items someone has. Some exemplars are shown in (122) and (123).

(122) How many book do you have?
(123) How many pens have you got?

According to PT (Pienemann, 2005), the word order 'AUX-2nd' is acquired at Stage 5 of L2 English development, and its acquisition necessitates the mastery of the Stage 4 structures 'yes/no inversion' and 'copula inversion'. Because, in Book 1, 'yes/no inversion' and 'copula inversion' were the grammatical foci in prior units, the instruction of 'AUX-2nd' in a later unit (Unit 6) follows the learning sequence as stipulated in PT (Pienemann, 2005).

Local analysis of Book 2. In this volume, the only new grammatical focus is 'do-2nd'. Four other structures ('words/formulas', 'canonical word order SV(O)', 'yes/no inversion', and 'copula inversion') are repeatedly present as incidental items.

In particular, incidental occurrences of 'canonical word order SV(O)', such as sentences (124) and (125), are shown in all units of this volume. The repetition of this structure in the texts provides an opportunity for students to contextualize the use of the teaching focus in the corresponding lessons. For example, in (124), the teaching focus is the use of the singular and plural forms of countable nouns. The use of 'canonical word order SV(O)' offers a context for students to practice the focal grammar instead of learning isolated items.

(124) I have two pens.

(125) We want some noodles.

The word order 'do-2nd' is the grammatical focus of Unit 4 and recurs in Units 5 and 8. Students are required to productively use WH-questions in which the second position is occupied by the auxiliary *do* to ask for specific information. Sentences (126) and (127) are exemplars from Unit 4.

(126) What do you want?

(127) When do you play baseball?

The previous analysis has revealed that the Stage 4 structures 'yes/no inversion' and 'copula inversion' were among the grammatical foci of Book 1. According to PT, the prerequisite for the acquisition of the Stage 5 word order 'do-2nd' is the mastery of the Stage 4 structures. Thus, the instruction of 'do-2nd' in Book 2 agrees with the hypothesized sequence as outlined in the processability hierarchy (Pienemann, 2005).

Local analyses of Books 3-4. The last two volumes, Books 3 and 4, do not include new grammatical foci. The syntactic structures taught in the first two volumes are repeatedly used as incidental items in Books 3 and 4.

The other syntactic structures, except for 'ADV-fronting' and 'cancel inversion', all recur as incidental items in Book 3. The following sentences are exemplars involving 'canonical word order SV(O)'.

(128) She plays soccer on Sunday.

(129) He is sleeping.

Six syntactic structures are repeatedly used in Book 4, including 'words/formulas', 'canonical word order SV(O)', 'yes/no inversion', 'copula inversion', 'do-2nd', and 'AUX-2nd'. Some examples involving 'copula inversion' are presented in (130) and (131).

(130) Is there any lemonade? Yes, there is.

(131) Are there any cookies? No, there aren't.

Summary of the findings. To sum up, the results of the analysis of the *Super Kids* textbook series reveal that the sequencing of the targeted syntactic items is mostly compatible with their sequencing as hypothesized in the PT-based processability hierarchy (Pienemann, 1998, 2005). The syntactic structures located at the initial three stages are introduced as grammatical foci in a learnable manner. In this textbook series, the pupils are required to start with the formulaic strings, and then to learn the category procedural skills at Stage 2 such as the SVO structure. Based on all the previous processing resources, the students need to acquire the NP procedural skills such as 'do-fronting' in Unit 4 of Book 1. However, the Stage 4 structure 'copula inversion' is taught in a premature way. The initial occurrence of 'copula inversion' locates the earliest point in time when the VP procedure is required in the whole series, namely, in Unit 2 of Book 1. The pedagogical teaching sequence that the VP procedural skills are developed before the NP procedural skills does not follow the PT-based learning sequence (Pienemann, 1998, 2005). For the word orders at Stage 5, the instruction of 'AUX-2nd' in Unit 6 of Book 1 marks the point in time when the S-procedural skills are obligatory for the students to develop for the first time. The students are expected to progress to the S-procedure stage after they have developed the VP procedural skills in this textbook series. Therefore, the teaching of 'do-2nd' and 'AUX-2nd' is presented in a learnable manner.

Based on the specific analysis of each book in this series, the sequencing of the focal syntactic items shows considerable consistency with the arrangement of lesson topics and required functions. The whole series starts with the instruction of formulaic expressions such as *What's your name?* and *I'm John*, since the lesson topic concerns 'Self-introduction'. The second word order 'copula inversion' is used in Unit 2 of Book 1 to fulfil the function of asking for information about family (*Is he your brother?*). The third syntactic focus 'canonical word order SV(O)' is taught in Unit 3 of Book 1, where students need to express their favourite colours as exemplified in *I like red*. Subsequently, 'do-fronting' is obligatorily provided in Unit 4 of Book 1; in this lesson, learners are required to request information about others' favourite things (*Do you like water?*). The following key sentence structure 'yes/no inversion' is called for in Unit 5 of Book 1, where students need to confirm specific information in relation to sports or activities (*Can you skate?*). Next, the focal instruction of 'AUX-2nd' is associated with the lesson topic in Unit 6 of Book 1, namely, students are required to request specific information in relation to the quantities of possessions (*How many books do you have?*). The final syntactic focus 'do-2nd' occurs in Unit 4 of Book 2, since the lesson context requires students to ask for specific information related to someone's agenda such as *When do you play baseball?*.

As shown above, the arrangement of lesson topics in *Super Kids* series contextualizes the use of necessary language functions. Given a variety of communicative situations, the required syntactic items are accordingly taught for students to achieve the functions.

5.3.2.4 Results—*Join in*

General findings of the textbook series. Table 5.15 lays out all occurrences of the targeted syntactic structures that are teaching objectives in the eight volumes of the *Join in* series. The top row refers to the six developmental stages of L2 English acquisition as hypothesized in PT (Pienemann, 1998, 2005). The second row shows the syntactic structures that are acquired at the corresponding stages. The symbol '?' indicates the occurrence of a structure that enjoys grammatical focus. Incidental occurrences of structures are marked by means of an 'x'. Empty cells indicate none of the relevant structures are used.

Table 5.15 Occurrences of PT-syntactic items in *Join in*

Stage	1	2	3	4			5		6
Syntax	words/ formulas	SV(O)	ADV-fronting	do-fronting	yes/no inversion	copula inversion	do-2nd	AUX-2nd	cancel inversion
Book 1	Δ	Δ							
Book 2	x	x		Δ		Δ			
Book 3	x	x		x	Δ	x		Δ	
Book 4	x	x		x	x	x	Δ	x	
Book 5	x	x		x	x		x	x	
Book 6	x	x				x	x	x	
Book 7		x		x	x		x	x	
Book 8		x		x	x	x			

Table 5.15 shows that, except for Stage 6, all the other developmental stages (Pienemann, 1998, 2005) are included in the *Join in* series. Except for 'ADV-fronting' and 'cancel inversion', all other syntactic structures are provided as learning objectives in this set of textbooks, including 'words/formulas', 'canonical word order SV(O)', 'do-fronting', 'yes/no inversion', 'do-2nd', and 'AUX-2nd'.

Focusing on the incidental occurrence of the structures (highlighted by '?'), we can find that: 1) in Book 1, there are two structures specified as teaching objectives, namely, 'words/formulas' and 'canonical word order SV(O)'; 2) In Book 2, two word order rules are introduced as grammatical foci: 'do-fronting' and 'copula inversion'; 3) Book 3 contains two teaching objectives 'yes/no inversion' and 'AUX-2nd'; 4) there is only one teaching focus—'do-2nd'—in Book 4; 5) Books 5-8 have no new teaching objectives.

With respect to the ordering of the structures in *Join in*, there are several preliminary findings to be concluded here. 1) Similar to the abovementioned three sets of textbooks, *Join in* series begins with the focal instruction of 'words/formulas'. The instruction of this Stage 1's item in *Join in* follows PT predictions (Pienemann, 1998). 2) 'Do-fronting', 'yes/no inversion', and 'do-2nd' are all taught as a teaching focus later than their previous-stage word order rules, which shows consistency with their sequencing as hypothesized in PT (Pienemann, 1998, 2005). 3) However, the ordering of three other word order rules appears to be vague. Specifically, 'canonical word order SV(O)' and 'copula inversion' are both taught as a grammatical focus in the same volume with their preceding-stage structures. The other word order 'AUX-2nd' (Stage 5) is introduced as a grammatical focus after one of the two structures at Stage 4 'copula inversion' but at the same volume with the other Stage 4 structure 'yes/no inversion'. Therefore, further insights into the corresponding volumes are called for in order to confirm the ordering of these structures.

Local analysis of Book 1. 'Words/formulas' is the grammatical focus of Unit 1 and recurs in Units 2, 3, 4, and 5. Students need to memorize and use a range of formulaic structures such as 'What's your name?' and 'I'm fine'. The word order SVO is the grammatical focus of Unit 2 and recurs in the following units. Students are expected to talk about the colours of different things by using simple SVO sentences such as (132) and (133).

(132) It's purple.
(133) The floor is brown.

According to the processability hierarchy for L2 English development, 'canonical word order SV(O)' is acquired at Stage 2, and its preceding stage is the first lemma access stage in which only formulaic expressions can be acquired. Thus, the sequencing of 'canonical word order SV (O)' and 'words/formulas' in Book 1 agrees with the sequencing outlined in the PT-based processability hierarchy (Pienemann, 1998).

Local analysis of Book 2. In this volume, 'do-fronting' is the grammatical focus of Unit 5. Students need to produce this structure to confirm specific information from others such as their favourite food or meal. Sentences (134) and (135) are extracted from Unit 5.

(134) Do you like milk?
(135) Do you love breakfast?

Since the 'canonical word order SVO' was a grammatical focus in Book 1, the teaching of the Stage 3 structure 'do-fronting' in Book 2 is consistent with the learning sequence as hypothesized in PT (Pienemann, 1998).

The other word order, 'copula inversion', is the grammatical focus of Unit 1 and recurs in Units 2, 5, and 6. Students are asked to confirm specific information through the use of yes-or-no questions in which the copula verb is placed in sentence-initial position, as exemplified in (136) and (137).

(136) Is it red?
(137) Are they white?

According to PT (Pienemann, 2005), 'copula inversion' is acquired at Stage 4, and its acquisition necessitates the mastery of Stage 3 structures such as 'do-fronting'. However, in *Join in*, Book 2, 'copula inversion' in Unit 1 is a grammatical focus before 'do-fronting' in Unit 5. The sequencing of these two structures violates their sequencing as hypothesized in PT-based processability hierarchy (Pienemann, 2005).

Local analysis of Book 3. 'Words/formulas', 'canonical word order SV(O)', 'do-fronting', and 'copula inversion' recur as incidental items in Book 3. Examples involving 'canonical word order SV(O)' are shown in (138) and (139).

(138) The mouse is tired.
(139) The dog is sad.

'Yes/no inversion' is the grammatical focus of Unit 2. Students are expected to formulate yes-or-no questions in which the auxiliary is fronted, such as (140) and (141).

(140) Can you play the piano?
(141) Can I play games?

According to PT (Pienemann, 2005), 'yes/no inversion' is acquired at Stage 4, and its acquisition requires the mastery of Stage 3 structures such as 'do-fronting'. As discussed above, the Stage 3 word order 'do-fronting' was a grammatical focus in Book 2. Thus, the instruction of the Stage 4 structure 'yes/no inversion' in Book 3 follows the learning sequence as stipulated in PT (Pienemann, 2005).

The Stage 5 word order 'AUX-2nd' is the grammatical focus of Unit 3 and recurs in Unit 4. Students are required to produce WH-questions in which the second position is occupied by the auxiliary verb to seek specific information relating, for instance, to outfits. Dialogue (142) is excerpted from Unit 3.

(142) A: What am I wearing?
B: A green shirt and blue jeans.

The previous analysis has shown that the Stage 4 structure 'copula inversion' was the grammatical focus of Unit 1 of Book 2. In addition, the other Stage 4 structure 'yes/no inversion' appears as the teaching objective of Unit 2 of Book 3. Therefore, the instruction of the Stage 5 structure 'AUX-2nd' in Unit 3 of Book 2 is consistent with the hypothesized learning sequence in which 'copula inversion' and 'yes/no inversion' should precede 'AUX-2nd', as stated in PT (Pienemann, 2005).

Local analysis of Book 4. The only grammatical focus, 'do-2nd', is taught in Unit 1. It is then recycled in Units 2 and 5. Students need to seek specific information, such as someone's routine, by using WH-questions in which the auxiliary *do* appears in second position. Sentences (143) and (144) are exemplars from Unit 1.

(143) What time do you get up?

(144) When do you go to school?

The prior analysis has demonstrated that the Stage 4 structures 'yes/no inversion' and 'copula inversion' were grammatical foci in previous volumes (Books 2 and 3). Thus, the instruction of the Stage 5 word order 'do-2nd' in Book 4 is consistent with the hypothesized learning sequence in which 'yes/no inversion' or 'copula inversion' should precede 'do-2nd'.

Local analysis of Books 5-8. In Books 5 to 8, there are no new grammatical foci. The syntactic structures taught in the previous volumes ('words/formulas', 'canonical word order SV(O)', 'do-fronting', 'yes/no inversion', 'copula inversion', 'do-2nd', and 'AUX-2nd') recur as incidental items in the last four volumes.

The Stage 2 word order SVO recurs as an incidental item most frequently in the last four volumes. As mentioned before, the incidental occurrences of 'canonical word order SV(O)' contextualize the use of other teaching foci, thus allowing students to learn and practice the latter in context instead of learning the foci as isolated items. For example, Unit 1 of Book 7 focuses on the use of the future tense ('*will* + V' and '*be going to*'). The target sentences are formed in the structure SVO that has been taught before, as exemplified in (145) and (146).

(145) I'm going to eat healthy food.
(146) I will drink more water.

Students are familiar with the sentence structure SVO, because it was taught as focal grammar in the previous lessons. When students learn new grammar such as the future tense, they may feel it is easier to understand this rule in a specific context. At the same time, students may review the 'old' structure SVO and reinforce its practice.

Summary of the findings. In conclusion, the analysis of the *Join in* textbook series indicates that the sequencing of the targeted syntactic structures is mostly compatible with their sequencing as hypothesized in the PT-based processability hierarchy (Pienemann, 1998, 2005). Similar to the other three sets of textbooks, the structures belonging to the first three stages in the *Join in* series are presented in a learnable pedagogical teaching sequence. The pupils need to learn some formulaic structures at the beginning. In the subsequent lesson they have to go up to Stage 2 to acquire the category procedural skills ('canonical word order SV(O)'). After developing all the previous processing resources, the students are expected to move to Stage 3 to learn the NP procedural skills ('do-fronting'). However, the instruction of 'copula inversion' is premature for the pupils. 'Copula inversion' is the grammatical focus of Unit 1 in Book 2, coming before the teaching of 'do-fronting' in Unit 5 of Book 2. The earliest point in time when the VP procedure is required in this textbook series precedes that of the NP procedure. According to PT (Pienemann, 1998, 2005), the learner is not able to acquire the VP procedural skills before he or she has developed the NP procedural skills. Therefore, 'copula inversion' in the

Join in series is not taught in a learnable manner. The word orders 'do-2nd' and 'AUX-2nd' at the S-procedure stage are introduced as the instructional foci after the teaching of the VP procedural skills. This teaching order agrees with the PT-based learning sequence (Pienemann, 1998, 2005).

From a processability perspective, most of the syntactic foci with the exception of 'copula inversion' in *Join in* textbook series are considered processable and learnable for the elementary-school students. Noteworthily, the learnability of sentence structures does not appear to be the primary concern in the textbook due to the premature teaching of 'copula inversion'. Based on the local analyses of individual volumes, there is evidence that those syntactic items are taught as structural consequences of necessary language functions in relation to specific topics in the lessons.

The whole textbook series introduces formulaic structures such as *What's your name?*, since the first lesson emphasizes the use of basic English expressions such as 'Greetings' and 'Self-introduction'. The second teaching focus 'copula inversion' is called for later in the context where students are expected to request specific information about the colours of entities (*Are they white?*). The next teaching objective 'canonical word order SV(O)' is produced in Unit 2 of Book 1 to discuss the colours of various things (*The floor is brown*). In the following, the focal instruction of 'do-fronting' appears in Unit 5, as learners need to learn how to confirm information about others' favourite food or meal (*Do you like milk?*). Subsequently, the provision of 'yes/no inversion' occurs in Unit 2 of Book 3; in this lesson, students are expected to ask for information about the activities or entertainment, as exemplified in *Can you play the piano?*. The following key word order 'AUX-2nd' is taught in Unit 3 of Book 3 to allow students to seek specific information relating to outfits, such as *What am I wearing?*. As the final syntactic focus, 'do-2nd' provided in Unit 1 of Book 4 is called for in the context where learners need to ask for someone's routine or agenda (*When do you go to school?*).

It appears that the topics and related language functions play a dominant role in the organization of textbook content and thus define the use of relevant syntactic foci in individual lessons. The sentence structures such as the *yes-or-no* questions and WH-questions are more frequent to be produced in the related communicative situations of general topics such as 'Activities' or 'School', since they are highly useful for students to request information in communication.

5.3.3 Comparison and summary: The main results of the four textbook series

The four textbook series, *New Standard English*, *PEP English*, *Super Kids*, and *Join in*, are currently used in mainland China on a nationwide scale for early EFL education starting from Grade Three to Grade Six in primary schools. In the following, the sequencing of grammatical structures that are taught in these four sets of textbooks are compared and summarized with regards to morphology and syntax.

(1) The ordering of morphological items

In the area of morphology, this study found that the ordering of the morphological items in these four textbook series shows partial agreement with the learning sequence as stipulated in PT (Pienemann, 1998, 2005). Overall, in all the four sets, the ordering of the morphological items at the first two stages, at least, is consistent with the PT-based learning sequence (Pienemann, 1998). Apart from that, there are some differences among these four textbook series regarding the extent to how much the ordering of those structures agrees with PT predictions.

Table 5.16 Ordering of morphological foci in *New Standard English*

Book	Lesson	Morphological items	Stage
1	1	words/formulas	1
	9	possessive determiner	2
2		3rd ps sg -s	5
3	3	V-ing	4
	8	phrasal plural -s	3
4		simple past -ed	2
6		lexical plural -s	2

Table 5.16 shows the sequencing of the morphological foci in the entire textbook series of *New Standard English* based on the previous textbook analysis. The third column lists the morphological foci taught as the teaching objectives. The first column presents which volume(s) those objectives are introduced. The second column indicates the specific lessons① where the objectives are obligatorily taught in order to determine the order between two different morphemes within the same volume. The fourth column refers to the developmental stages that the morphological items belong to.

As can be seen from Table 5.16, in *New Standard English*, the morphological structures belonging to the first three stages are sequenced as grammatical foci in accordance with the PT-based processability hierarchy for L2 English development (Pienemann, 1998, 2005). The Stage 4 morpheme 'V-ing' and the Stage 5 morpheme '3rd ps sg -s' both precede their previous-stage structures, which is contradictory to the sequenced development of the VP procedural skills and the S-procedural skills as stipulated in PT predictions (Pienemann, 1998, 2005). Thus, while the ordering of the morphological items at the initial three stages achieves an agreement with PT predictions, teaching and learnability are adjusted in a poor way in terms of the higher-stage morphemes including 'V-ing' (Stage 4) and '3rd ps sg -s' (Stage 5).

① For a better understanding of ordering, different expressions such as 'module' and 'unit' in the four sets of textbooks are unified into 'lesson', namely, a study unit in educational instruction, as shown in Tables 5.16-5.23.

Table 5.17 Ordering of morphological foci in *PEP English*

Book	Lesson	Morphological items	Stage
1	1	words/formulas	1
	6	phrasal plural -s	3
2	2	possessive determiner	2
	5	lexical plural -s	2
3		3rd ps sg -s	5
4		V-ing	4

The layout of Table 5.17 is identical to that of Table 4.16. As shown in Table 5.17, in *PEP English*, 'words/formulas', 'possessive determiner', and 'lexical plural -s' (Stages 1 and 2) and the VP morpheme 'V-ing' (Stage 4) are introduced as grammatical foci in line with the PT-based learning sequence (Pienemann, 1998, 2005). However, the introduction of structures belonging to Stage 3 ('phrasal plural -s') and Stage 5 ('3rd ps sg -s') are provided earlier than the provision of their preceding-stage morphemes, which is not consistent with the L2 learning sequence as hypothesized in PT (Pienemann, 1998, 2005).

Table 5.18 Ordering of morphological foci in *Super Kids*

Book	Lesson	Morphological items	Stage
1	1	words/formulas	1
	2	possessive determiner	2
	6	V-ing	4
2	5	simple past -ed	2
	6	lexical plural -s	2
	7	phrasal plural -s	3
	8	3rd ps sg -s	5

Similarly, Table 5.18 reveals the entire ordering of morphological foci in *Super Kids*. As shown above, 'words/formulas', 'simple past -ed', 'possessive determiner', 'lexical plural -s', and 'phrasal plural -s' (Stages 1 to 3) and the grammatical morpheme '3rd ps sg -s' (Stage 5) are introduced as grammatical foci in keeping with the learning sequence as hypothesized in PT (Pienemann, 1998, 2005). Nevertheless, the instruction of the Stage 4 morpheme 'V-ing' is premature in the whole textbook series, since it precedes the Stage 3 morpheme 'phrasal plural -s'. Thus, it can be concluded that the sequencing of morphological foci in *Super Kids* mostly agrees with the PT's hypotheses with the only exception of 'V-ing' at Stage 4.

Table 5.19 Ordering of morphological foci in *Join in*

Book	Lesson	Morphological items	Stage
1	1	words/formulas	1
	4	possessive determiner	2
	4	lexical plural -s	2
	4	simple past -ed	2
	4	phrasal plural -s	3
2	2	3rd ps sg -s	5
	3	V-ing	4
	4	V-en	4

Table 5.19 provides an overview of how the morphological foci are ordered in the whole series of *Join in*. The items at the first two stages including 'words/formulas', 'simple past -ed', 'possessive determiner', and 'lexical plural -s' and the VP morphemes 'V-ing' and 'V-en' (Stage 4) are presented as teaching foci in accordance with their sequencing as outlined in PT-based processability hierarchy (Pienemann, 1998, 2005). However, the introduction of 'phrasal plural -s' (Stage 3) and '3rd ps sg -s' (Stage 5) appears to be premature: 1) 'phrasal plural -s', which should come after the Stage 2's lexical morphemes, is taught simultaneously with 'possessive determiner', 'lexical plural -s', and 'simple past -ed' in Lesson 4; and 2) the Stage 5 morpheme '3rd ps sg -s' precedes the VP morphemes 'V-ing' and 'V-en'. Therefore, except for the morphemes belonging to Stage 3 ('phrasal plural -s') and Stage 5 ('3rd ps sg -s'), the ordering of all the other morphological items agrees with the PT's predictions.

Generally speaking, the ordering of the morphological features at the first two stages under investigation is similar in these four sets of textbooks, namely, their ordering agrees with the hypothesized sequencing as stated in PT (Pienemann, 1998, 2005). The introduction of the morphological structures at the higher stages, however, differs in the four textbook series. *Super Kids* presents the highest agreement with the PT's predictions and seems more appropriate in terms of learnability than the other three textbook series. *PEP English* and *Join in* both show a modest agreement with PT-based learning sequence (Pienemann, 1998, 2005) with respect to the ordering of most of morphological features except for the morphemes belonging to Stage 3 and Stage 5. Compared to the other three series, *New Standard English* presents a partial agreement with PT's hypotheses; the prominent issue is implied in the ordering of the morphemes that are located at Stages 4 to 5 of the processing hierarchy (Pienemann, 1998, 2005), such as 'V-ing' and '3rd ps sg -s'.

(2) The ordering of syntactic items

In the area of syntax, the analyses reveal that the ordering of the syntactic structures in these four textbook series shows a high consistency with the learning sequence as stated in PT.

Except for that, the agreement of the ordering of target structures with PT predictions is slightly different among the four sets of textbooks.

Table 5.20 Ordering of syntactic foci in *New Standard English*

Book	Lesson	Syntactic items	Stage
1	1	words/formulas	1
	4	canonical word order SV(O)	2
	8	copula inversion	4
2	4	Do-fronting	3
	5	yes/no inversion	4
	6	do-2nd	5
3		AUX-2nd	5

Table 5.21 Ordering of syntactic foci in *PEP English*

Book	Lesson	Syntactic items	Stage
1	1	words/formulas	1
	5	canonical word order SV(O)	2
2	2	copula inversion	4
	5	Do-fronting	3
3	1	ADV-fronting	3
	4	yes/no inversion	4
	5	AUX-2nd	5
	6	do-2nd	5

Table 5.22 Ordering of syntactic foci in *Super Kids*

Book	Lesson	Syntactic items	Stage
1	1	words/formulas	1
	2	copula inversion	4
	3	canonical word order SV(O)	2
	4	Do-fronting	3
	5	yes/no inversion	4
	6	AUX-2nd	5
2		do-2nd	5

Table 5.23 Ordering of syntactic foci in *Join in*

Book	Lesson	Syntactic items	Stage
1		words/formulas	1
2	1	copula inversion	4
	2	canonical word order SV(O)	2
	5	Do-fronting	3
3	2	yes/no inversion	4
	3	AUX-2nd	5
4		do-2nd	5

Tables 5.20-5.23 individually reveal the entire ordering of the syntactic features that are taught as teaching objectives in the four textbook series. For each table, the syntactic foci are provided in the third column; the first column lists the volumes where those features are taught, and the second column refers to the specific lessons where their focal instruction appear.

As presented in Table 5.20 and Tables 5.22-5.23, an identical ordering is found in the instruction of the syntactic structures in *New Standard English*, *Super Kids*, and *Join in*. 'Words/formulas', 'canonical word order SV(O)', and 'do-fronting' (Stages 1 to 3), 'yes/no inversion' (Stage 4), and the two word orders 'do-2nd' and 'AUX-2nd' (Stage 5) are all introduced as grammatical foci in line with the PT-based processability hierarchy (Pienemann, 1998, 2005). However, the other word order at Stage 4 'copula inversion' is taught before its preceding-stage structure, which does not agree with its ordering as hypothesized in PT (Pienemann, 2005).

For *PEP English*, as shown in Table 5.21, 'words/formulas', 'canonical word order SV (O)', 'ADV-fronting', and 'do-fronting' (Stages 1 to 3), 'yes/no inversion' (Stage 4), and the two structures 'do-2nd' and 'AUX-2nd' (Stage 5) are provided as grammatical foci in accordance with the processability hierarchy for L2 English development. Nevertheless, similar to the other three sets of textbooks, 'copula inversion' (Stage 4) appears as a teaching objective in a premature manner.

Overall, the ordering of the syntactic foci in all the four sets of textbooks shows a considerable agreement with the PT's predictions. The syntactic items at all the other stages under investigation except for Stage 4 ('copula inversion') are ordered in line with learnability constraints. The only word order which is not taught in a learnable manner in this study is 'copula inversion', since it precedes the instruction of the NP procedural skills and is taught too early in the entire textbook series.

Apart from the sequencing of grammatical structures, a minor finding in the previous local analyses of individual volumes may need to be mentioned here, namely, incidental items. As defined in Section 5.1, an incidental item refers to re-occurrence of a grammatical structure in the textbooks. Such an item is not instructed as the teaching objective. It is merely the repetition of a grammatical structure which has been taught as the instructional focus in a previous lesson. For instance, in *New Standard English* series, from Books 4 to 8, no new syntactic features are provided as teaching objectives, while the targeted word orders that were the focus of previous volumes repeatedly occur in the texts. Take 'canonical word order SV(O)' for example. In *New Standard English* Book 4, one teaching focus is the use of specific adjectives such as *nice*, *shy*, and *big*. Through the presentation of simple sentences of the SV(O) type, students can contextualize the use of these adjectives, as exemplified in *She's very nice. But she's a bit shy.* It seems that students may also be able to implicitly reinforce the practice of the SV(O) structure, which has been taught as a grammatical focus in the previous lessons, when they manage to produce such sentences. However, since the current study only focuses on the sequencing of grammatical foci, thus incidental items are not considered as primary concern here. This issue will remain for future research, such as theoretical and learnability implications of re-occurrences of grammatical structures.

In the next chapter, I will discuss the main findings in regards to the grading of grammar in the compilation of these textbooks. I will also discuss the possible consequences of a deviant introduction of grammatical structures from a processability perspective. The discussion will take in the current state of grammar instruction in English textbooks in China. Suggestions for promoting an ESL grammatical syllabus will also be made on the basis of the developmental schedules as developed in Processability Theory. This will provide an insight into how SLA research can be utilized in L2 teaching practice.

Chapter 6

Discussion: Learnability and Pedagogical Implications

This chapter discusses the results of the textbook analysis undertaken in Chapter 5 within a broader context of second language acquisition, taking into account L2 learners' developmental readiness and other pedagogical issues. The results of the analyses of the grading of grammatical structures in the textbook series are discussed based on Processability Theory (PT) (Pienemann, 1998, 2005) and compared with the findings of established ESL research (e. g., Lenzing, 2008). The sequencing of grammar exhibited in the textbook analysis are further discussed in a wider context of ESL instruction in China, considering pedagogical approaches that inspire textbook design. Some suggestions will also be provided in regards to developing a learnable grammatical introduction in English textbooks.

6.1 Summary of the key findings

The present textbook evaluation investigates the research question: whether or not the sequencing of the grammatical structures introduced as the teaching objectives in the four sets of English textbooks used in primary schools in China is compatible with the sequenced development that the learners go through in acquiring English as an L2 as hypothesized in PT (Pienemann, 1998, 2005). On the positive side, the results show that the grammatical sequencing in these four textbook series is partially compatible with the learning sequence as stipulated in PT. For all four textbook series, the morpho-syntactic structures at Stages 1 and 2 are graded in accordance with the hypothesized learning sequence (Pienemann, 1998, 2005). Despite this, the ordering of the grammatical structures at the later stages slightly differs among the four sets of textbooks and within the areas of morphology and syntax.

In the area of morphology, *Super Kids* has shown the highest consistency with the learning sequence as stipulated in PT (Pienemann, 1998, 2005). The other morphological items taught as teaching objectives are introduced in an order that is processable and learnable for students, with the only exception of the VP morpheme 'V-ing' (Stage 4) which is taught in a premature manner. 'V-ing' appears before 'phrasal plural -s' (Stage 3) in the whole textbook series; this does not agree with the PT's hypothesis (Pienemann, 1998, 2005) that the learner can acquire the VP procedural skills only when they have developed all the previous NP procedural skills.

PEP English and *Join in* have been found to achieve a similar pedagogical teaching order of the morphological items. The morphological items located at the first two stages are taught as grammatical foci in line with the PT-based learning sequence (Pienemann, 1998, 2005). The pupils are required to begin with the single words or invariant forms; subsequently, they need to develop the category procedural skills (the SVO structure). However, the instruction of 'phrasal plural -s' is not presented in a learnable way. It is taught as an instructional focus either before (in *PEP* English) or simultaneously with (in *Join in*) the lexical morphemes. Such pedagogical teaching orders are not consistent with the PT's hypothesis (Pienemann, 1998) that the category procedure is a necessary prerequisite for the NP procedure. The instruction of Stage 4 morphemes 'V-ing' and 'V-en' are learnable for the pupils, since the two sets of textbooks follow the L2 sequenced development, namely, the learner has to develop the NP procedural skills before he or she moves to the VP procedure stage. Nevertheless, '3rd ps sg -s' is conversely instructed as a teaching objective before the VP morphemes in these two textbook series. This violates the sequenced development of L2 processing skills, namely, the learner is not able to acquire the S-procedural skills before he or she has developed the VP procedural skills.

New Standard English presents a partial agreement with PT' predictions and does not coordinate the ordering of the morphological items at Stages 4-5 with learnability in an effective way; but at least, the morphological items at the initial three stages are ordered in accordance with the hypothesized sequencing (Pienemann, 1998, 2005). The pedagogical teaching sequence in this textbook series shows that: at first the pupils only need to learn invariant forms, and then they are expected to progress to the category procedure stage (lexical morphemes), and afterwards they have to acquire the NP procedural skills ('phrasal plural -s'). However, the instruction of 'V-ing' and '3rd ps sg -s' is not presented in a learnable manner. They precede their prior-stage morphemes in the textbook series. The pupils cannot acquire these two morphemes due to that they have not developed all the previous processing resources (the NP procedure and the VP procedure) at that point.

The situation in the area of syntax seems less complex. The ordering of the syntactic structures taught as teaching objectives is highly similar among these four sets of textbooks. Overall, except for 'copula inversion' (Stage 4) which is taught before the Stage 3 word orders, the other syntactic features under investigation are ordered in line with the PT-based processability hierarchy (Pienemann, 1998, 2005). For these four textbook series, the students are required to start with some formulaic structures such as *how are you*?; later, they are expected to learn the SVO structure through using the category procedure. After developing all the previous processing skills, the students need to acquire the NP procedural skills ('ADV-fronting' and 'do-fronting'). However, 'copula inversion' is taught too early in the whole series. The teaching order that the VP procedural skills are developed prior to the NP procedural skills goes against the PT-based learning sequence (Pienemann, 1998, 2005). The instruction of 'do-2nd' and 'AUX-2nd' is considered learnable in these four sets of textbooks, since the students are required to acquire the S-procedural skills after they have developed the VP procedural skills.

Apart from the ordering of grammatical structures, the presence of several structures at the same developmental stages differs in the four textbook series. One contrast exists between 'V-ing' and 'V-en'. These two morphemes are both processed through the VP procedures and can be acquired at Stage 4 of ESL morphological development. However, 'V-ing' is included in all the four sets of textbooks, while 'V-en' only appears in *Join in*. Similarly, 'Do-fronting' and 'ADV-fronting' forms the other contrast. These two word orders are hypothesized to be acquired at Stage 3 of ESL syntactic development through the process of the NP procedure. Nevertheless, the previous textbook analysis reveals a difference between their presence, namely, 'Do-fronting' is introduced in all the four sets of textbooks but 'ADV-fronting' merely appears in *PEP English*.

6.2 The ordering of grammatical structures and learners' developmental readiness

The acquisition-based ordering of the structures at the initial two stages indicates that the textbook writers' idea of early-stage grammatical development follows the developmental trajectory as stipulated in Processability Theory; therefore, the introduction of morpho-syntactic structures at Stages 1 and 2 is processable and learnable for L2 students.

According to Processability Theory (Pienemann, 1998, 2005), learning a L2 equates to acquiring the skills to process L2 grammatical structures. L2 processing skills are developed in a sequence that follows the order of activation of processing procedures (Pienemann, 1998, p. 7). The sequenced activation of L2 processing procedures allows for the production of grammatical structures. A processing procedure can be activated and the corresponding grammatical structure can be produced only if all the previous processing skills have been developed (Pienemann, 1998). For instance, if a L2 learner can apply the category procedure (Stage 2), he or she will be able to produce the word order 'canonical word order SV(O)'. Next, if the learner is able to use the NP procedure to produce the word order 'do-fronting', he or she is already capable of using the preceding procedure—the category procedure—and producing the word order 'canonical word order SV(O)'. Accordingly, the process of acquiring L2 processing procedures and grammatical features is cumulative. The activation of the various processing procedures is sequenced, so that L2 learners, in the course of their L2 acquisition, must go through a series of stages (Pienemann, 1998). Each earlier-stage procedure in this sequential progression is a prerequisite for what is acquired at a later stage. In other words, less complex grammatical structures processed at an earlier developmental stage constitute the precondition for the more complex ones at later stages (Mansouri & Duffy, 2005).

From a processability perspective, L2 learners at any level of development are able to produce only those grammatical structures which the current state of their language processing procedures can process (Pienemann, 1998, pp. 4-5). That is, L2 learners are able to learn the structures only when they are developmentally ready to process them. Being 'ready' refers to that the learners have developed the L2 processing procedures required for the acquisition of a grammatical structure situated at the next stage. Here, the key point of learnability is the learners' developmental readiness.

Applied to this textbook evaluation, the sequencing of the morpho-syntactic structures at Stages 1 and 2 in all four sets of textbooks is in full agreement with the learners' developmental readiness. That is, before teaching a grammatical structure such as 'canonical word order SV (O)', which is situated at the category procedure stage (Stage 2), single words or formulaic expressions that are acquired at the lemma access stage (Stage 1) are taught as obligatory learning items in the textbooks. This finding indicates that the authors of these four textbook series have taken into account the learners' developmental readiness in their sequencing of structures at the initial two stages. They have perceived single words or formulaic expressions such as 'How are you?' as less complex items than a canonical word order SVO such as 'I like you'. In other words, since the word order SVO is considered more difficult for L2 students, this structure is introduced as a grammatical focus after formulaic expressions, which are considered less difficult to learn.

However, our findings also reveal that the ordering of several grammatical structures in the four textbook series is different compared to the L2 learning sequence as stipulated in PT. In all four sets of textbooks, there is only one syntactic structure ('copula inversion') taught in a premature manner; two of them present two morphological structures (either 'phrasal plural -s' or '3rd ps sg -s') in a deviant pedagogical teaching sequence, whereas two of them present one morphological structure ('V-ing') in a deviant teaching order. These forms are introduced as grammatical foci before the structures at their previous stages have been presented. The findings imply that the authors of the four series may consider these four structures less difficult for L2 students and thus these forms are taught earlier than others. However, from a processability perspective, the early instruction of these four structures in the textbooks does not take into consideration L2 learners' developmental readiness.

For instance, the Stage 4-word order 'copula inversion' is taught prior to the Stage 3-word order 'do-fronting' in all four textbook series. The inversion of the NP procedural skills and the VP procedural skills violates their sequencing as hypothesized in the PT-based processability hierarchy. According to PT (Pienemann, 1998, 2005), the acquisition of 'copula inversion' calls for the activation of the VP procedure at Stage 4, and the acquisition of 'do-fronting' necessitates the activation of the NP procedure at Stage 3. Since the NP procedure is the prerequisite for the VP procedure, the processing of 'do-fronting' is deemed less complex than that of 'copula inversion'. For L2 learners, it is more difficult to acquire 'copula inversion' than 'do-fronting'. Thus, it is more realistic for them to learn the less complex structure 'do-fronting' first and then learn the more complex one 'copula inversion' later. The authors may not have considered the processing complexity of 'copula inversion' in the four textbook series.

6.3 Presence of the structures within a same stage: Two pairs of contrasts

Apart from the ordering of the focal morpho-syntactic structures in the textbooks, two interesting findings in the present study may also draw our attention. First, as reported in Chapter 5, one of the two VP morphemes at Stage 4—'V-ing'—is taught as a focal grammatical item in all the four sets of textbooks, whilst the other Stage 4 morpheme 'V-en' does not appear in all the other three textbook series with the only exception of *Join in*. Second, 'do-fronting' (Stage 3) is introduced as a teaching objective in all the four textbook series, but the other word order at Stage 3—'ADV-fronting'—only appears in *PEP English*.

For the contrast between 'V-ing' and 'V-en', it could be argued that the contrast between 'V-ing' and 'V-en' in the four textbook series does not appear to be problematic, since the underlying linguistic rule 'auxiliary SV-agreement' can account for these two structural outcomes. According to Pienemann's *Rapid Profile* (cf. Pienemann & Mackey, 1993), 'Auxiliary SV-agreement' refers to Subject-Verb agreement in sentences containing an auxiliary verb. Interphrasal information exchange is required to process this rule (Pienemann, 1998). L2 learners need to learn to choose the auxiliary according to a range of temporal, aspectual or modal motivations (e. g., *be*, *have*, *modal*), and then unify these features with the corresponding ones in the lexical verbs (e. g., *V-ing*, *V-en*, *V*). Therefore, two of the structural outcomes are progressive *be* + *V-ing* and perfective *have* + *V-en*. In another word, the introduction of either 'V-ing' or 'V-en' indicates that the underlying rule 'auxiliary SV-agreement' which requires interphrasal exchange information at Stage 4 (VP procedure) has been taught as a teaching objective in the four sets of textbooks. Similarly, Lenzing (2008) did not distinguish these two VP forms in her textbook analysis; instead, she grouped these two VP morphemes into the same morphological category at Stage 4—'Auxiliary SV-agreement' (Lenzing, 2008, p. 226; cf. Lenzing, 2004, p. 73). In Lenzing (2008), the results only indicated that 'auxiliary SV-agreement' was taught as a learning objective in *Playway* 3, *Playway* 4, and *Ginger* 1, but her analysis did not show whether the two structural outcomes of this rule—'V-ing' and 'V-en'—both occurred in all the books. It should be noted that, however in the present study, there appears to remain vague about why 'V-en' is not explicitly taught in the other three textbook series except for *Join in*. This issue will remain for future research and may be addressed based on the interviews with the textbook writers and a deeper investigation into their compilation guidelines or primary concerns.

With respect to 'ADV-fronting' and 'do-fronting', based on the previous local analyses of each textbook series, a possible explanation for the contrast between these two syntactic structures is related to the communicative aspects of language learning specified in the four textbook series. First, 'do-fronting' is one type of the *yes-or-no* questions which are frequently used to confirm or request specific information in English communication (Celce-Murcia &

Larsen-Freeman, 1999). The following sentences are extracted from the four textbook series and have been presented in the textbook analysis of Chapter 4.

(88) Do you like meat? (from *New Standard English*)

(105) Do you want pears? (from *PEP English*)

(119) Do you like water? (from *Super Kids*)

(134) Do you like milk? (from *Join in*)

As analysed in Chapter 5, these sentences containing the word order 'do-fronting' are used by students to ask and confirm others' favourite things, hobbies, or demands, which is associated with the theme (or topics) of the corresponding lessons. Therefore, it could be argued that the writers of the four textbook series consider 'do-fronting' as a commonly-used question to achieve effective communication. Second, the only focal instruction of 'ADV-fronting' in *PEP English* (Unit 1 of Book 3) also seems to be related to the specific theme (or topics) of the lesson, namely, activities on weekends. The students need to emphasize the time and talk about their activities, as exemplified in the following sentences (cf. Chapter 5).

(109) Sometimes I go hiking.

(110) On Sunday I go shopping.

As we can see, the exemplars focus more on the use of adverbs or adverbials that refer to time, such as 'sometimes' and 'on Sunday'. The rest of the sentences is the canonical word order SV(O), which has been introduced in Book 1 of *PEP English*. Therefore, it could be argued that in the case of 'ADV-fronting' in *PEP English*, the teaching focus seems to more concern the vocabulary (or phrases) that specifies the time rather than the combination of 'ADV +SVO'. Furthermore, it does not appear to be problematic that 'ADV-fronting' is not taught in the other three textbook series, since this structure may not be closely related to their communicative aspects.

6.4 Explanation for the ordering of grammatical structures: Theme-based textbook design

Is it possible that the design of grammar instruction in the four textbook series analysed in this study follows other concepts of L2 learning and teaching? One question worth asking is whether the acquisition-based ordering of structures at the initial first stages and the deviant introduction of structures at the intermediate and high levels (Stages 3 to 5), reported in the present study, is inspired by the textbook writers' consideration of the context of English education in China.

6.4.1 Theme-based compilation in the four textbook series

According to the prefaces of the four textbook series, a theme-based teaching approach pervaded the compilation guidelines adopted by the authors. For example, in the preface of the *New Standard English* series, the authors Chen and Ellis stated:

> 每册 内容以题材(theme)为纲,以功能、结构、运用任务(task of using English)为目。同一题材在全套教材中重复出现,但其内容逐步扩展加深,螺旋上升。词汇、语法项目和功能用语的选择和安排,均以题材为出发点,以运用英语的任务为载体。
>
> (*New Standard English*, Book 1, Chen & Ellis, 2012, p. 2)

> The contents of each volume follow a theme-based syllabus, considering functions, grammatical structures, and tasks of using English as learning objectives. One overall theme is pervasive in the whole textbook series, but the contents associated with that theme are gradually extended and enriched—'spiralled'. The vocabulary, grammatical items and functions (or notions) are selected and arranged on the basis of themes, and they are implemented through tasks of using English.
>
> (*New Standard English*, Book 1, Chen & Ellis, 2012, p. 2; my translation)

Similarly, the preface of the *PEP English* series indicates that this textbook series is designed according to a theme-based syllabus.

> 我们比较和研究了多套国内外小学英语教材,博采众长,形成了本套教材特有的编写体系。本套教材的编写思路是以话题为纲,以交际功能和语言结构为主线,逐步引导学生运用英语完成有实际意义的语言任务。
>
> (*PEP English*, Book 1, Wu, 2012, p. I)

> After comparing and investigating several series of domestic and international English textbooks for primary-school education, we established a compilation system that was tailored to this textbook series. This textbook series is designed according to a theme-based syllabus, focusing on language functions and grammatical structures. It is expected to gradually guide the students in their use of English for the purpose of completing practical language tasks.
>
> (*PEP English*, Book 1, Wu, 2012, p. I; my translation)

A similar claim is provided in the preface of the *Super Kids* series.

本套教材以话题为纲，融汇功能、词汇和语法等语言要素，系统编排学习内容。教材围绕和真实生活相关的话题展开学习活动，通过会话恰当地引入功能学习项目，并有序呈现、训练、巩固基础词汇和句型。

(*Super Kids*, Book 1, Liu et al., 2012, p. I)

This textbook series is designed according to a theme-based syllabus. It incorporates the key components of language such as functions, vocabulary and grammar into the selection and arrangement of learning contents. The series focuses on themes that are related to our real life and implements a variety of learning activities. Through the use of conversation, this series appropriately introduces language functions, and also presents, practices and reinforces the basic vocabulary and sentence structures.

(*Super Kids*, Book 1, Liu et al., 2012, p. I; my translation)

The *Join in* series also uses its preface to address the criteria used for textbook compilation.

本教材以主题开展教学。教程所涉及的话题贴近学生的实际日常生活，如：问候、告别、学校生活、购物、家庭、喜欢和不喜欢、询问时间、节日问候等。根据学生认知特点，着重听说演唱玩等活动设计。

(*Join in*, Book 1, Zhang, 2014, p. I)

This textbook series provides language instruction based on themes. The series includes topics that are closely associated with the students' real life, such as greetings, farewell, school life, shopping, family, like or dislike, asking the time, festival greetings, etc. In line with the students' cognitive abilities, this series emphasizes the design of learning activities such as listening, speaking, role-play, games, etc.

(*Join in*, Book 1, Zhang, 2014, p. I; my translation)

As shown above, all four textbook series are designed around themes. Theme-based approaches (also termed topic-based approaches) are a form of content-based instruction that aims to deliver content and language integrated teaching (Alptekin, Erçetin, & Bayyurt, 2007). Content refers to the subject matter the students learn through the use of the target language (Richards & Rodgers, 2001). L2 is regarded as the medium of conveying content and information instead of being taught in an isolated way without the integration of particular content (Khranke, 1987). Focusing on the content, the theme-based approach integrates different objectives of L2 learning such as functions, vocabulary, and grammar around a theme or specific topics closely related to the students' interests, needs, personal experiences and daily life (Met,

1999).

Motivated by a theme-based approach, the writers of the four textbook series consider the theme or topics as the primary concern in the compilation. For example, the writers of the *New Standard English* series indicate that they follow the "'题材－功能－结构－任务'的多步法编写大纲"('theme—function—structure—task' multi-procedure for syllabus design; the author's translation) (*New Standard English* Book 1, Chen & Ellis, 2012, p. 1). The themes of individual lessons (or units) determine what kinds of target grammar and vocabulary need to be utilized to achieve the use of corresponding functions or notions.

6.4.2 Explanation for acquisition-based orderings at the initial two stages

In relation to the current textbook analysis, the acquisition-based ordering of the structures belonging to Stages 1 and 2 in the four sets of textbooks may be associated with theme-based textbook compilation.

In *New Standard English*, the theme of the first module is "Greetings" and thus there are two related categories of functions: "greeting and saying farewell" and "introducing oneself". The grammar and vocabulary needed for this context are provided accordingly, such as words or formulas "Hello / Hi, I'm …", "Goodbye / Bye-bye", "Good morning", "How are you?", and "I'm fine, thank you". Therefore, the Stage 1's item 'words/formulas' is taught as the grammatical focus in Module 1. Later, in Module 9, the theme is "Family" and the required function is that students need to learn how to introduce their or each other's family members. In this context, the Stage 2 morpheme 'possessive determiner' is obligatorily provided as the teaching focus to fulfil the function, such as 'This is my mother' and 'This is his/her father'. In Module 9 of Book 4, the theme is "Weekend" and students are required to describe activities that happened in the past such as what they did at school or home during the previous weekend. Accordingly, the lexical morpheme 'simple past -ed' is specified as the grammatical objective. The similar explanation applies to the provision of 'lexical plural -s' and 'canonical word order SV(O)'. 'Lexical plural -s' appears as the grammatical focus in Module 4 of Book 6 because students need to come up with generalizations of things in the library. To refer to a whole category, both the generic plural form of the noun, with no article, and the construction '*the* + plural noun' are used. In Book 1, 'Canonical word order SV(O)' is instructed as the grammatical focus of Module 4. The theme of this module is 'We love animals'. Students are required to make simple statements about animals. The basic word order SVO is thus provided to achieve this required function. Therefore, there is evidence that the ordering of structures at Stages 1 and 2 in *New Standard English* is closely related to the arrangement of theme and required functions in the textbooks.

In *PEP English*, the focal instruction of 'word/formulas' in the first unit of Book 1 can be attributed to the theme "Hello!" and necessary functions "greetings and farewells". As a result, students need to memorize and reproduce a certain range of single words and semi- or fully formulaic expressions such as *many thanks*, *hello / hi*, and *goodbye / bye*. In Book 2, the theme of Unit 2 is "My family", and students are required to introduce others and define the relationship. Thus, possessive determiners (or adjectives) such as *my* or *our* are taught as the grammatical focus in Unit 2. The other morpheme, 'lexical plural -s', is introduced as the teaching focus of Unit 5, since the theme is "Where is my ruler" and students need to guess what the lost thing is and identify its quantity. In Unit 5 of Book 1, the theme is "Let's eat!", and students are required to describe their favourite foods or offer food to someone. The canonical word order SV(O) is thus called for as an obligatory item. Therefore, based on the theme and required functions of the corresponding lessons, the structures at Stage 2 including 'possessive determiner', 'lexical plural -s' and 'canonical word order SV(O)' are ordered after the instruction of Stage 1's item 'words/formulas' in *PEP English*.

In *Super Kids*, 'words/formulas' is taught as the grammatical focus of Unit 1 in Book 1 because students need to learn basic greetings such as Hello/Hey, *How are you* and *Many thanks*. Subsequently, the theme of Unit 2 in Book 1 focuses on relatives and acquaintances. Students are required to introduce their family, teachers or schoolmates and also to identify their relationship to others. To fulfil this function, 'possessive determiner' is accordingly provided as a grammatical focus in the context. In Book 2, 'simple past -ed' is the grammatical focus of Unit 5, where students are expected to discuss their activities or those of others in the past. The other lexical morpheme, 'lexical plural -s', is introduced as the grammatical focus of Unit 6, because the required function is to describe the things by specifying their quantity. For the provision of 'canonical word order SV(O)' in Unit 3 of Book 1, students are required to express their favourite colours. Thus, target sentences such as *I like red* are taught as a teaching focus in this unit. Motivated by the lesson theme and related functions, the instruction of Stage 1's item 'word/formulas' precedes that of structures at Stage 2 in this textbook series.

A similar correlation between the theme (or topics) and the grammar is revealed in the analysis of *Join in*. In Unit 1 of Book 1, 'words/formulas' is specified as the grammatical focus since students need to memorize and use some basic greetings such as 'goodbye', 'hello', or 'many thanks'. In Unit 4 of Book 1, the topics of this unit are about 'school things'. Students are required to identify specific possessions and answer the question 'what's this?' or 'what are they?'. In this context, 'possessive determiner' and 'lexical plural -s' are provided as the teaching foci. In Unit 2 of Book 1, the word order SVO is taught as the grammatical focus since students are expected to describe the colours of a variety of things such as 'The floor is brown'.

In conclusion, the ordering of structures belonging to Stages 1 and 2 in all the four sets of textbooks conforms to PT predictions; this may be associated with the theme (or topics) and related functions specified in the corresponding lessons. The theme-based compilation may determine which structure is obligatorily used in a context to fulfil the required functions.

6.4.3 Explanation for deviant orderings at later stages

Theme-based textbook compilation may also account for the deviant grading of several structures at the intermediate or high stages in the four textbook series.

For example, the morpheme '3rd ps sg -s' (Stage 5) is introduced prior to the Stage 4 structures, or it appeared too early in the initial volumes of three of the four textbook series. The early introduction of '3rd ps sg -s' may be associated with the early occurrence of a related theme (or topics) such as favourite things or routines. In the *New Standard English* textbook series, it is the grammatical focus of Book 2. The theme of Module 5 in Book 2 is "Activities", and the related function is "talking and asking about activities on weekdays and weekends". Students are required to describe, in the present tense, what one of their acquaintances or friends (or relatives) normally does at those times. The third person singular inflection *-s* is obligatory if the subject is a third person singular pronoun (e. g., *she*) or a singular proper name (e. g., *Amy*). Similar themes in *PEP English*, Book 3 and *Join in*, Book 2 also provide the context for the instruction of '3rd ps sg -s'. In *PEP English*, Book 3, the theme of Unit 3 is 'My friends'. In *Join in*, Book 2, the theme of Unit 2 is 'My classmates'. Students are required to talk in the present tense about what one of their friends or classmates usually does or likes. Therefore, '3rd ps sg -s' is introduced as the grammatical focus very early in these textbook series.

Similar explanations apply to the untimely introduction of 'V-ing' and 'phrasal plural -s' in the textbook series. In *New Standard English*, Book 3, the theme of Module 3 is 'What are they doing?', and students are required to talk about their present activities. In *Super Kids*, Book 1, the theme of Unit 6 is 'My classroom', and students need to talk about what is happening in their classroom, such as 'we are having English'. The morpheme 'V-ing' is thus provided as the grammatical focus in a specific context in these two books. Similarly, in *PEP English*, Book 1, the theme of Unit 6 is 'Happy birthday!', and students need to talk about a birthday party and count things they see around them, such as how many candles there are on the tables. In *Join in*, Book 1, the theme of Unit 4 is 'School things', and students are expected to talk about school-related things and specify, for instance, how many chairs there are in a classroom. Therefore, taking context into consideration, 'phrasal plural -s' is an early grammatical focus in these two books.

The early instruction of 'copula inversion' in all the four series may also be related to the themes or topics in the corresponding lessons. 'Copula inversion' is one type of *yes-or-no* questions in English. *Yes-or-no* questions are very important structures for L2 learners in English communication. They are mainly used to request or query specific information (Celce-Murcia & Larsen-Freeman, 1999). As shown in the present textbook analysis (see Chapter 5), students are required to query an entire proposition or seek a piece of missing information pertaining to a specific theme (or topics). *Yes-or-no* questions are one of the most useful expressions within such contexts. For instance, in Module 8 of *New Standard English*, Book 1, the theme is "Ask friends". The function students are expected to learn is "Asking about objects and talking about location". To ask their friends about some things that are not nearby or about unfamiliar places, students have to know how to seek information in the form of *yes-or-no* questions. Thus, 'copula inversion' is introduced as the grammatical focus in the module. Similar themes in the other three textbook series also mean that students need to use *yes-or-no* questions to request specific information in a given context. Therefore, 'copula inversion' is specified as the grammatical focus in a premature manner in these textbook series.

6.5 Implication of premature instruction on L2 acquisition

As discussed above, the selection and sequence of grammatical structures may be related to the arrangement of themes (or topics) and relevant functions in the analysed textbook series. It seems that, in these textbooks, the concern with usefulness of a grammatical form (what kind of grammatical expression is needed in a given context) takes precedence over learnability considerations (whether the structure is learnable for L2 students). Although the overall ordering of the grammatical structures shows positive evidence that the introduction of the structures at the initial two stages may take the learners' developmental readiness into account. However, the premature teaching of those structures that are not processable and learnable at a given point may result in two possible negative consequences for a learner's acquisition process.

6.5.1 'Avoidance' or 'omission' strategy

One possible negative consequence is that students probably avoid or omit the use of the structures they have already acquired at the earlier developmental stages. For example, Pienemann (1986, 1989) conducted a teaching experiment in which he observed the acquisition by L2 learners of four German word order rules—'canonical order (SVO)', 'adverb preposing (ADV)', 'verb separation (SEP)', and 'inversion (INV)'. These word order rules were hypothesized to emerge at different stages of the L2 German acquisition process: Stage X (SVO), Stage X+1 (ADV), Stage X+2 (SEP), Stage X+3 (INV). Two of the informants were at Stage X+1 (ADV). After the untimely introduction of the structure INV, which should normally occur at Stage X+3, these two informants were found to reduce their frequency of use of the structure ADV by 75% (Pienemann, 1989, p. 72).

A further investigation carried out by Pienemann (1989) showed that, since these two informants were at a lower stage (Stage X+1), they had not developed the processing procedures required for the higher stage (Stage X+3). They merely knew that an element (e. g., an adverb) other than the subject could be preposed while they learned ADV. They did not know that the subject and the verb must be inverted (this information was included in the process of INV at Stage X+3). Therefore, the informants performed violations in the use of INV. When they realised that they were not able to process INV, they attempted to avoid the use of this non-learnable structure and stopped using ADV as well. Such an 'avoidance' or 'omission'-strategy does not contribute to facilitating the acquisition process, but confines the expressiveness of the learner's language (Pienemann, 1989, p. 76). A similar finding was revealed in Lightbown's (1982, 1983, 1985) empirical research on L2 English acquisition of adolescent learners who were primarily exposed to classroom input of English. The L2 learners were found to give up using some structures they had learned and replace them with less complex structures such as the use of progressive *-ing* (cf. Lightbown, 1985).

If the learners who are not developmentally ready constantly apply the 'avoidance' or 'omission' strategy in their L2 acquisition, this may result in the temporary stagnation and their being 'left behind' in L2 development (cf. Pienemann, 1998, 2005). Pienemann (2005) provides an explanation of this phenomenon: "when a learner accumulates many inferior choices, each of which becomes generatively entrenched, one can predict that further development is structurally impeded" (p. 51). Here, 'inferior choice' refer to the use of omission strategy. A longitudinal SLA study (Clahsen, Meisel, & Pienemann, 1983, cited in Pienemann, 2005) attested that a constant use of omission strategy might hinder further progress in L2 development even after a long period of exposure to the target language. The informants who had been stick with a highly simplified interlanguage did not progress in their grammatical development despite seven to fifteen years of exposure and seemed to be less possible to achieve native-like competence in their interlanguage. Noteworthily, the correlation between cumulative omission strategy and low levels of acquisition after long-term exposure still remained for further research (Pienemann, 2005, p. 52).

6.5.2 Rote-learned formulae

The other possible negative consequence is that the students may simply use those structures which go beyond their processing capacities as rote-learned formulae. According to the Teachability Hypothesis (Pienemann, 1984, 1987, 1989), stages of L2 acquisition cannot be skipped through formal intervention. Pienemann (1998) accounted for why 'skipping' a stage through teaching was impossible within the theoretical framework of PT:

> Each stage requires processing procedures which are developed at the previous stage. 'Skipping stages' in formal instruction means there would be a gap in the processing procedures required for the learner's language acquisition. Since all processing procedures underlying a structure are required for the processing of the structure, the learner would simply be unable to produce the structure. (Pienemann, 1998, p. 13)

Consequently, teaching structures that students are unable to process at their current stage probably leads to students' non-acquisition and merely using structures as fixed formulae. As reported in Pienemann's (1984) empirical study on L2 acquisition of a German word order rule 'INVERSION', one of the two informants—Teresa—failed to actually acquire this learning objective. According to a number of longitudinal and cross-sectional studies by ZISA research group (see Section 4.1.2; cf. Clahsen, 1980; Meisel, Clahsen, & Pienemann, 1981; Clahsen, Meisel, & Pienemann, 1983; Pienemann, 1980, 1981), the L2 development of German word order rules follows a five-stage sequential progression: canonical word order (Stage 1), adverb preposing (ADV) (Stage 2), particle shift (PARTICLE) (Stage 3), inversion (INVERSION) (Stage 4), and verb-final (V-END) (Stage 5). In Pienemann's (1984) experiment, Teresa was found to locate at Stage 2 (ADV) of her interlanguage at the onset of the formal instruction. After a period of focal instruction of the word order INVERSION, Teresa seemed to 'apply' this structure successfully in her oral production.

However, a further analysis of the learner's data revealed that Teresa did not actually acquire the use of INVERSION. In Teresa's so-called production, one out of three corresponding sentences was a formulaic structure which had been provided in the formal instruction, and all other sentence with the application of INVERSION were copied from the sentences which had been drilled in the teaching experiment (Pienemann, 1984, p. 195). Therefore, Teresa's formulaic application of INVERSION could not be considered as systematic and productive use of this syntactic rule. In another word, the introduction of INV had not added it to Teresa's interlanguage system. Pienemann (1984) offers evidence that the premature teaching of a structure (INVERSION at Stage 4) for unready students (Teresa was at Stage 2) cannot result in actual acquisition of the rule without prior acquisition of the developmentally earlier structure (PARTICLE at Stage 3).

6.6 Reconsidering instructed SLA and textbook development

SLA research on developmental sequences such as PT (Pienemann, 1998, 2005) provides insights into how the learners gradually acquire a second language in a sequential manner and brings our attention to the learner's developmental readiness, namely, the learner's current state of L2 processing capacity at a given point. Here is a question: how can such an understanding of L2 acquisition make a contribution to optimizing the formal instruction on SLA and textbook design?

Research on language acquisition has confirmed the importance of input as prerequisite in L2 learning (Cook, 1991; Krashen, 1977, 1981, 1982, 1985; Swain, 1985; White, 1987, 1989). In particular, for learners in FL settings such as Mainland China, not only is there limited or no natural exposure to a foreign language such as English, but the majority of the input comes from classroom instruction, where language textbooks serve as the basis for FL learning and teaching and offer the practical guidelines for students and teachers. Thus, it is not easy to design and compile the textbooks. To select the textbook which suits the learners' interest and needs best and promotes more efficient teaching bears much considerations as well.

The current textbook analysis has revealed that, for the purpose of engaging the school children's interest and needs, all the four textbooks under investigation adopted a theme-based approach in their compilation and emphasized the communicative aspects of the target language. The themes (or topics) structure the whole course and determine what kind of language functions to be achieved in a specific context and thus control the selection of relevant grammatical structures based on which one is called for to fulfil effective communication. For instance, the previous analysis of *New Standard English* Book 1 has showed that the NP morpheme 'phrasal plural -s' was taught as a grammatical focus since the topic of Unit 6 is 'birthday party' and thus students need to learn how to count or describe the relevant stuff in someone's birthday party. When describing countable entities, the nominal plural maker -s is produced, as exemplified in *Two cakes. Three candles.* Since the selection of themes emphasizes their interest potential and appropriateness for children, thus it may enable those young learners to obtain more motivations and facilitate effective learning. This is because the children are more likely to attempt harder to understand and to keep focused when the lesson content is relevant and interesting (Brinton, Snow, & Wesche, 2003; Freeman & Freeman, 2006). Thus, the careful arrangement of curricular themes (or topics) based on children's experiences or interests in the current four sets of textbooks can provide students a contextual, purposeful and enjoyable learning opportunity in the FL formal instruction.

While young learners may achieve better learning if motivated, no matter how much motivations they can receive from pedagogical intervention such as the textbooks, they may not be capable of acquiring those grammatical structures that are located at a high stage of L2 development. During the analysis of a beginner-level Italian coursebook widely used in Austria, Zipser (2012) found that the order and distribution of grammatical structures were highly random and did not follow the natural sequence of L2 development. The subsequent analysis of oral speech production of the students who had been using the selected coursebook provided evidence that the students could not productively use the Stage 4 structure such as *Le susine sono molto buone* 'The plums are very good' (Zipser, 2012, p. 59), even though this structure was previously taught as a teaching objective in the beginning lessons. Although the Italian coursebook focused on the communicative aspects of language in specific cultural situations and engaged a variety of topics related to daily life, the students still felt difficult to productively use the structures that ranked high in the processability hierarchy at the start of their L2 process (Zipser, 2012). Therefore, for the purpose of a more efficient learning and effective teaching, it is also significant to shape our understanding of L2 learning process and pay attention to the learner's actual capacity. This can be incorporated into theme-based textbooks which emphasizes communicative and contextual factors in language use through differentiating learning objectives and general input.

Applied to L2 English classrooms, the untimely introduction of grammatical structures in a textbook may lead to wasted time and frustration when the teacher attempts to teach a structure that the learner is not capable of learning. A possible solution to the issue of premature instruction is to consider learnability constraints in the arrangement of textbook content. Pienemann (1985), Lenzing (2004), and Zipser (2012) all suggested that we should incorporate the principles of learners' developmental readiness when selecting textbook content and sequencing the textbook's syllabus. Therefore, from a processability perspective, grammar should be hierarchically arranged in accordance with the developmental sequence of the L2 acquisition process. Here are two suggestions.

Firstly, the structures located at the early developmental stages as hypothesized in PT should be introduced prior to those predicted to occur at the later stages. Secondly, the introduction of grammar should concentrate on the structures that are either just within the learner's current stage, or at the stage immediately above, rather on those too far ahead of the learners' current level. For example, grammatical structures at low stages, such as 'canonical word order SV(O)', should be introduced as foci in the initial volumes of a full textbook series, or first modules of a textbook. The structures located at higher developmental stages, such as 'do-2nd', should be emphasised only in later books or units.

Some scholars have questioned the idea that grammatical input should be arranged according to the developmental sequence of L2 acquisition. Their concerned was with the heterogeneity of classes. For example, Krashen (1982) and Lightbown (1998) pointed out possible limitations in regards to the implementation of teaching lessons based on the developmental sequence in L2 classrooms. According to Krashen (1982), the claim that grammatical input could be sequenced was based on the assumption that each student in a L2 classroom was at the same stage of L2 development. He further claimed that it was unlikely for students to stay at the same level of acquisition due to individual differences such as the amount of exposure to the target language outside of class. Lightbown (1998) stated that "the heterogeneity of classes is a well-known reality, one that would make developmentally targeted teaching very difficult to organize" (p. 179). She made a crucial point that teaching should not—and does not need to—organize and structure according to stages of L2 acquisition (Lightbown, 1998). In 2000, Lightbown further asserted that "the developmental sequences research should help teachers identify progress in ways other than an increase in target form accuracy" (p. 443). However, a number of classroom-based studies (e. g., Bonilla, 2016; Di Biase, 2007, 2008; Mansouri & Duffy, 2005) have provided evidence that progression of lessons in line with L2 development sequences contributes to a higher grammatical accuracy and a faster rate of L2 acquisition. As far as the issue of the heterogeneity of L2 classes is concerned, Pienemann (1984) suggested that applying the developmental research agenda was not a mere matter of writing acquisition orders into new curricula, but that, instead, variational features reflected in L2 learning also needed to be considered, such as different types of learners and learning problems.

> [...] if teaching is intended to be based on the process of natural acquisition it has to be taken into account that—depending on the learner-type—learning problems which appear at a given acquisitional stage can be solved in different structural ways ranging between 'deviant' and standard-oriented [...] Thus it has to be decided which of these transitional solutions of learning tasks has to be adopted for instruction. (Pienemann, 1984, p. 209)

In addition, in order to benefit, at least, the majority of students in the same class, abundant communicative input containing a variety of target grammatical structures should be provided through well-designed activities or tasks. Assuming the students in a L2 classroom are at different levels from Stage 3 to Stage 5 in their interlanguage development, a possible method to organize grammatical input is to introduce new structures that the learners are ready to integrate into their current stage of L2 development. Based on the previous discussion, the grammatical input is expected to include those structures which are either within the learner's current level or just one step beyond the stage. In this case, the structures that are located at Stage 3 to Stage 6 can be considered in the provision of grammatical input. Moreover, as Pienemann (1985) pointed out, in the grammatical input, the structures that are learnable should not appear only once; instead, those structures should be 'emphasized' at the right point in the learners' L2 development, and they should continue to appear (or review) in a later track. Therefore, the grammatical input in L2 formal instruction should not only cover a broad selection of carefully-chosen target structures in line with the developmental readiness of different learners, but also recycle them through activities or tasks.

6.7 Suggestions for grammar instruction in textbooks

How can we, in a feasible manner, arrange grammatical input in textbooks according to the developmental path of L2 acquisition? I will propose three suggestions. They are based on the previous discussion, the current textbook analysis and SLA theory such as PT.

First of all, the textbooks should provide abundant input. L2 acquisition cannot occur without input. In FL settings such as those that prevail in mainland China, L2 students have little opportunities to receive natural exposure to English. The school education is the dominant environment where the students access the input. Textbooks serve as the basis for English learning and teaching in China. They provide the main source of linguistic exposure to English for students. Therefore, the textbooks should offer full and rich input, to support all or the majority of students within the classroom in acquiring those target grammatical structures that the students are developmentally ready to process. As found in this textbook evaluation, almost all of the targeted grammatical structures that were presented as teaching foci in the previous lessons appear repeatedly in subsequent material. Repetition of those structures in a variety of texts such as songs, rhymes, dialogues, and games can provide an opportunity for students to 'pick up' the structures they are ready to learn as focal grammar.

Second, in terms of sequencing grammatical structures in textbooks, L2 learning sequence and communicative needs should be both taken into account. To balance these two aspects, Pienemann (1985) proposed three inspiring guidelines:

> 1. Do not demand a learning process which is impossible at a given stage (i. e., ordering of teaching objectives be in line with stages of acquisition).
> 2. But do not introduce deviant forms.
> 3. The general input may contain structures which were not introduced for production. (Pienemann, 1985, p. 63)

To be specific, the developmental sequence of L2 acquisition as stipulated in PT should be implemented into the grading of grammatical structures that are taught as teaching objectives. Within the area of general input such as activities or exercises, the grading of structures does not need to be strictly arranged in accordance with L2 learning sequence. For communicative-based textbooks such as the four sets of textbooks investigated in the current study, the primary concern of textbook compilation is on the introduction of theme (or topics) related to naturally occurring conversation and the achievement of required language functions (or notions). Thus, the structures for general input should be provided in line with communicative needs, namely, which structure is needed to communicative effectively in a given context.

Therefore, the grammatical items integrated in the textbooks, including exercises and tasks, should be subdivided into two categories: the obligatory structures and the optional structures. The obligatory structures refer to the learning objectives required to be learned and produced by students. The obligatory structures should be selected and graded in accordance with the L2 acquisition process as stipulated in PT. 1) A structure at an earlier stage should be introduced before a structure at a later stage. For example, single words or formulaic expressions need to be taught as teaching foci prior to lexical morphemes at Stage 2 such as 'simple past -ed' and 'lexical plural -s'. 2) structures at the intermediate or high levels should not be introduced as obligatory structures in the initial volumes of a textbook series or the beginning units of a textbook. For instance, the Stage 5 structures such as '3rd ps sg -s' should not be introduced as a teaching objective in the first lesson of the initial volume, earlier than its previous-stage structures.

The optional structures refer to those features that are not required for production but that appear as structural consequences of the structures that are obligatory to achieve the communicative needs within the textbook theme (or topics). The current textbook analysis has found that incidental occurrences of the targeted structures appear in almost all textbooks. Although those structures are not considered to be the grammatical foci (the obligatory learning items) in a particular lesson, their repetition is still of interest. For example, Unit 1 of *Join in*, Book 7, focuses on the use of the future tense such as 'will + V' and 'be going to'. The target sentences are formed in the structure SVO that has been taught before, as exemplified in 'I'm going to eat healthy food'. The word order SVO appears as a structural consequence of the obligatory structure such as 'be going to'. In this case, students are familiar with the structure SVO, since it was focal grammar in previous lessons. When students learn new grammar, such as the future tense, they may feel it easier to understand this rule in a specific context. In the meantime, students are provided with an opportunity to revise the 'old' structure SVO and reinforce its practice.

Then, how can we determine which structure to be added into the list of obligatory items and which one to be grouped into optional items? Here is an example. As Table 5.1 shows, in Book 8 of *New Standard English*, the theme of Module 4 is "Incidents" and the function is "talk about ongoing events". As a result, at least three structures can be selected for fulfilling the required function in this context: the canonical word order SV(O), progressive be + V-ing, and WH-question with an auxiliary. According to L2 learning sequence as hypothesized in PT, SV(O) is located at Stage 2, 'V-ing' is located at Stage 4, and 'AUX-2nd' is located at Stage 5. In line with their progression in L2 acquisition process, SV(O) should be taught as the obligatory items at first in the lesson, while 'V-ing' and 'AUX-2nd' can also occur as the optional items.

Another suggestion for grammar instruction in textbooks is that a variety of pedagogical tasks should be provided in textbooks to meet heterogeneous demands of students in a L2 classroom. Numerous SLA researchers have considered pedagogical tasks to be a feasible way of combining communicative language skills with beneficial grammar instruction (e.g., Bygate, Skehan, & Swain, 2001; Crookes & Gass, 1993; Ellis, 2001, 2003; Ke? ler, 2008; Nunan, 1991). A pedagogical task is defined in Breen (1987, p. 23) as:

> [...] any structured language learning endeavour which has a particular objective, appropriate content, a specified working procedure, and a range of outcomes for those who undertake the task. 'Task' is therefore assumed to refer to a range of workplans which have the overall purposes of facilitating language learning—from the simple and brief exercise type, to more complex and lengthy activities such as group problem-solving or simulations and decision-making. (Breen, 1987, p. 23)

In contrast with normal exercises such as 'cloze tests', pedagogical tasks have a better chance of identifying different levels of developmental readiness in students and of addressing student needs (Johnson, 2003; Keßler, 2008; Seedhouse, 2005). Once teachers have a general understanding of the current developmental stage of individual students through a task test, they can focus on the instruction of the obligatory structures that all or the majority of the students are developmentally ready to acquire next. In the meantime, teachers can also use tasks in which all or the majority of students can use those grammatical items that are available to them for communicative practice (Keßler et al., 2011). Therefore, textbook writers should design a certain range of pedagogical tasks (e.g., Spot-the-difference task, Story-completion task) in the teaching units (or lessons) of their textbooks. Pienemann (1998, p. 280) applied a few task types to elicit production containing a high density of target structures, such as the task 'Habitual Actions' for elicitation of '3rd ps sg -s', which he defines as follows:

> Habitual Actions: third person singular *-s*
> This task involved a set of photographs depicting "a day in the life of someone such as a librarian or a police officer". Learners were asked questions such as "what does a librarian do every day?" (Pienemann, 1998, p. 280)

The feasibility of these established tasks has been confirmed in various empirical studies on the developmental sequence of L2 English acquisition (Keßler, 2007; Mansouri & Duffy, 2005; Pienemann, 1998). These tasks may contribute to the design of pedagogical tasks in ESL teaching materials. For example, at the beginning of a teaching unit in the textbook, spot-the-difference task can be used to detect the current state of the students' interlanguage development. Two pictures which share similarities and also possess slight differences are respectively presented for the students. They need to describe their own pictures and ask each other's differences. During this task, different students may apply their individual strategies to achieve the goal—to pinpoint the differences between two pictures. Based on the oral production of the students, the teacher may have a general understanding of the learner's developmental readiness. In a later lesson, the task 'Habitual Actions' can be utilized to practice the use of '3rd ps sg -s' as the obligatory item in a communicative-based classroom, if the students are developmentally ready for this morpheme at Stage 5.

6.8 Summary

Based on the analysis results reported in the previous chapter, this chapter discusses several issues of grammar instruction in L2 classrooms from a processability perspective and within a broader context of ESL pedagogical implications. The findings demonstrate positive evidence that a partial agreement exists between the grammatical sequencing in these four textbook series and the L2 learning sequence as outlined in the PT-based processability hierarchy. In general, the acquisition-based ordering of the grammatical items that are acquired at Stages 1 and 2 in all the four sets of textbooks provides evidence that the textbook authors have taken the learner's developmental readiness into consideration in the introduction of those structures at a low level. However, several structures at a higher stage were not introduced as grammatical foci in a way that is processable and learnable for L2 students.

The findings also reveal that the premature instruction of several structures in the textbooks is possibly associated with pedagogical considerations of the textbook writers within the context of English education in China. The design of those textbooks is based around themes. Since the themes are perceived as the primary concern in textbook writing and compilation, the introduction of grammatical items is related to whether they are useful expressions in regards to the fulfilment of communication within a specific theme (or topics). The level of a learner's developmental readiness might not be taken into account in the selection and order of grammatical items in the textbook design.

Empirical evidence from previous SLA research (e. g. , Pienemann, 1984, 1989) shows that the premature instruction of grammatical structures could have two negative consequences on the acquisition process. One possible consequence is that students may avoid or omit the use of those structures they have already acquired in previous developmental stages. The other one is that students who are developmentally unready may be 'left behind' in their L2 acquisition process. Therefore, to avoid these potential negative effects the principles of developmental readiness should be incorporated into the grading of grammar.

Finally, three suggestions for grading the grammatical items in the textbooks are proposed on the basis of developmental readiness of learners, communicative needs, and heterogeneity of L2 classrooms. Textbooks should provide abundant input with a variety of carefully chosen contexts. The grammatical items specified as obligatory learning items should be graded in line with the developmental sequence of L2 acquisition as stipulated in PT. Pedagogical tasks should be provided in textbooks, allowing teachers to identify different levels of developmental readiness in individual learners and to emphasize the items that the majority of students are developmentally ready to acquire.

Chapter 7

Conclusion and Comment

This study achieved its aim to conduct an acquisition-based evaluation of four English textbook series (28 books altogether) for primary school education in China: *New Standard English* (Chen & Ellis, 2012), *People's Education Press English* (Wu, 2012), *Super Kids* (Liu et al., 2012), and *Join in* (Zhang, 2014). The textbook evaluation has examined the following research question: whether the sequencing of the grammatical structures introduced as the teaching objectives in these four textbook series is compatible with the sequenced development that the learners go through in acquiring English as an L2 as hypothesized in Processability Theory (PT; Pienemann, 1998, 2005). In the textbook analysis, the grammatical structures introduced as teaching objectives were documented and categorized against the processability hierarchy for ESL development as stipulated in PT. Their selection and ordering in the textbook series was compared with the sequence of corresponding items outlined in the processability hierarchy. The main findings of the analysis are listed below.

7.1 Summary of findings

The grammatical sequencing in these four textbook series reveals partial agreement with the processability hierarchy for L2 English development as stipulated in PT, in both areas of morphology and syntax. Generally speaking, in all four textbook series, the sequencing of the morphological items that are acquired at Stages 1 and 2 is consistent with their ordering as outlined in the hypothesized processability hierarchy. Compared to the morphological sequencing, the sequencing of syntactic structures in the four sets of textbooks shows a higher consistency with the PT-based learning sequence. In all four textbook series, the sequencing of the syntactic items at the first three stages and Stage 5 is found to agree with their sequencing as presented in the PT-based processability hierarchy.

Considering both areas of morphology and syntax, the grammatical structures that are acquired in the first two developmental stages are introduced as teaching foci in accordance with their sequencing as outlined in the PT-based processability hierarchy. This finding indicates that the textbook writers' idea of low-level structures follows the L2 developmental trajectory as stipulated in PT.

The instruction, in the four textbook series, of several grammatical structures that are only able to be acquired at an intermediate or high level (Stages 3 to 5) does not show strong consistency with the PT progression. Those structures are introduced as grammatical foci before structures associated with earlier stages. The findings imply that the writers of the four series might consider these structures less difficult for L2 students than they really are, and these structures were therefore taught earlier than other, easier ones. From a processability perspective, the premature instruction of these four structures in the textbooks does not take into consideration L2 learners' developmental readiness.

In contrast to previous ESL studies on SLA-based textbook analysis (e. g. , Lenzing, 2008; Zipser, 2012), in which the ordering of grammatical structures was found to be rather random, the present study reveals less of a discrepancy between the English textbooks selected for scrutiny and the staged L2 development as hypothesized in PT: the highlighted issue is reflected in the deviant instruction of only four grammatical structures: 'phrasal plural -s', 'V-ing', '3rd ps sg -s' and 'copula inversion' (a maximum of two in each textbook series).

Given the premature instruction of the four structures as observed, the question arises as to whether such phenomena might be related to textbook writers' considerations in regards to textbook compilation. The answer to the issue is presented in the following.

The analysed textbooks were compiled according to a theme-based approach, as demonstrated in the textbook prefaces. The textbook writers considered the themes or topics closely related to student interests and needs to be their primary concern in the course of textbook compilation. The themes of individual lessons (or units) determine what kinds of target grammar and vocabulary need to be utilized to achieve the use of corresponding language functions. As far as the analysed textbooks is concerned, the selection and sequence of grammatical items at intermediate or high stages might be associated with the design of theme (or topics) and necessary functions. Usefulness of grammatical items in a given context was the primary concern for those textbook writers, rather than whether the grading of grammar is learnable for L2 learners.

However, the premature instruction of grammatical structures might have negative effects on the learning process of L2 learners. Two possible consequence that were addressed in the current study, based on empirical evidence from SLA research on developmental sequences (Pienemann, 1984, 1986, 1989; Lightbown, 1982, 1983, 1985) are that 1) students might avoid or omit the use of grammatical structures they have acquired before due to possible frustration triggered by their failure to acquire non-learnable new structures; and 2) developmentally unready students might simply use those 'unlearnable' structures as rote-learned formulae.

To address such problems and facilitate a more effective teaching, this study has proposed three suggestions for developing a learnable grammar instruction in English textbooks in a feasible manner. Developmental readiness and pedagogical issues such as the issue of heterogeneity in L2 classes were taken into account.

First, the textbooks should provide full and rich input. Second, the grammatical items in the textbooks should be grouped into obligatory and optional structures, and the obligatory structures should be selected and ordered in keeping with the developmental sequence of L2 English acquisition as stipulated in PT. Third, pedagogical tasks designed for determining the level of L2 learners' developmental readiness should be provided in the textbooks, to deal with the issue of heterogeneity in L2 classrooms.

7.2 Significance and contribution

First of all, given the findings as reported, the present study contributes to filling a 'gap' in previous research within the SLA field. As reviewed in Chapter 3, established studies on textbook evaluation do not pay attention to the sequencing of grammatical structures in teaching materials for early English education within the context of mainland China. Following previous ESL studies on PT-based assessment (c. g., Lenzing, 2004, 2008), this study shows only partial agreement between what is learnable and what is taught in current textbooks; it does so through the analysis of a broader range of textbooks (four series including 28 textbooks).

Second, the current study looks into the ordering of structures introduced as teaching objectives through differentiating between the initial occurrence and the incidental occurrence. This is based on a processing view of L2 development (Pienemann, 1998, 2005), namely, learning an L2 in fact is learning a set of L2 processing skills, and the learner produces a grammatical structure only when the implicit skill-based procedure becomes available. The initial occurrence of a structure locates the point in time when the underlying processing procedure is obligatory for the students to learn for the first time in the textbook series. Therefore, the ordering of the initial occurrence of grammatical structures shows the sequence of the underlying processing skill development required in the sets of textbooks. The incidental items (or occurrences) refer to all the later reoccurrences of a structure after the first introduction in the textbook series. They indicate how many times a structure reoccurs in the textbooks. This study differs from the previous textbook studies (e. g., Lenzing, 2004, 2008) that applied a quantitative analysis and focused on percentage of occurrence of structures. The distinction between 'initial occurrence' and 'incidental occurrence' may enrich our understanding of acquisition-based textbook evaluation by adding a qualitative perspective.

Third, the proposed suggestions may serve as a reference for the design of grammatical syllabi and English curriculum in a L2 communicative setting. For future syllabus construction, it will be a good attempt to integrate three aspects, namely, the developmental path of L2 acquisition, communicative aspects of L2 learning, and the issue of heterogeneity. The grammatical objectives can be grouped into the obligatory items and the optional items. The grading of obligatory structures that are required to be produced by students should be organized within the constraints of learnability. The selection and sequence of optional items can be adjusted according to communicative needs of L2 learners; the repetition of certain structures are also needed in order to fulfil necessary functions and contextualize the practice of focal grammar. As an important component of a grammatical syllabus, the design of activities or exercises can take pedagogical tasks into account. This kind of tasks may be helpful for teaching practitioners to focus on specific structures in line with the needs of individual students.

7.3 Limitations and suggestions for future improvement

Some weaknesses associated with limitations beyond the control of the researcher within the restricted timeframe need to be identified. The first one relates to the selection of the analysed textbooks. Although this study relies on a broader range of data (in comparison with the established studies, e.g., Lenzing, 2004, 2008 and Zipser, 2012, more textbooks and complete series were taken into consideration), the selection of textbooks was still limited in quantity. Since the primary intention of this study was to examine the sequencing of grammar in current English textbooks, insights gained through the analysis of more textbooks that are widely used in China are needed to extend the generalizability of the findings in this study.

The second limitation is that the present study did not obtain any 'first-hand' information in regards to the writers of the analysed textbook series. Due to limitations of communication and negotiation, as well as a tight research schedule, the researcher failed to get the opportunity to interview the textbook writers in person. Although information on textbook design was collected in an acceptable way (in the absence of better alternatives), interviews with textbook writers (or editors) seems to be highly desirable to make the current discussion more convincing and informative. Such interviews could look into the writers' or editors' primary concerns with respect to textbook compilation, their perception of grammar instruction in textbooks, the optimal way of sequencing grammar from their perspectives, and limitations of textbook design beyond their control. Reliance on such interviews, the presence of few structures in different textbook series may be accounted for in a more reliable way, such as the issue of why 'V-en' is not included in some of the textbooks.

Another limitation is the lack of a component which compares the textbooks with primary data on acquisition. Due to the limited timeframe, the researcher could not conduct a longitudinal study on the classroom learners (Grade 3 to Grade 6 in primary schools) who have been using the analysed four ESL textbook series. A comparison between those textbooks and those L2 learners is needed in order to address a range of specific issues. For instance, whether or not those limited textbooks might make a difference to actual learning. More specifically, whether or not a textbook that did conform to the L2 learning sequence as hypothesized in Processability Theory (PT) achieved better learning. A comparison of the learners' production between pre- and post-use of those textbooks is also required, in order to examine whether those learners acquire the teaching objectives specified in those textbooks according to the PT stage sequencing. My future research will focus on these issues and seek to further illuminate the relationship between learnability (what the learners did actually learn given those textbooks) and teachability (as proposed by the textbooks).

In addition, this study did not investigate in a thorough way the overall input provided by textbooks, such as exercises and activities. Although the textbook analysis incorporated a fairly superficial look into the incidental occurrences of certain structures in the textbooks, it did not provide a comprehensive understanding of these items. Since this study only focuses on the sequencing of grammatical foci rather than the presentation of all the grammatical structures in the textbooks, issues related to grammatical presentation and general input remain a matter for further investigation. In future research, I intend to combine other SLA approaches such as input frequency or input processing with the PT-based approach.

Finally, the current study showed that some structures were introduced in one textbook series for the first and second years of English education (Grades 3 and 4) while those structures were taught in other textbook series for later years of English teaching (e. g. , Grades 5 and 6). This issue may need further investigation into the difference in the four sets of textbooks regarding when to start a next-stage grammatical structures. Future research may consider a comparison between the target textbooks and English curriculums (or educational references). A standard criterion of L2 proficiency is needed in order to examine whether a specific structure is taught too early in a textbook series or too late in another textbook series according to the progress of L2 learning and teaching. This may provide a broader understanding of the learner's development readiness.

The limitations of this study can be regarded as suggestions for future improvement. Although many issues and aspects related to textbooks were not addressed and solved, the present study has provided some preliminary insights into the sequencing of grammar in L2 textbooks in terms of learnability and teachability. The four suggestions proposed here may contribute to developing a SLA-based grammatical syllabus and improving the design of L2 textbooks for more efficient learning and more effective teaching.

Bibliography

Al Fraidan, A. (2012). Evaluation of two ESP textbooks. *English Language Teaching*, 5(6), 43-47.

Adams, M. (1978). Methodology for examining second language acquisition. In E. Hatch (Ed.), *Second language acquisition*. Rowley, Mass: Newbury house.

Adamson, B. (2004). *China's English: A history of English in Chinese education*. Hong Kong: Hong Kong University Press.

Akakura, M. (2012). Evaluating the effectiveness of explicit instruction on implicit and explicit L2 knowledge. *Language Teaching Research*, 16 (1), 9-37.

Allen, H. W. (2008). Textbook materials and foreign language teaching: Perspectives from the classroom. *NECTFL Review*, 62, 5-28.

Ambridge, B., et al., (2008). The effect of verb semantic class and verb frequency (entrenchment) on children's and adults' graded judgements of argument structure overgeneralization errors. *Cognition*, 106 (1), 87-129.

Andersson, A.-B. (1992). *Second Language Learners' Acquisition of Grammatical Gender in Swedish*. (Doctoral), University of Göteborg.

Aski, J. M. (2003). FL textbook activities: Keeping pace with second language acquisition research. *Foreign Language Annals*, 36, 57-65.

Bagarić, V., & Mihaljević-Djigunović, J. (2007). Defining communicative competence. *Metodika*, 8 (1), 94-103.

Bailay, N., Madden, C., & Krashen, S. D. (1974). Is there a 'natural sequence' in adult second language learning? *Language Learning*, 24, 235-243.

Banciu, V., & Jireghie, A. (2012). Communicative language teaching. *The Public Administration and Social Policies Review*, 1(8), 94-98.

Barnes, S., Gutfreund, M., Satterly, D., & Wells, G. (1983). Characteristics of adult speech which predict children's language development. *Journal of Child Language*, 10(1), 65-84.

Bernsten, S. G. (2002). *Using Conversation Analysis to evaluate pre-sequences in invitation, offer and request dialogues in ESL textbooks*. (Master), University of Illinois, Urbana-Champaign.

Bettoni, C. & Di Biase, B. (2015). *Grammatical development in second languages: exploring the boundaries of processability theory*. European Second Language Acquisition.

Bettoni, C., Di Biase, B., & Nuzzo, E. (2009). Postverbal subject in Italian L2: a processability theory approach. In J.-U. Kessler & D. Keatinge (eds.), *Research in Second Language Acquistion: Empirical Evidence Across Languages.*

Bley-Vronman, R. (1989). What is the logical problem of foreign language learning? In S. M. Gass & J. Schachter (Eds.), *Linguistic perspectives on second language acquisition* (pp. 41-68). Cambridge [England]; New York: Cambridge University Press.

Bloom, L., & Lahey, M. (1978). *Language development and language disorders.* New York: Wiley.

Bloomfield, L. (1933). *Language.* New York: Holt, Rinehart and Winston, Inc.

Boss, B. (1996). German grammar for beginners - the Teachability Hypothesis and its relevance to the classroom. In J. C. Arbonés, J. Rolin-Ianziti, & R. Sussex (Eds.), *Who's Afraid of Teaching Grammar* (pp. 93-103). Brisbane: University of Queensland.

Bonilla, C. L. (2014). From number agreement to the subjunctive: Evidence for Processability Theory in L2 Spanish. *Second Language Research*, 31, 53-74.

Bonilla, C. L. (2015). Instruction Stages of Processability Theory in L2 Spanish: Next or Next + 1?. In K. Baten, A. Buyl, K. Lochtman, & M. V. Herreweghe (Eds.), *Theoretical and methodological developments in Processability Theory* (pp. 205-238). Amsterdam/Philadelphia: John Benjamins Publishing Company.

Bragger, J. D., & Rice, D. B. (2000). FL materials: Yesterday, today, and tomorrow. In F. W. Medley & R. M. Terry (Eds.), *Agents of change in a changing age* (pp. 107-140). Lincolnwood, IL: National Textbook Company.

Breen, M. p. (1987). Learner contributions to task design. In C. Candlin & D. Murphy (Eds.), *Language Learning Tasks* (pp. 23-46). Englewood Cliffs, NJ: Prentice-Hall.

Breen, M. P., & Candlin, C. N. (1987). Which materials? A consumer's and designer's guide. In L. E. Sheldon (Ed.), *ELT textbooks and materials: problems in evaluation and development. ELT Documents* 126. London: Modern English Publications and the British Council.

Bresnan, J. (2001). *Lexical-functional syntax* (Vol. 16.): Blackwell.

Bresnan, J., & Kanerva, J. M. (1989). Locative inversion in Chichewa: a case study of factorization in grammar. *Linguistic Inquiry*, 20(1), 1-50.

Brinton, D. M., Snow, M. A., & Wesche, M. (2003). *Content-based second language instruction.* Ann Arbor: The University of Michigan Press.

Brooks, L., & Swain, M. (2009). Languaging in collaborative writing: Creation of and response to expertise. In A. Mackey & C. Polio (Eds.), *Multiple perspectives on interaction in SLA* (pp. 58-89). Mahwah, NJ: Lawrence Erlbaum.

Brown, R. W. (1973). *A first language: the early stages*. Cambridge, Mass: Harvard University Press.

Bulté, B., & Housen, A. (2012). Defining and operationalising L2 complexity. In A. Housen, F. Kuiken & I. Vedder (Eds.). *Dimensions of L2 performance and proficiency: complexity, accuracy and fluency in SLA*. Amsterdam: Hohn Benjamins Publishing.

Butterworth, G., & Hatch, E. (1978). A Spanish-speaking adolescent's acquisition of English syntax. In E. Hatch (Ed.), *Second language acquisition*. Rowley, Mass: Newbury house.

Bygate, M., Skehan, P., & Swain, M. (2001). *Researching Pedagogic Tasks: Second Language Learning, Teaching, and Testing*. Oxford, UK: Routledge.

Campbell, C., Laanemets, U., Lillepea, M., Loog, T., Kammiste, T., Kartner, P., . . . Truus, K. (1998). Survey Review: ELT Coursebooks for Secondary Schools. *ELT Journal*, 52(4), 337-352.

Canale, M. (1981). From communicative competence to communicative language pedagogy. In J. C. Richards & R. Schmidt (Eds.), *Language and communication* (pp. 2-27). New York: Longman.

Canale, M., & Swain, M. (1980). Theoretical bases of communicative approaches to second language teaching and testing. *Applied Linguistics*, 1, 1-47.

Cardoso, W., John, P., & French, L. (2008). The Variable Perception of /s/ + Coronal Onset Clusters in Brazilian Portuguese English. In B. Baptista and M. A. Watkins (Eds.), *Proceedings of the Symposium on the Acquisition of Second Language Speech (New Sounds)* (pp. 86-106).

Carroll, S. (2001). *Input and Evidence: The Raw Material of Second Language Acquisition*. Amsterdam: John Benjamins Publishing.

Cazden, C. B., Cancino, H., Rosansky, E., & Schumann, J. (1975). *Second language acquisition sequences in children, adolescents and adults: Final report*. Washington, DC: National Institute of Education.

Celce-Murcia, M. (2007). Rethinking the role of communicative competence in language teaching. In E. A. Soler & M. P. Jorda (Eds.), *Intercultural Language Use and Language Learning* (pp. 41-57). Berlin: Springer.

Celce-Murcia, M., & Larsen-Freeman, D. (1999). *The Grammar Book: An ESL/EFL Teacher's Course* (2nd ed.). Boston: Heinle & Heinle.

Celce-Murcia, M., Dörnyei, Z., & Thurrell, S. (1995). Communicative competence: A pedagogically motivated model with content specifications. *Issues in Applied Linguistics*, 6 (2), 5-35.

Chau, T. C. (1975). Error analysis, contrastive analysis and students' perception: a study of difficulty in second language learning. *International Review of Applied*

Linguistics, 13, 119-143.

Charters, H., Jansen, L., & Dao, L. (2012). Think of a number: learning to make nouns plural in second language acquisition. *Association Francaise de Linguistique Cognitive*, 8.

Chen, L., & Ellis, p. (Eds.). (2012). *New Standard English* (1st ed.). Beijing: Foreign Language Teaching and Research Press.

Chomsky, N. (1959). Review: Verbal behaviour by B. F. Skinner. *Language*, 35(1), 26-58. Retrieved from http://www.jstor.org.virtual.anu.edu.au/stable/411334.

Chomsky, N. (1965). *Aspects of the theory of syntax*. Cambridge, Mass: MIT Press.

Chomsky, N. (1980). *Rules and representations*. Oxford: Blackwell.

Chomsky, N. (1981a). *Lectures on Government and Binding*. Cambridge, Mass: MIT Press.

Chomsky, N. (1981b). Principles and parameters in syntactic theory. In N. Hornstein & D. Lightfoot (eds.), *Explanation in Linguistics: The Logical Problem of Language Acquisition*. London: Longman.

Chomsky, N. (2007). Approaching UG from below. In U. Sauerland & H. Gartner (Eds.), *Interfaces + Recursion = Language?: Chomsky's Minimalism and the View from Syntax-Semantics* (pp. 1-29). Berlin/ New York: Mouton de Gruyter.

Clahsen, H. (1980). Psycholinguistic aspects of L2 acquisition. In S. Felix (ed.), *Second Language Development* (pp. 57-79). Tubingen: Narr.

Clahsen, H. (1984). The acquisition of German word order: A test case for cognitive approaches to second language acquisition. In R. Andersen (ed.), *Second Language*. Mass: Rowley.

Clahsen, H. (1988). Parametrized grammatical theory and language acquisition: a study of the acquisition of verb placement and inflection by children and adults. In S. Flynn & W. O'Neil (Eds.), *Linguistic Theory in Second Language Acquisition* (pp. 47-75). Dordrecht: Kluwer.

Clashen, H. (1984). The acquisition of German word order: a test case for cognitive approaches to L2 development. In A. R. (Ed.), *Second languages: a cross-linguistic perspective* (pp. 219-242). Rowley, Mass: Newbury House.

Cook, V. & M. Newson. (1996). *Chomsky's Universal Grammar: An Introduction*. Oxford: Blackwell.

Cook, V. (1991). *Chomsky's Universal Grammar: An Introduction*. Oxford: Blackwell.

Cook, V. (2013). *Second language learning and language teaching*. New York, NY: Routledge.

Cook, V., & Newson, M. (2007). *Chomsky's universal grammar: An introduction*. Malden, MA/ Oxford: Blackwell Pub.

Corder, S. p. (1967). The significance of learner's errors. *IRAL - International Review of Applied Linguistics in Language Teaching*, 5(1-4), 161-170.

Corder, S. p. (1971). Idiosyncratic dialects and error analysis. *International Review of Applied Linguistics in Language Teaching*, 9(2), 147-160. 209-232.

Cortazzi, M., & Jin, L. (1996). English teaching and learning in China. *Language teaching*, 29 (2), 61-80.

Crandall, E. & Basturkmen, H. (2004). Evaluating pragmatics-focused materials. *ELT Journal*, 58 (1), 38-49.

Crookes, G. & Gass, S. (1993). *Task in a pedagogical context: integrating theory and practice*. Clevedon, Avon: Multilingual Matters.

Cunningsworth, A., & Kusel, p. (1991). Evaluating teachers' guides. *ELT Journal*, 45 (2), 128-139.

Dai, B. (2008).《新视野大学英语》教材评估 (a textbook evaluation of *New Horizon College English*). *Journal of Capital Normal University (Social Sciences Edition)*, (S4), 129-131.

Dai, Q. et al. (2000). *Applied studies of Chinese minority nationality languages and orthographies*. Kunming: Yunnan Nationalities Press.

Dalkey, N. C. (1969). An experimental study of group opinion: The Delphi method. *Futures*, 1(5), 408-426.

Daoud, A.-M., & Celce-Murcia, M. (1979). Selecting and Evaluating A Textbook. In M. Celce-Murcia & L. McIntosh (Eds.), *Teaching English as a second or foreign language* (pp. 302-307). Rowley, Mass: Newbury House Publishers.

Davison, W. F. (1976). Factors in Evaluating and Selecting Texts for the Foreign-Language Classroom. *English Language Teaching Journal*, 30(4), 310.

De Bot, K. (2015). *A history of applied linguistics: From 1980 to the present*. London/New York: Routledge.

De Houwer, A. (1995). Bilingual language acquisition. In P. Fletcher & B. MacWhinney (Eds.), *The handbook of child language* (pp. 219-250). Oxford, UK: Blackwell.

De Keyser, R. M. (2005). What makes learning second-language grammar difficult? A review of issues. *Language Learning*, 55 (Supplement 1), 1-25.

de Villiers, J. G., & de Villiers, P. A. (1973). A cross-sectional study of the acquisition of grammatical morphemes in child speech. *Journal of Psycholinguistic Research*, 2(3), 267-278.

DeKeyser, R. M. (2005). What makes learning second-language grammar difficult? A review of issues. *Language Learning*, 55 (S1), 1-25.

Deng, Z., Duan, F., & Zhang, p. (2002). 大学英语教材难度比较研究 (a comparison study of difficulty of university English textbooks). *China University Teaching*,

(7), 57-62.

Di Biase, B. (2007). *A processability approach to the acquisition of Italian as a second language: Theory and applications.* (Ph. D.), Australian National University, Canberra.

Di Biase, B. (2008). Focus-on-form and development in L2 learning. In J.-U. Ke? ler (Ed.), *Processability approaches to second language development and second language learning* (pp. 197-220). Newcastle upon Tyne: Cambridge Scholars Publishing.

Di Biase, B., Kawaguchi, S., & Yamaguchi, Y. (2015). The development of English as a second language. In C. Bettoni & B. D. Biase (Eds.), *Grammatical development in second languages: Exploring the boundaries of Processability Theory* (pp. 85-116): European Second Language Association.

Dougill, J. (1987). Not so obvious. In L. E. Sheldon (Ed.), *ELT Textbooks and Materials: Problems in Evaluation and Development. ELT Documents* 126. Oxford: Modern English Publications / The British Council.

Dulay, H., & Burt, M. K. (1973). Should we teach children syntax? *Language Learning*, 23(2), 245-258.

Dulay, H., & Burt, M. K. (1974). Natural sequences in child second language acquisition. *Language Learning*, 24(1), 37-53.

Dulay, H., & Burt, M. K. (1975). Creative construction in second language learning and teaching In M. Burt & H. Dulay (Eds.), *New directions in second language learning, teaching, and bilingual education* (pp. 21-32). Washington, DC: TESOL.

Dyson, B. (1996). The debate on form-focused instruction: a teacher's perspective. *Australian Review of Applied Linguistics*, 19(2), 59-78.

Dyson, B. (2009). Processability Theory and the role of morphology in ESL development: A longitudinal study. *Second Language Research*, 25, 355-376.

Dyson, B. (2010). Learner language analytic methods and pedagogical implications. *Australian Review of Applied Linguistics*, 33. 3, 30. 1-30. 21.

Educational Testing Service. (2004). *Scoring Guides (Rubrics) for Writing Responses.* Retrieved from www. ets. org.

Ellis, N. (1995). Consciousness in second language acquisition: A review of field studies and laboratory experiments. *Language Awareness*, 4, 121-146.

Ellis, N. (2002). Frequency effects in language processing: A review with implications for theories of implicit and explicit language acquisition. *Studies in Second Language Acquisition*, 24, 143-188.

Ellis, R. & Yuan, F. (2004). The effects of planning of fluency, complexity, and accuracy in second language narrative writing. *Studies in Second Language*

Acquisition, 26 (1), 59-84.

Ellis, R. (1984). *Classroom second language development*. Oxford: Pergamon.

Ellis, R. (1985). *Understanding second language acquisition*. Oxford: Oxford University Press.

Ellis, R. (1989). Are classroom and naturalistic acquisition the same? A study of the classroom acquisition of German word order rules. *Studies in Second Language Acquisition*, 11(3), 303-328.

Ellis, R. (1994). *The study of second language acquisition*. Oxford: Oxford University Press.

Ellis, R. (1997). The empirical evaluation of language teaching materials. *ELT Journal*, 51(1), 36-42.

Ellis, R. (2001). Non-reciprocal tasks, comprehension and second language acquisition. In M. Bygate, P. Skehan, & M. Swain (eds.), *Researching pedagogical tasks: second language learning, teaching, and testing* (pp. 49-74). Harlow: Longman.

Ellis, R. (2002). Does form-focused instruction affect the acquisition of implicit knowledge? *Studies in Second Language Acquisition*, 24(2), 223-236.

Ellis, R. (2003). *Task-based language learning and teaching*. Oxford: Oxford University Press.

Ellis, R. (2006). Current issues in the teaching of grammar: an SLA perspective. *TESOL Quarterly*, 40(1), 83-107.

Ellis, R. (2008). *The study of second language acquisition*. Oxford: Oxford University Press.

Ellis, R., Basturkmen, H., & Loewen, S. (2001). Preemptive focus on form in the ESL classroom. *TESOL Quarterly*, 35, 407-432.

Fabiano-Smith, L., & Goldstein, B. A. (2010). Phonological acquisition in bilingual Spanish-English speaking children. *Journal of Speech, Language, and Hearing Research*, 53, 160-178.

Feng, A. (2007). *Bilingual education in China: Practices, policies and concepts*. Clevedon/ Buffalo/ Toronto: Multilingual Matters Ltd.

Fathman, A. (1975). The relationship between age and second language productive ability. *Language Learning*, 25(2), 245-253.

Fraidan, A. A. (2012). Evaluation of Two ESP Textbooks. *English Language Teaching*, 5(6), 43.

Freeman, D. E., & Freeman, Y. S. (2006). Teaching language through content themes: Viewing our world as a global village. In T. A. Young & N. L. Hadaway (Eds.), *Supporting the literacy development of English learners: Increasing success in all classrooms* (pp. 61-78). Newark, Del.: International Reading Association.

Fries, C. C. (1945). *Teaching and learning English as a foreign language*. Ann Arbor, MI: University of Michigan Press.

Fries, C. C. (1957). Structural linguistic and language teaching. *The Classical Journal*, 52(6), 265-268.

Furrow, D., Nelson, K., & Benedict, H. (1979). Mothers' speech to children and syntactic development: Some simple relationships. *Journal of Child Language*, 6 (3), 423-442.

Gao, C. Z. (2001). Second language learning and the teaching of grammar. *Education*, 122 (2), 326-336.

Gao, X. D. (2005). *Noun phrase morphemes and topic development in L2 Mandarin Chinese: A processability perspective*. (Ph. D.), University of Wellington, Victoria, New Zealand.

Gao, X., Barkhuizen, G., & Chow, A. W. K. (2011). Research engagement and educational decentralisation: problematising primary school English teachers' research experiences in China. *Educational Studies*, 37(2), 201-219.

Gao, X., Liao, Y., & Li, Y. (2014). Empirical studies on foreign language learning and teaching in China (2008-2011): A review of selected research Language Teaching, 47(01), 56-79.

Gao, Y. (2009). Sociocultural contexts and English in China: Retaining and reforming the cultural habitus. In J. L. Bianco, J. Orton & Y. Gao (Eds.), *China and English: Globalisation and dilemmas of identity* (pp. 56-78). Clevedon: Multilingual Matters.

Gass, S. (2003). Input and interaction. In C. Doughty & M. Long (Eds.), *Handbook of second language acquisition* (pp. 224-255). Oxford: Blackwell Publishers.

Gass, S. M., & Selinker, L. (1994). *Second language acquisition: an introductory course*: L. Erlbaum Associates.

Gass, S., & Lakshmanan. (1991). Accounting for interlanguage subject pronouns. *Second Language Research*, 7, 181-203.

Gass, S., & Varonis, E. (1994). Input, interaction and second language production. *Studies in Second Language Acquisition Research*, 16, 283-302.

Gathercole, V., & Thomas, E. (2009). Bilingual first-language development: Dominant language takeover, threatened minority language take-up. *Bilingualism: Language and Cognition*, 12, 213-237.

Genesee, F., Paradis, J., Crago, M. (2004). *Dual Language Development and Disorders: A Handbook on Bilingualism and Second Language Learning*. Baltimore: Brookes Publishing.

Goldschneider, J. M., & DeKeyser, R. M. (2001). Explaining the "natural order of L2 morpheme acquisition" in English: A meta-analysis of multiple determinants.

Language Learning, 51 (1), 1-50.

Goldstein, B. A. (2004). *Bilingual language development and disorders in Spanish-English Speakers*. Baltimore, MD: Brookes Publishing Company.

Guasti, M. T. (2002). *Language acquisition: The growth of grammar*. Cambridge, MA: MIT Press.

Guilani, M. A., Yasin, M. S. M., & Hua, T. K. (2011). Authenticity of Iranian English Textbooks for Schools. *English Language and Literature Studies*, 1(2), 25.

Haegeman, L. (1991). *Introduction to Government and Binding Theory*. Oxford: Blackwell.

Hakansson, G & Norrby, C. (2010). Environmental influence on language acquisition: comparing second and foreign language acquisition of Swedish. *Language Learning*, 60 (3), 628-650.

Hakuta, K. (1974). A preliminary report on the development of grammatical morphemes in a Japanese girl learning English as a second language. *Working Papers on Bilingualism*, 3, 18-43.

Hale, T., & Budar, E. (1970). Are TESOL classes the only answer? *Modern Language Journal*, 54, 487-492.

Halliday, M., McIntosh, A., & Strevens, p. (1964). *The linguistic sciences and language teaching*. London: Longmans.

Hamayan, E., & Tucker, G. (1980). Language input in the bilingual classroom and its relationship to second language achievement. *TESOL Quarterly*, 14 (4), 453-468.

Harley, B. & Swain, M. (1984). The interlanguage of immersion students and its implications for second language teaching. In A. Davies, C. Criper & A. P. R. Howatt (Eds.), *Interlanguage* (pp. 291-311). Edinburgh, Scotland: Edinburgh University Press.

Harmer, J. (1991). *The Practice of English Language Teaching*. New York: Longman Publishing.

Hoffmann, C. (1991). *An introduction to bilingualism*. Longman.

Housen, A. & F. Kuiken. (2009). Complexity, accuracy, and fluency in second language acquisition. *Applied Linguistics*, 30 (4), 461-473.

Housen, A., Pierrard, M., & Daele, S. V. (2005). Structure complexity and the efficacy of explicit grammar instruction. In A. Housen & M. Pierrard (Eds.), *Investigations in instructed second language acquisition* (pp. 235-270). Berlin/New York: Mouton de Gruyter.

Hu, G. (2002). Potential cultural resistance to pedagogical imports: The case of communicative language teaching in China. *Language, Culture, and Curriculum*, 15 (2), 93-105.

Hulstijn, J. H. , Ellis, R. , & Eskildsen, S. (Eds.) (2015). Orders and sequences in the acquisition of L2 morphosyntax, 40 years on: An introduction to the special issue. *Language Learning*, 65, 1-5.

Hutchby, I. & Wooffitt, R. (1998). *Conversation Analysis*. Cambridge: Polity Press.

Hutchinson, T. , & Torres, E. (1994). The textbook as agent of change. *ELT Journal*, 48(4), 315-328.

Hutchinson, T. , & Waters, A. (1987). *English for specific purposes: a learning-centered approach*. New York: Cambridge University Press.

Hyltenstam, K. (1977). Implicational patterns in interlanguage syntax variation. *Language Learning*, 27(2), 383-410.

Hymes, D. H. (1967). Models of the interaction of language and social setting. *Journal of Social Issues*, 23(2), 8-38.

Hymes, D. H. (1972). On communicative competence. In J. B. Pride & J. Holmes (Eds.), *Sociolinguistics: Selected readings* (pp. 269-293). Harmondsworth: Penguin.

Ishihara, N. & Paller, D. L. (2016). Research-informed materials for teaching pragmatics: the case of agreement and disagreement in English. In B. Tomlinson (ed.), *SLA Research and Materials Development for Language Learning* (pp. 87-102). New York: Routledge.

Jaén, M. M. , & Basanta, C. p. (2009). Developing conversational competence through language awareness and multimodality: the use of DVDs. *ReCALL*, 21(03), 283-301.

Jansen, L. (2008). Acquisition of German Word Order in Tutored Learners: A Cross - Sectional Study in a Wider Theoretical Context. *Language Learning*, 58(1), 185-231.

Jansen, L. M. (1991). The development of word order in natural and formal German second language acquisition. *Australian Working Papers in Language Development*, 5, 1-42.

Johnson, D. , & Johnson, R. (1999). *Learning together and alone: Cooperative, competitive, and individualistic learning*. Boston: Allyn & Bacon.

Johnson, K. (2003). *Designing language teaching tasks*. Basingstoke: Palgrave MacMillan.

Johnson, R. (1986). Selecting a coursebook: a realistic approach. In S. Holden (Ed.), *Techniques of teaching from theory to practice* (pp. 54-57). Oxford: Modern English Publications/ The British Council.

Johnson, R. T. , & Johnson, D. W. (1999). Cooperative learning and assessment. In D. Kluge, S. Mcguirc, D. Johnson, & R. Johnson (Eds.), JALT applied materials cooperative learning (pp. 164- 178).

Johnston, M. (1985). *Syntactic and morphological progression in learner English*. Canberra: Department of Immigration and Ethnic Affairs.

Kaplan, R., & Bresnan, J. (1982). Lexical-Functional Grammar: a formal system for grammatical representation. In J. Bresnan (Ed.), *The mental representation of grammatical relations* (pp. 173-281). Cambridge, MA: The MIT Press.

Kawaguchi, S. (2005a). Argument structure and syntactic development in Japanese as a second language. In M. Pienemann (Ed.), *Cross-linguistic aspects of Processability Theory* (pp. 253-298). Amsterdam: John Benjamins.

Kawaguchi, S. (2005b). Processability theory and Japanese as a second language. *Acquisition of Japanese as a second language*, 8, 83-115.

Kawaguchi, S. (2011). Japanese as a second language: A test case for the typological plausibility of PT. In M. Pienemann & J.-U. Keßler (Eds.), *Studying Processability theory: An introductory textbook* (pp. 99-105). Amsterdam/Philadelphia: John Benjamins Publishing Company.

Kempen, G., & Hoenkamp, E. (1987). An Incremental Procedural Grammar for Sentence Formulation. *Cognitive Science*, 11(2), 201-258.

Keßler, J.-U. (2006). *Englischerwerb im Anfangsunterricht diagnostizieren. Linguistische Profilanalysen und der übergang von der Primar- in die Sekundarstufe I.* (Giessener Beiträge zur Fremdsprachendidaktik). Tübingen: Gunter Narr.

Keßler, J.-U. (2007). Assessing EFL-development online: A feasibility study of Rapid Profile. In F. Mansouri (Ed.), *Bilingualism and theory-driven second language acquisition research* (pp. 119-143). Newcastle upon Tyne: Cambridge Scholars Press.

Keßler, J.-U. (2008). Communicative tasks and second language profiling: Linguistic and pedagogical implications. In J. Eckerth & S. Siekmann (Eds.), *Task-Based Language Learning and Teaching* (pp. 291-310). Frankfurt am Main: Peter Lang GmbH.

Keßler, J.-U., & Plesser, A. (2011). *Teaching Grammar*. Paderborn: Verlag Ferdinand Schöningh.

Keßler, J.-U., Liebner, M., & Mansouri, F. (2011). Teaching. In M. Pienemann & J.-U. Kessler (Eds.), *Studying processability theory: an introductory textbook* (Vol. 1., pp. 149-156). Philadelphia: John Benjamins Publishing Company.

Khranke, K. (1987). *Approaches to Syllabus Design for Foreign Language Teaching* (Language in Education: Theory and Practice 67). Washington, D.C.: Centre for Applied Linguistics.

Kidd, E., et al., (2007). Object relatives made easy: A cross-linguistic comparison of the constraints influencing young children's processing of relative clauses.

Language and Cognitive Processes, 22, 860-897.

Klima, E., & Bellugi, U. (1966). Syntactic regularities in the speech of children. In J. Lyons & R. Wales (Eds.), *Psycholinguistic Papers* (pp. 183-208). Edinburgh: Edinburgh University Press.

Krashen, S. D. (1976). Formal and informal linguistic environments in language acquisition and language learning. *TESOL Quarterly*, 10, 157-169.

Krashen, S. D. (1977). Some issues relating to the Monitor Model. In H. D. Brown, C. A. Yorio, & R. H. Crymes (Eds.), *On TESOL '77: Teaching and Learning English As a Second Language: Trends in Research and Practice* (pp. 144-158). Washington, D. C.: Teachers of English to Speakers of Other Languages.

Krashen, S. D. (1981). *Second Language Acquisition and Second Language Learning*. Oxford: Pergamon Press.

Krashen, S. D. (1982). *Principles and practice in second language acquisition*. Oxford: Pergamon Press.

Krashen, S. D. (1985). *The input hypothesis: issues and implications*. New York; London: Longman.

Krashen, S. D., & Seliger, H. W. (1976). The role of formal and informal environments in second language learning: A pilot study. *Linguistics*, 172, 15-21.

Krashen, S. D., & Scarcella, R. (1978). On routines and patterns in language acquisition and performance. *Language Learning*, 28(2), 283-300.

Krashen, S. D., Butler, J., Birkbaum, R., & Robertson, J. (1978). Two studies in language acquisition and language learning. *ITL: Review of Applied Linguistics*, 39(40), 73-92.

Krashen, S. D., Madden, C., & Bailey, N. (1975). Theoretical aspects of grammatical sequencing. In M. Burt & H. Dulay (eds), *Second language learning, teaching and bilingual education*. Washington: TESOL. 44-54.

Lado, R. (1957). *Linguistics across cultures: applied linguistics for language teachers*. Ann Arbor: University of Michigan Press.

Lan, J., & Meng, H. (2009). Multidimensional approach to the evaluation of New College English. *Journal of Kashgar Teachers College*, 30(4), 85-88.

Lanza, E. (2001). Bilingual first language acquisition: A discourse perspective on language contact in parent-child interaction. In J. Cenoz & F. Genesee (Eds.), *Trends in bilingual acquisition* (pp. 201-230). Amsterdam: John Benjamins.

Lapkin, S., Hart, D., & Swain, M. (1991). Early and middle French immersion programs—French language outcomes. *Canadian Modern Language Review*, 48 (1), 11-40.

Lapkin, S., & Swain, M. (1996). Vocabulary teaching in a grade 8 French immersion classroom: A descriptive case study. *Canadian Modern Language Review*, 53(1),

242-256.

Larsen, D. (1975). A re-evaluation of grammatical structure sequencing. *On TESOL' 74* (pp. 151-161). Washington: TESOL.

Larsen-Freeman, D. E. (1976). An explanation for the morpheme acquisition order of second language learners. *Language Learning*, 26(1), 125-134.

Larsen-Freeman, D. E. (2003). *Teaching language: From grammar to grammaring*. Boston: Thomson/ Heinle.

Larsen-Freeman, D. E. (2015). Research into practice: Grammar learning and teaching. *Language Teaching*, 48 (2), 263-280.

Larsen-Freeman, D. E., & Long, M. H. (1991). *An introduction to second language acquisition research*. New York: Longman.

Lenzing, A. (2004). Textbooks and teachability: An analysis of primary school textbooks in terms of Processability Theory. (M. A. Master Thesis), Universität Paderborn.

Lenzing, A. (2008). Teachability and learnability: An analysis of primary school textbooks. In J.-U. Kessler (Ed.), *Processability approaches to second language development and second language learning* (pp. 221-241). Newcastle, UK: Cambridge Scholars Publishing.

Lenzing, A. (2013). *The Development of the Grammatical System in Early Second Language Acquisition: The Multiple Constraints Hypothesis*. Amsterdam: John Benjamins Publishing Company.

Lenzing, A. (2014). Rapid Profile: A Screening Procedure for Second Language Acquisition Assessment Manual.

Levelt, W. J. M. (1981). The speaker's linearization problem. *Philosophical Transactions of the Royal Society of London* (Series B, Biological Sciences), 295 (1077), 305-315.

Levelt, W. J. M. (1982). Linearization in describing spatial networks. In S. Peters & E. Saarinen (Eds.), *Processes, Beliefs, and Questions* (pp. 199-220). Dordrecht, Reidel: D. Reidel Publishing Company.

Levelt, W. J. M. (1983). Monitoring and self-repair in speech. *Cognition*, 14, 41-104.

Levelt, W. J. M. (1989). *Speaking: from intention to articulation*. Cambridge, Mass: MIT Press.

Lewis, M. p. (2009). *Ethnologue languages of the world*. Dallas, Tex: SIL International.

Li, S. (2010). The effectiveness of corrective feedback in SLA: A meta-analysis. *Language Learning*, 60(2), 309-365.

Liamkina, O., & Ryshina-Pankova, M. (2012). Grammar dilemma: Teaching grammar as a resource for making meaning. *The Modern Language Journal*, 12, 270-289.

Lieven, E. (2010). Input and first language acquisition: Evaluating the role of frequency.

Lingua, 120, 2546-2556.

Lightbown, P. M. (1982). Classroom language as input to second language acquisition. Paper presented at the Second European-North American Workshop on Second Language Acquisition Research. Gohrde, West Germany. August.

Lightbown, P. M. (1983). Exploring relationships between developmental and instructional sequences in L2 acquisition. In H. Seliger & M. Long (Eds.), *Classroom-oriented research in language acquisition* (pp. 217-243). Rowley MA: Newbury House.

Lightbown, P. M. (1985). Great expectations: second language acquisition research and classroom teaching. *Applied Linguistics*, 6 (2), 74-90.

Lightbown, P. M. (1998). The importance of timing in focus on form. In C. Doughty & J. Williams (Eds.), *Focus on Form in Classroom Second Language Acquisition* (pp. 177-196). Cambridge; New York: Cambridge University Press.

Lightbown, P. M. (2000). Classroom SLA research and second language teaching. *Applied Linguistics*, 21 (4), 431-462.

Lightbown, P. M., & Spada, N. (1990). Focus-on-form and corrective feedback in communicative language teaching. *SSLA*, 12, 429-448.

Liu, B. (2016). *A processability approach to the L2 acquisition of Chinese syntax*. (Ph. D.), Australian National University, Canberra.

Liu, D., Krause, A., & Cossu, G. (Eds.). (2012). *Super Kids* (1st ed.). Beijing: People Education Press & Pearson Longman Publishing Group.

Loewen, S., & Reinders, H. (2011). *Key Concepts in Second Language Acquisition*. UK: Palgrave Macmillan.

Loewen, S., Li, S., Fei, F., Thompson, K., Nakatsukasa, S., & Chen, X. (2009). Second language learners' beliefs about grammar instruction and error correction. *The Modern Language Journal*, 93, 91-104.

Long, M. H. (1981). Input, interaction and second language acquisition. In H. Winitz (Ed.), *Native language and foreign language acquisition. Annals of the New York Academy of Sciences* 379 (pp. 259-278).

Long, M. H. (1983). Does second language instruction make a difference? A review of research. *TESOL Quarterly*, 17(3), 359-382.

Long, M. H. (1991). Focus on form: A design feature in language teaching methodology. In K. de Bot, R. Ginsberg & C. Kramsch (Eds.), *Foreign language research in cross-cultural perspective* (pp. 39-52). Amsterdam: Benjamins.

Long, M. H., & Robinson, p. (1998). Focus on form: Theory, research and practice. In C. Doughty & J. Williams (Eds.), *Focus on form in classroom language acquisition* (pp. 15-41). Cambridge: Cambridge University Press.

Lyster, R. (2001). Negotiation of form, recasts and explicit correction in relation to error types and learner repair in immersion classrooms. *Language Learning*, 51(S1), 265-301.

Lyster, R., & Ranta, L. (1997). Corrective feedback and learner uptake: Negotiation of form in communicative classrooms. *Studies in Second Language Acquisition*, 19(1), 37-66.

Mackey, A., & Goo, J. (2007). Interaction research in SLA: A meta-analysis and research synthesis. In A. Mackey (Ed.), *Input, interaction, and corrective feedback in L2 learning* (pp. 379-452). New York: Oxford University Press.

MacLeod A., Laukys, K., & Rvachew, S. (2011). The impact of bilingual language learning on whole-word complexity and segmental accuracy among children aged 18 and 36 months. *International Journal of Speech-Language Pathology*, 13, 490-499.

MacLeod, A., Fabiano-Smith, L., Boegner-Pagé, S., & Fontolliet, S. (2013). Simultaneous bilingual language acquisition: The role of parental input on receptive vocabulary development. *Child Lang Teach Ther*, 29 (1), 131-142.

Makino, T. Y. (1979). English morpheme acquisition order of Japanese secondary school students. *The Japan Association of College English Teachers (JACET)*, 10, 21-46.

Mansouri, F. (2005). Agreement morphology in Arabic as a second language. In M. Pienemann (Ed.), *Cross-linguistic aspects of Processability Theory* (pp. 117-153). Amsterdam: John Benjamins Publishing Company.

Mansouri, F., & Duffy, L. (2005). The pedagogic effectiveness of developmental readiness in ESL grammar instruction. *Australian Review of Applied Linguistics*, 28(1), 81-99.

Mason, C. (1971). The relevance of intensive training in English as a foreign language for university students. *Language Learning*, 21(2), 197-204.

Matthews, D., et al., (2007). French children's use and correction of weird word orders: A constructivist account. *Journal of Child Language*, 34, 381-409.

McDonough, J., & Shaw, C. (1993). *Materials and methods in ELT: A teacher's guide*. Oxford: Blackwell.

McDonough, K., & Mackey, A. (2008). Syntactic priming and ESL question development. *Studies in Second Language Acquisition*, 30(1), 31-47.

McGrath, I. (2002). *Materials evaluation and design for language teaching*. Edinburgh: Edinburgh University Press.

Meisel, J. M., Clahsen, H., & Pienemann, M. (1981). On determining developmental stages in natural second language acquisition. *Studies in Second Language Acquisition*, 3(2), 109-135.

Meng, L. (2011). 从跨文化交际视角改进大学英语教材(to improve college English materials from a cross-cultural communication perspective). *Journal of Southwest University for Nationalities*, 32(7), 192-194.

Met, M. (1999). *Content-Based Instruction: Defining Terms, Making Decisions* (NFLC Reports). Washington, D. C.: The National Foreign Language Centre.

Milon, J. p. (1974). The Development of Negation in English by a Second Language Learner. *TESOL Quarterly*, 8(2), 137-143.

Ministry of Education (MOE). (2001). *Guidelines for Promoting English Language Instruction in Primary Schools*. Beijing: Ministry of Education.

Ministry of Education (MOE). (2011). *Standard English Curriculum in Compulsory Education*. Beijing: Ministry of Education.

Mori, J. (2005). Why Not Why? The Teaching of Grammar, Discourse, Sociolinguistic and Cross-Cultural Perspectives. *Japanese Language and Literature*, 39(2), 255-289.

Mukundan, J., Hajimohammadi, R., & Nimehchisalem, V. (2011). Developing an English Language Textbook Evaluation Checklist: A Focus Group Study. *International Journal of Humanities and Social Science*, 1(12), 100-106.

Nassaji, H. (1999). Towards integrating form-focused instruction and communicative interaction in the second language classroom: Some pedagogical possibilities. *The Canadian Modern Language Review*, 55, 385-402.

Nassaji, H. (2016). Research timeline: Form-focused instruction and second language acquisition. *Language Teaching*, 49 (1), 35-62.

Nassaji, H., & Fotos, S. (2010). *Teaching grammar in second language classrooms: Integrating form-focused instruction in communicative context*. New York: Routledge.

Neumann, H. (2014). Teacher assessment of grammatical ability in second language academic writing: a case study. *Journal of Second Language Writing*, 24, 83-107.

Newport, E. L., Gleitman, H., & Gleitman, L. R. (1977). Mother I'd rather do it myself: The contribution of selected child listener variables. In C. E. Snow & C. A. Ferguson (Eds.), *Talking to Children* (pp. 109-149). London: Cambridge University Press.

Nguyen, M. T. T. (2011). Learning to Communicate in a Globalized World: To What Extent Do School Textbooks Facilitate the Development of Intercultural Pragmatic Competence? *RELC Journal*, 42(1), 17-30.

Norris, J., & Ortega, L. (2000). Effectiveness of L2 instruction: A research synthesis and quantitative meta-analysis. *Language Learning*, 50(3), 417-528.

Norris, J., & Ortega, L. (2001). Does types of instruction make a difference?

Substantive findings from a meta-analytic review. *Language Learning*, 51, 157-213.

Nunan, D. (1991). Communicative tasks and the language curriculum. *TESOL Quarterly*, 25(2), 279-295.

O' Grady, W. D., Dobrovolsky, M., & Katamba, F. (1996). *Contemporary linguistics: An introduction*. New York: Longman.

Ozdemir, B. (2004). Language development in Turkish-German bilingual children and implications for English as a third language. M. A. thesis, University of Paderborn.

Pallotti, G. (2014). A simple view of linguistic complexity. *Second Language Research*, July.

Paradis, J. (2007). Tense as a clinical marker in child L2 English: Comparing English language learners with and without SLI. In E. Gavruseva & B. Haznedar (Eds.), *Current trends in child second language acquisition: A generative perspective*. Amsterdam: John Benjamins.

Pérez-Leroux, A. T., Cuza, A., and Thomas, D. (2011). Clitic placement in Spanish/English bilingual children. *Bilingualism: Language and Cognition*, 14 (1), 221-232.

Pesetsky, D. (1999). Linguistic universals and Universal Grammar. In R. A. Wilson & F. C. Keil (Eds.), *The MIT Encyclopedia of the Cognitive Sciences* (pp. 476-478). Cambridge, Massachusetts: MIT Press.

Petraki, E., & Bayes, S. (2013). Teaching oral requests: an evaluation of five English as a second language coursebooks. *Pragmatics*, 23(3), 499-517.

Pica, T. (1983). Adult acquisition of English as a second language under different conditions of exposure. *Language Learning*, 33(4), 465-497.

Pica, T. (1985). Linguistic simplicity and learnability: Implications for language syllabus design. In K. Hyltenstam & M. Pienemann (Eds.), *Modelling and assessing second language acquisition* (pp. 137-151). Clevedon: Multilingual matters.

Pica, T. (1994). Research on negotiation: what does it reveal about second-language learning conditions, processes, and outcomes? *Language Learning*, 44(3), 493-527.

Pienemann, M. (1984). Psychological constraints on the teachability of languages. *Studies in Second Language Acquisition*, 6(2), 186-214.

Pienemann, M. (1985). Learnability and syllabus construction. In K. Hyltenstam & M. Pienemann (Eds.), *Modelling and assessing second language acquisition* (pp. 23-75). Clevedon: Multilingual matters.

Pienemann, M. (1986). The effect of instruction on learners' orientation in L2 acquisition. In A. Ramat (Ed.), *L'apprendimiento non guidato di una seconda lingua* (pp. 307-326). Bologna: Mulino.

Pienemann, M. (1987). Determining the influence of instruction on L2 speech processing. *Australian Review of Applied Linguistics*, 10(2), 83-113.

Pienemann, M. (1989). Is Language Teachable? Psycholinguistic Experiments and Hypotheses. *Applied Linguistics*, 10(1), 52-79.

Pienemann, M. (1990). *LARC research projects* 1990. Sydney, NSW: Language Acquisition Research Centre.

Pienemann, M. (1992). COALA-A computational system for interlanguage analysis. *Second Language Research*, 8(1), 59-92.

Pienemann, M. (1998). *Language processing and second language development: processability theory* (Vol. 15.). Philadelphia: J. Benjamins.

Pienemann, M. (2005). *Cross-linguistic aspects of Processability Theory*. Amsterdam: Benjamins.

Pienemann, M. (2015). An outline of Processability Theory and its relationship to other approaches to SLA. *Language Learning*, 65(1), 123-151.

Pienemann, M., & Johnston, M. (1987). *Towards an explanatory model of second language acquisition*. Paper presented at the Interlanguage Conference, La Trobe University, Melbourne.

Pienemann, M., & Mackey, A. (1993). An empirical study of children's ESL development and rapid profile. In P. McKay (Ed.), *ESL development: Language and literacy in schools* (Vol. 2, pp. 115-259): Commonwealth of Australia & National Languages and Literacy Institute of Australia.

Pienemann, M., Di Biase, B., & Kawaguchi, S. (2005). Extending Processability Theory. In M. Pienemann (Ed.), *Cross-linguistic aspects of Processability Theory* (pp. 199-251). Amsterdam: John Benjamins Publishing Company.

Pienemann, M., Keßler, J.-U., & Roos, E. (Eds.) (2006). *Englischerwerb in der Grundschule. Ein Studien- und Arbeitsbuch*. Paderborn: Schöningh/UTB.

Pienemann, M., & Keßler, J.-U. (2011). *Studying Processability Theory: An Introductory Textbook* (Vol. 1). Philadelphia: John Benjamins Publishing Company.

Pine, J. M., et al. (2008). Tense over time: Testing the agreement/ tense omission model as an account of the pattern of tense-marking provision in early child English. *Journal of Child Language*, 35(1), 55-75.

Ping, W. (2013). Perspectives on English teacher development in rural primary schools in China. Journal of Pedagogy, 4(2), 208-219.

Polio, C. (1997). Measures of linguistic accuracy in second language writing research. *Language Learning*, 47 (1), 101-143.

Prabhu, N. S. (1987). *Second Language Pedagogy*. Oxford: Oxford University Press.

Qi, Y. (2016). The importance of English in primary school education in China: Perceptions of students. *Multilingual Education*, 6 (1), 1-18.

Rao, Z. (1996). Reconciling communicative approaches to the teaching of English with traditional Chinese methods. *Research in the Teaching of English*, 30, 458-471.

Ravem, R. (1968). Language acquisition in a second language environment. *IRAL - International Review of Applied Linguistics in Language Teaching*, 6(1-4), 175-186.

Ravem, R. (1970). The Development of Wh-Questions in First and Second Language Learners. *ERIC*, 16-41.

Reagan, T. (2004). Objectification, positivism and language studies: a reconsideration. *Critical Inquiry in Language Studies: An International Journal*, 1(1), 41-60.

Riasati, M. J., & Zare, p. (2010). Textbook Evaluation: EFL Teachers' Perspectives on "New Interchange". *Studies in Literature and Language*, 1(8), 54-60.

Richards, J. C. (2001). *Curriculum Development in Language Teaching*. New York: Cambridge University Press.

Richards, J. C. (2010). Series editor's preface. In N. Harwood (Ed.), *English language teaching materials: Theory and practice*. New York, NY: Cambridge University Press.

Richards, J. C. (2012). The role of textbooks in a language program. Retrieved from http://www. professorjackrichards. com/wp-content/uploads/role-of-textbooks. pdf

Richards, J. C., & Rodgers, T. S. (2001). *Approaches and methods in language teaching* (2nd ed.). Cambridge; New York: Cambridge University Press.

Ringbom, H., & Akademi, A. (1980). On the distinctions between second-language acquisition and foreign-language learning. *Papers in Language Learning and Language Acquisition*, 37-44.

Roberts, J. T. (1996). Demystifying materials evaluation. *System*, 24, 375-389.

Roos, J. (2007). *Spracherwerb und Sprachproduktion: Lernziele und Lernergebnisse im Englischunterricht der Grundschule*. Tübingen: Gunter Narr.

Rosansky, E. J. (1976). Methods and morphemes in second language acquisition research. *Language Learning*, 26(2), 409-425.

Saaty, T. L. (1980). *The analytical hierarchical process: Planning, priority setting, resource allocation*. New York: McGraw-Hill.

Sadownik, J. (2003). Minimalist faculty of language, computational system and logic. *Poznań Studies in Contemporary Linguistics*, 38, 167-185.

Sakai, H. (2008). An analysis of Japanese university students' oral performance in English using processability theory. *System*, 36(4), 534-549.

Schegloff, E. A., Koshik, I., Jacoby, S., & Olsher, D. (2002). 1. Conversation analysis and applied linguistics. *Annual Review of Applied Linguistics*, 22, 3-31.

Schmidt, R. (1990). The role of consciousness in second language learning. *Applied Linguistics*, 11, 129-158.

Schmidt, R. (1994). Deconstructing consciousness in search of useful definitions for applied linguistics. *AILA Review*, 11, 11-26.

Schwartz, B. D. (1993). On explicit and negative data effecting and affecting competence and linguistic behavior. *Studies in Second Language Acquisition*, 15, 147-163.

Scotton, C. M., & Bernsten, J. (1988). Natural Conversations as a Model for Textbook Dialogue. *Applied Linguistics*, 9(4), 372-384.

Seedhouse, p. (2004). *The interactional architecture of the language classroom: a conversation analysis perspective*. Malden, MA: Blackwell Pub.

Seedhouse, p. (2005). "Task" as research construct. *Language Learning*, 55(3), 533-570.

Selinker, L. (1972). Interlanguage. *IRAL; International Review of Applied Linguistics in Language Teaching*, 10(3).

Sert, O., & Seedhouse, p. (2011). Introduction: Conversation analysis in applied linguistics. *Novitas-ROYAL (Research on Youth and Language)*, 5(1), 1-14.

Sheldon, L. E. (1988). Evaluating ELT textbooks and materials. *ELT Journal*, 42(4), 237-246.

Shi, J., & Ji, R. (2011). 英语视听说教材评估体系的建构及应用 (The construction and application of evaluation system for English visual and verbal teaching materials). *Education Research Monthly*, (05), 68-74.

Shintani, N., & Ellis, R. (2010). The incidental acquisition of English plural *-s* by Japanese children in comprehension-based and production-based lessons. *Studies in Second Language Acquisition*, 32, 607-637.

Skinner, B. F. (1957). *Verbal Behaviour*. New York: Appleton-Century-Crofts.

Skinner, B. F. (1968). *The technology of teaching*. New York: Appleton-Century-Crofts.

Slobin, D. (1970). Universals of grammatical development in children. In G. F. d. Arcais & W. Levelt (Eds.), *Advances in Psycholinguistics* (pp. 174-186). Amsterdam: North-Holland Publishing.

Smith, N. (2004). *Chomsky: ideas and ideals*. New York: Cambridge University Press.

Song, J., & Sardegna, V. G. (2014). EFL learners' incidental acquisition of English prepositions through enhanced extensive reading instruction. *RELC Journal*, 45(1), 67-84.

Song, X., & Cheng, L. (2011). Investigating primary English immersion teachers in China: Background, instructional contexts, professional development, and perceptions. *Asia-Pacific Journal of Teacher Education*, 39, 1-16.

Spada, N., & Lightbown, P. M. (1999). Instruction, first language influence and developmental readiness in second language acquisition. *Modern Language Journal*, 83(1), 1-22.

Stein, M., Stuen, C., Carnine, D., & Long, R. M. (2001). Textbook evaluation and adoption. *Reading & Writing Quarterly: Overcoming Learning Difficulties*, 17 (1), 5-23.

Swain, M. (1985). Communicative competence. Some roles of comprehensible input and comprehensible output in its development. In S. M. Gass & C. Madden (Eds.), *Input and second language acquisition* (pp. 235-253). Rowley, Mass: Newbury House.

Swain, M. (1988). Manipulating and complementing content teaching to maximise second language learning. *TESL Canada Journal*, 6(1), 68-83.

Swain, M. (1995). Three functions of output in second language learning. In G. Cook and B. Seidlhofer (Eds.), *Principle and practice in applied linguistics* (pp. 125-144). Oxford: Oxford University Press.

Swain, M. (2000). French immersion research in Canada: Recent contributions to SLA and applied linguistics. *Annual Review of Applied Linguistics*, 20, 199-212.

Swain, M. (2005). The output hypothesis: theory and research. In E. Heinkel (Ed.), *Handbook of research in second language teaching and learning* (pp. 471-483). Mahwah, NJ: Lawrence Erlbaum Associates.

Swain, M., & Lapkin, S. (1998). Interaction and second language learning: Two adolescent French immersion students working together. *The Modern Language Journal*, 82(3), 320-337.

Tang, D. & Absalom, D. (1998). Teaching across cultures: Considerations for western EFL teachers in China. *Hong Kong Journal of Applied Linguistics*, 3 (2), 117-132.

Theakston, A. L., et al. (2004). Semantic generality, input frequency and the acquisition of syntax. *Journal of Child Language*, 31, 61-99.

Theakston, A. L., et al. (2005). The acquisition of auxiliary syntax: BE and HAVE *Cognitive Linguistics*, 16, 247-277.

Thorndike, E. L. (1975). *A Teacher's word book of the twenty thousand words found most frequently and widely in general reading for children and young people* (Rev. New York, Bureau of Publications, Teachers College, Columbia University. ed.). Detroit: Gale Research.

Tomlinson, B. (2003). *Developing materials for language teaching*. New York: Continuum.

Tomlinson, B., Dat, B., Masuhara, H., & Rubdy, R. (2001). Survey review. EFL courses for adults. *ELT Journal*, 55(1), 80-101.

Towell, R. (1987). A discussion of the psycholinguistics bases for communicative language teaching in a foreign language situation. *British Journal of Language Teaching*, 25(2), 91-99.

Tucker, C. A. (1975). Evaluating beginning textbooks. *English Teaching Forum*, 13, 335-361.

Upshur, J. A. (1968). Four experiments on the relation between foreign language teaching and learning. *Language Learning*, 18(1-2), 111-124.

VanPatten, B., & Williams, J. (2007). *Theories in second language acquisition: an introduction*. Mahwah, N.J: Lawrence Erlbaum Associates.

VanPatten, B., Williams, J., Rott, S., & Overstreet, M. (2004). *Form-meaning connections in SLA*. Mahwah, NJ: Lawrence Erlbaum.

Vellenga, H. (2004). Learning pragmatics from ESL & EFL textbooks: How likely?. *TESL-EJ*, 8 (2).

Wang, Q. (2007). Evaluation and Analysis of the Textbook. *Journal of Guizhou University for Ethnic Minorities (Philosophy and Social Science)*, (6), 185-187.

Wang, W., & Gao, X. (2008). English language education in China: A review of selected research. *Journal of Multilingual and Multicultural Development*, 29, 280-299.

Wang, X. (2011). *Grammatical development among Chinese L2 learners: From a processability account*. (Ph. D.), Newcastle University, New Castle Upon Tyne, United Kingdom.

Wang, X., & Yang, Y. (2012). Research and Design of English Textbook Evaluation Based on Readability and FAHP. *Foreign Languages in China*, 9(3), 67-77.

Weinreich, U. (2010). *Languages in contact: Findings and Problems*. Stuttgart, DEU: Walter de Gruyter.

Wells, G. (1985). *Language development in the pre-school years*. Cambridge: Cambridge University Press.

Wen, Q. (2012). Teaching English as an international language in mainland China. In A. Kirkpatrick & R. Sussex (Eds.), *English as an international language in Asia: Implications for language education* (pp. 79-93). Dordrecht: Springer Verlag.

Wen, Q., & Gao, X. (2007). Dual publication and academic inequality. *International Journal of Applied Linguistics*, 17, 221-225.

White, L. (1987). Against comprehensible input: the input hypothesis and the development of second language competence. *Applied Linguistics*, 8 (2), 95-110.

White, L. (1989). *Universal Grammar and Second Language Acquisition*. Amsterdam/Philadelphia: Hohn Benjamins Publishing Company.

White, L. (1991). Adverb placement in second language acquisition: some effects of positive and negative evidence in the classroom. *Second Language Research*, 7(2),

133-161.

Whitman, R. L., & Jackson, K. L. (1972). The unpredictability of contrastive analysis. *Language Learning*, 22(1), 29-41.

Wigglesworth, G. & Storch, N. (2009). Pair versus individual writing: effects on fluency, complexity and accuracy. *Language Testing*, 26 (3), 445-466.

Williams, D. (1983). Developing criteria for textbook evaluation. *ELT Journal*, 37(3), 251-255.

Williams, J. (2005). Form-focused instruction. In E. Hinkel (Ed.), *Handbook on research in second language teaching and learning* (pp. 671-691). Mahwah, NJ: Lawrence Erlbaum Associates.

Wode, H. (1978). The L1 vs. L2 acquisition of English negation. *Working Papers on Bilingualism*, 15, 37-57.

Wode, H. (1981). *Learning a second language I: an integrated view of language acquisition*. Tübingen: Gunter Narr.

Wolfe-Quintero, K., Inagaki, S., & Kim, H. (1998). *Second language development in writing: measures of fluency accuracy & complexity*. Honolulu, HI: University of Hawaii.

Wong, J. (2002). "Applying" conversation analysis in applied linguistics: Evaluating dialogue in English as a second language textbooks1. *IRAL, International Review of Applied Linguistics in Language Teaching*, 40(1), 37.

Wong, J. (2007). Answering my call: A look at telephone closings. In H. Bowles & P. Seedhouse (Eds.), *Conversation Analysis and Language for Specific Purposes* (pp. 271-304). Bern: Peter Lang AG, International Academic Publishers.

Wu, X. (Ed.). (2012). *People's Education Press English*. Beijing: People's Education Press.

Xie, J. (2008). 基于语料库的英语教材词汇评估(a corpus-based evaluation of vocabulary in English textbooks). *Journal of Basic English Education*, 10(3), 21-25.

Yamaguchi, Y. (2008). The early syntactic development in child L2 acquisition: What happens after "canonical order"?. In J-U. Keβler (Ed.). *Processability Approaches to Second Language Development and Second Language Learning* (pp. 247-268). Newcastle, UK: Cambridge Scholars Publishing.

Yamaguchi, Y. (2009). The development of plural marking and plural agreement in child English L2 acquisition. In J-U. Keβler & D. Keatinge (Eds.). *Research in Second Language Acquisition: Empirical Evidence across Languages* (pp. 9-39). Newcastle, UK: Cambridge Scholars Publishing.

Yang, B. (1992). A review of the contrastive analysis hypothesis. 19, 133-149. Retrieved from http://fonetiks.info/bgyang/db/92cah.pdf.

Yang, C. C. R. (2009). Theme-based teaching in an English course for primary ESL students in Hong Kong. *Electronic Journal of Foreign Language Teaching*, 6 (2), 161-176.

Yang, H. (24 May 2001). *Towards improving marker reliability*. University of Hong Kong.

Yavas, M. (2014). *Unusual productions in phonology*. New York, NY: Psychology Press.

Yoshioka, K. & Doi, T. (1988). Testing the Pienemann-Johnston model with Japanese: a speech-processing view of the acquisition of particles and word order. Paper presented at the 8th Second Language Research Forum, University of Hawaii at Manoa, Honolulu, March 3-6.

Yu, Q., Fan, W., & Li, N. (2008). A Study of China's College English Textbooks for Non-English Majors-On the Match Between College English Textbooks and English Learners' Topic Interest. *Foreign Languages in China*, 5(3), 60-65.

Zhang, E., & Adamson, B. (2007). Implementing language policy: Lessons from primary school English. In A. Feng (Ed.), *Bilingual education in China: Practices, policies and concepts* (pp. 161-181). Clevedon/ Buffalo/ Toronto: Multilingual Matters Ltd.

Zhang, S. (Ed.). (2014). *Join in*. Beijing: Foreign Language Teaching and Research Press.

Zhang, X. & Lantolf, J. p. (2015). Natural or artificial: Is the route of L2 development teachable?. *Language Learning*, 65 (1), 152-180.

Zhang, Y. (2001). *Second language acquisition of Chinese grammatical morphemes: A processability perspective*. (Ph. D.), Australian National University, Canberra.

Zhang, Y. (2005). Processing and formal instruction in the L2 acquisition of five Chinese grammatical morphemes. In M. Pienemann (Ed.), *Cross-linguistic Aspects of Processability Theory* (pp. 155-178). Amsterdam: Benjamins.

Zhang, Y. (2007). Testing the topic hypothesis: The L2 acquisition of Chinese syntax. In F. Mansouri (Ed.), *Second Language Acquisition Research: Theory-Construction and Testing* (pp. 145-171). Newcastle, UK: Cambridge Scholar Publishing.

Zhang, Y. & Widyastuti, I. (2010). Acquisition of L2 English morphology: A family case study. *Australian Review of Applied Linguistics*, 33(3), 29.1-29.17.

Zhang, Y., Zhang, Y., Peng, Y., & Tang, L. (2011). 教材评估理论指导下的《开放英语》教材分析 (a textbook analysis of <Open English> under the guidance of textbook evaluation theory). *Distance Education in China*, (9), 77-82.

Zhou, M. L. (2001). Language policy and illiteracy in ethnic minority communities in China. *Journal of Multilingual and Multicultural Development*, 21 (2), 129-148.

Zipser, K. (2012). Processability theory and pedagogical progression in an Italian textbook. *Linguistica*, 52(1), 55-68.

Zou, Q. (2009). 基于性别视角评价商务英语教材编写 (an evaluation of business English textbooks from a gender perspective). *Journal of Changsha University*, 23(4), 154-155.

Appendix A: Analysed version of focal grammar in *New Standard English* Book 2

Module	Grammatical structures
1	grapheme: alphabet (a, b, c, d,…) formulaic structure: Here you are. SVO: This colour is yellow. It is blue.
2	SVO: This man is tall. This woman is thin. copula + S(X): Is it a tiger? Are they in zoo?
3	SVO: I like football. We like basketball. I ride bike. I don't ride bike.
4	*Do*-fronting: Do you like meat? Yes, I do/No, I don't.
5	possessive determiner: your mum/my dad/our teacher. 3rd ps sg -s: Amy goes to school on Monday. Tom plays football on Saturday. AUX + SVO: Does Lingling like fish? Yes, she does/No, she doesn't.
6	*Wh*-word + *do* + SVO: What do you do on Sunday/Saturday? possessive determiner: my bike/your book/her music class. SVO: I ride my bike.
7	semi-formulaic structure: It's spring/summer/autumn/winter. It's warm/cold/cool/hot today. SVO: We fly kites in spring. I ride my bike in summer.
8	possessive determiner: your desk/their classroom/his bedroom. 3rd ps sg -s/SVO: Daming flies a kite in the park. Amy goes fishing near the lake.
9	semi-formulaic structure: I've got a new book/a new shirt/a new dress. AUX + SVO: Have you got a new sweater? Yes, I have/No, I haven't. Does Amy have a bike? Yes, she does. /No, she doesn't.
10	semi-formulaic structure: Here's a hat/a skirt/a photo. words: red/yellow/blue/black.

Appendix B: Analysed version of focal grammar in *New Standard English* Book 3

Module	Grammatical structures
1	Numerals: Numbers 13-29 SVO: Twenty and one is twenty-one.
2	imperatives: Go straight on. Turn right/Left.
3	present continuous tense V-ing/SVO: She's watching TV. He's writing a letter.
4	present continuous tense V-ing/SVO: They're rowing a dragon boat. We're drinking water. *Wh*-word + AUX + SVO: What are they doing? What are you drinking?
5	present continuous tense V-ing/SVO: I'm making dumplings. They're eating fast food. *Do*-fronting: Do you want some?
6	modal verb + S(X): Can you run fast? Would you come here? Yes, I can. /No, I can't.
7	future tense with 'be going to'/SVO: We're going to go to Hainan.
8	future tense with 'be going to'/SVO: I'm going to run the 100 metres. *Wh*-word + AUX + SVO: What are you going to do? What will they do? phrasal plural marker -s: 100 metres/5 kilometres/200 centimetres.
9	modal verb + SVO: Can I have some sweets? Could you bring some water? Yes, you can. /Sorry, you can't.
10	'There + be' sentence: There is/are… phrasal plural marker -s: twelve months/three years/five days.

Appendix C: Analysed version of focal grammar in *New Standard English* Book 4

Module	Grammatical structures
1	adjectives: nice, shy, friendly, warm-hearted… She's very nice. But she's a bit shy.
2	adjectives: big, huge, small… London is the capital of England. And it's very big.
3	AUX + SVO: Will you take a kite tomorrow? Yes, I will. /No, I won't. SVO: I will take a kite and a ball on Saturday.
4	SVO: It can walk! I will do housework on Sunday.
5	SVO: Amy's taller than Lingling. You're shorter than me.
6	SVO: This boy is better than the girl. Tom is worse than the girl.
7	SVO: Washington D. C. is the capital of the U. S. A. It's in the east/west/south/north.
8	SVO: They were young then. I was two, then.
9	simple past tense *-ed*: I cooked fish. She laughed a lot.
10	SVO: We bought a watermelon. And then…?

Appendix D: Analysed version of focal grammar in *New Standard English* Book 5

Module	Grammatical structures
1	*Wh*-word + *do* + SVO: When did you come back? When do they come here? SVO: We came back…/They come here… AUX + SVO: Did you…? Yes, I did. /No, I didn't.
2	*Do*-fronting: Do you like…? *Wh*-word + *do* + SVO: How many/How much…do you want? phrasal plural marker -s: three boxes/five bottles/two kilos.
3	*Wh*-word + *do* + SVO: What did you do at the weekend? Where did you go? When/how…?
4	SVO: It's yours. They're mine.
5	'There + be' sentence: There are enough/not enough…
6	SVO: You can catch it well. I can't control it well. modal verb + SVO: Can you catch it well? Yes, I can. /No, I can't.
7	SVO with modal verbs: He/She/They can/can't…
8	simple present tense: I go to school today. We drink coffee together. 3rd ps sg -s in present tense: She skips the class. He does exercises in the playground.
9	AUX + SVO: Are you feeling sad/bored/angry? Does she feel happy? Yes, I am. /No, I am not. SVO: I feel happy/sad/tired. I don't feel angry.
10	'should/shouldn't'

Appendix E: Analysed version of focal grammar in *New Standard English* Book 6

Module	Grammatical structures
1	SVO: We lived…many years ago. /We live…now. simple past *-ed*: we lived…/I stayed… 'There + be' sentences: There were/weren't…There are…
2	simple past -ed: retired (retire), learned (learn)… simple present continuous V-ing/SVO: I'm learning…/She's dancing…
3	SVO: She had a sandwich. We drank some water. *Wh*-word + *do* + SVO: What did she have for breakfast yesterday? What did you drink?
4	lexical plural *-s*: two weeks/three months… copula verb + S(X): Is my book here? *Wh*-word + AUX + SVO: Where can you find…? When will you tell me…?
5	Adjectives: light, broken, heavy, hard…
6	SVO: It's in…/They're under… *Wh*-word + *do* + SVO: Where/when/what/who did you…?
7	imperative forms; simple future tense 'will'
8	*Wh*-word + *do* + SVO: What do you suggest? Why don't you…?
9	simple future tense 'be going to' irregular verb forms in past tense: wore (wear), told (tell)…
10	*Wh*-word + *do* + SVO: How did you arrive…? Where did she take a taxi? *Wh*-word + AUX + SVO: When are you going to the airport? When can you arrive…?

Appendix F: Analysed version of focal grammar in *New Standard English* Book 7

Module	Grammatical structures
1	copula verb: *be* SVO: This postcard is great! It's a picture of the Great Wall.
2	'There + *be*' sentence: There's a China town in New York! There's a…
3	possessive determiner: our/her/his/my/your… lexical plural -s: the stamps/posts… phrasal plural -s: lots of/some/ten stamps/posts… nouns
4	SVO: Thanksgiving is a fantastic festival. We always have a special meal.
5	modal verb + SVO: Can you speak English? Can I write to your friend?
6	semi-formulaic structure (*I've got*…): I've got a Chinese kite. /I've got a knife…
7	3rd ps sg *-s* in present tense: The elephant eats a lot. The lizard drinks a little. simple present tense: Pandas eat for twelve hours a day.
8	simple present tense: I always/often/sometimes/never…
9	semi-formulaic structure (*I want to*…): I want to visit the UN building in New York. I want to visit….
10	imperatives (*please* and *don't*): Don't talk in the library. Please stand in line.

Appendix G: Analysed version of focal grammar in *New Standard English* Book 8

Module	Grammatical structures
1	words: food items; cardinal numbers. formulaic structure: What do you want to eat? semi-formulaic structure: I want a [hot dog/a hamburger/a cola].
2	simple future tense (*be going to*). SVO: We're going to eat at half past twelve. It's going to snow in Harbin.
3	present continuous tense/SVO: The sun is shining. The bird is singing in the tree. The duck is eating the picnic.
4	present continuous tense V-ing: I'm making Daming's birthday card. SVO with modal verb: I can help you. He can make it.
5	present continuous tense/SVO: Daming is having a birthday party. Daming is playing the trumpet, but the phone is ringing.
6	SVO/simple past tense with irregular verb form: I bought you this book. Simon's family gave it to me.
7	SVO/simple past tense (regular and irregular forms): Shenzhou V flew into space with Yang Liwei. He spent about twenty-one hours in space. He made a video and now he is very famous. We laughed at him.

Appendix G: Analysed version of focal grammar in *New Standard English* Book 8(continued)

Module	Grammatical structures
8	SVO/simple past tense with irregular verb form: Helen Keller became blind and deaf. She wrote a book about herself. *Wh*-word + *do* + SVO: What does she write about? When did she become famous? copula verb + S(X): Was she deaf? Is he famous now? *Wh*-word + AUX + SVO: Why is he becoming famous now?
9	*Wh*-word + AUX + SVO: Why are you laughing? Why are you wearing a raincoat? present continuous tense V-ing: They're laughing. He's wearing a raincoat.
10	simple future tense (*be going to*): I'm going to go to the middle school this year. SVO: I'm really excited. /I'm worried.

Appendix H: Analysed version of focal grammar in *PEP English* Book 2

Unit	Grammatical structures
1	chunks: good morning/good evening/hi SVO: She's my mother. /I like hamburgers.
2	possessive determiner: my mother/our teacher/her brother. copula verb + S(X): Is he your father? Yes, he is.
3	semi-formulaic structure: what about…?
4	copula verb + S(X): Is my cap under the desk? No, it isn't.
5	lexical plural -s: two bananas/three mandarins/two oranges. *Do*-fronting: Do you want pears? Do you like bananas?
6	phrasal plural marking (NP agreement) -s: some apples/some cakes. *Wh*-word + *do* + SVO: How many pencils do you have? What do you have at school?

Appendix I: Analysed version of focal grammar in *PEP English*, Book 3

Unit	Grammatical structures
1	chunks/formulas: welcome! /Nice to meet you. SVO: I'm from the UK. We have new friends today. We like to play.
2	SVO: I'm the Easter Bunny. The man is the father.
3	SVO: It has a long nose. It's so fat! It's so tall! copula verb + S(X): Is it short? Is it fat? 3rd ps sg -s: My friend goes to school on Monday. David plays soccer in the afternoon.
4	semi-formulaic structure: Where is [Zip/Jack/Anne…]? SVO: It's under the desk. They're on the chair. copula verb + S(X): Is it on the desk? Are they under the chair? imperatives: put your foot under your chair. Put your arm in your desk. prepositions: under, on, in…

Appendix I: Analysed version of focal grammar in *PEP English*, Book 3(continued)

Unit	Grammatical structures
5	*Wh*-word + AUX + SVO: What will you eat for lunch? words (fruit items): orange, banana, apple, pear… SVO: I like apples. We eat grapes.
6	numerals: one, two, three… SVO: The black one is a bird! The white one is a cat. copula verb + S(X): Does she have balloons? Can you see birds? 3rd ps sg -s: It bits my little finger on the right.

Appendix J: Analysed version of focal grammar in *PEP English*, Book 4

Unit	Grammatical structures
1	possessive determiner: my schoolbag/your fish bowl/our classroom. formulaic structure: Where is it?
2	semi-formulaic structure: It's [green/red/black…]. words (colours): red, white, black, green…
3	lexical plural -s: He has glasses. His shoes are blue. possessive determiner: your T-shirt/my skirt. imperatives: Put on your T-shirt. Hang up my skirt.
4	present continuous tense V-ing: I am wearing a T-shirt. That man is holding an umbrella. AUX + SVO: Can you tell me…? Will they grow up? copula verb + S(X): Are these carrots? Is it a watermelon? Are they hens? *Wh*-word + AUX + SVO: How many horses can you have?
5	semi-formulaic structure (I'd like=I would like): I'd like [beef/water/rice/fish…]. copula verb + S(X): Is this beef? Are they vegetables?
6	phrasal plural -s: My family has six members. Three brothers. copula verb + S(X): Are those cows? Are these donkeys? *Wh*-word + *do* + SVO: How many babies do you have? What do you see in the picture?

Appendix K: Analysed version of focal grammar in *PEP English*, Book 5

Unit	Grammatical structures
1	SVO: She's quiet. She's very hard-working. He's very clever. copula verb + S(X): Is she strict? Is he very kind? possessive determiner: our new Chinese teacher/their maths teacher. phrasal plural -s: two teachers/thirty students.
2	copula verb + S(X): Are you at school? *Wh*-word + *do* + SVO: What do we have on Mondays? possessive determiner: my English class/ our Chinese course… SVO: We have Moral Education on Tuesdays. My English class is on Wednesday. lexical plural -s: on Mondays/Tuesdays/Wednesdays…

Appendix K: Analysed version of focal grammar in *PEP English*, Book 5 (continued)

Unit	Grammatical structures
3	SVO: The sandwich is delicious. It's healthy. copula verb + S(X): Is it tender? Are they spicy? *Wh*-word + *do* + SVO: What do you want to eat?
4	SVO: I can dance. I can sing. We can play ping-pong. AUX + SVO: Can you have a try? Can you play ping-pong? *Wh*-word + AUX + SVO: What can you do for the party?
5	SVO: My father can draw very well. copula verb + S(X): Is that a table beside the bed/ phrasal plural -s: many pretty flowers. So many pictures.
6	SVO: I'm hungry. I have some food.

Appendix L: Analysed version of focal grammar in *PEP English*, Book 6

Unit	Grammatical structures
1	possessive determiner: my clothes/our new classroom. ADV + SVO: Sometimes I go hiking. On Sunday I go shopping. lexical plural -s: classes, exercises, sports. 3rd ps sg -s: My mum does morning exercises at 7 o' clock. *Wh*-word + *do* + SVO: When do you do get up? When does your mum do morning exercises?
2	lexical plural -s: the colours, beautiful flowers. SVO: I like spring best. The colours are pretty! copula verb + S(X): Is it cold today?
3	SVO: It's in July and August. My mum will make *zongzi* then. copula verb + S(X): Is the singing contest in May? Is the school trip this year?
4	*Wh*-word + AUX + SVO: When do you celebrate Mid-Autumn Day this year? When do we celebrate Mother's Day? expressions of dates: April 1st, May 4th…
5	phrasal plural -s: three rabbits, five carrots. present continuous tense V-ing: It is jumping. It is playing with the carrot. SVO: It's your dog. That's my cat! *Wh*-word + AUX + SVO: What can they eat? What are they eating?
6	SVO/present continuous tense V-ing: She's listening to music. He's eating lunch.

Appendix M: Analysed version of focal grammar in *PEP English*, Book 7

Unit	Grammatical structures
1	semi-formulaic structure: Where is the [cinema/bookstore/museum/post office…]? SVO: it's near the library. It's over there.
2	SVO: You must pat attention to the traffic lights. I often go by subway. copula verb + S(X): Is this your bike? Is that the bus stop? *Wh*-word + *do* + SVO: How do we get there? How does she get to the bus stop? preposition phrases: by bus/taxi/plane/ship…
3	possessive determiner: his favourite comic book/her favourite movie. lexical plural -s: some pictures/ some beautiful leaves. SVO/present continuous tense V-ing: I'm checking a new comic book. We are going to the book store.
4	possessive determiner/lexical plural -s: your hobbies, his activities, her likes. 3rd ps sg -s: SVO: I like reading stories. We like singing and doing kung fu. AUX + SVO: Does he live on the South Island? Does she like swimming?
5	SVO: He's a businessman. She's a nurse. *Wh*-word + *do* + SVO: What does he do? Where does he work?
6	SVO: It was so good. We should share. *Wh*-word + AUX + SVO: What should I do? How could you eat all the popcorn?

Appendix N: Analysed version of focal grammar in *PEP English*, Book 8

Unit	Grammatical structures
1	SVO: I'm 1.61 metres. You're older than me.
2	simple past -ed: I stayed at home and watched TV. possessive determiner: your weekend/my room. SVO: I cleaned my room on Saturday. We played football on Sunday. *Wh*-word + *do* + SVO: What did you do last weekend? What does Zhang Peng do on Sunday?
3	simple past tense (regular and irregular forms): rode (ride), went (go), washed (wash), watched (watch), happened (happen). SVO: I fell off my bike. I saw lots of grapes. AUX + SVO: Can I come and visit you? Did you go to Turpan?
4	adverbs for time: *then* and *now*. 'There + be' sentence: There were no computers then. There is a gym now. possessive determiner: your father/our school.
5	simple past -ed/SVO: I looked at the school gym. He showed one picture. comparative sentence: It's bigger than the elephant. The tiger is smaller than the whale.
6	3rd ps sg -s/SVO: Mike sometimes plays football or exercise in the gym. He likes to speak English with his friends.

Appendix O: Analysed version of focal grammar in *Super Kids*, Book 2

Unit	Grammatical structures
1	formulaic structure: Thanks! Have a good time! SVO: This is a clock/This isn't a computer. It's a robot. noun phrases: a backpack/a suitcase/a computer/a window/a clock/a space shuttle…
2	formulaic structure: What's your name? I'm pluto. How old are you? I'm 10. SVO: That's a sofa. He's my dad. copula verb + S(X): Is this a closet? Is that a chair? Yes, this is. No, that isn't.
3	noun phrases: a house/a school/a station/an airport. formulaic structure: nice to meet you. imperatives: Stand up! Touch your head.
4	phrasal plural -s: We want some noodles. I want two bananas/two pencils. *Wh*-word + *do* + SVO: What do you want? When do you play baseball? imperatives: Get out of bed. Take off your shirt. Put on your shirt.
5	food items: a hamburger/hot dog/sandwich/salad/pancake… phrasal plural -s/SVO: I have two pens. We want some noodles. *Wh*-word + *do* + SVO: What do you want? What do they have? imperatives: Go inside. Sit down. Pick up the menu. Open the menu. Read the menu.
6	lexical plural -s: I like puppets. I like model cars. AUX + SVO: Does she like snakes? No, she doesn't. Can I have a puppy? Yes, you can. 3rd ps sg -s/SVO: She likes lizards. He likes kites. formulaic structure: Thank you. Excuse me.
7	numerals: Numbers 10-20. lexical plural -s/SVO: These are paintbrushes. Those are maps. They're pens. copula verb + S(X): Are they pens? Are these paintbrushes? Are those maps? Yes, they are….
8	weekdays and weekends: Monday, Tuesday, Wednesday, Thursday, Friday, Saturday, Sunday. SVO: I want to sing. I go to English class on Sunday. *Wh*-word + *do* + SVO: When do you go to piano class? When do you play baseball? imperatives: Get on the bike. Ride the bike. Ring the bell. Put on the brakes. Get off the bike.
9	regular past tense -ed/SVO: I played soccer yesterday. I cooked dinner. AUX + SVO: Did you play soccer? Did you cook dinner? Yes, I did. / No, I didn't.

Appendix P: Analysed version of focal grammar in *Super Kids*, Book 3

Unit	Grammatical structures
1	form of address (relatives): brother/sister/aunt/uncle. SVO: This is my friend. I like to play the guitar. I like to run. Do-fronting: Do you like to run? Do you like to sing? Yes, I do. /No, I don't. /Yes, we do. /No, we don't.
2	formulaic structure: Nice to meet you. See ya! SVO: I like English. These are my friends. AUX + SVO: Does he go to cram school on Friday? Does she play basketball on Friday? Yes, he does. /No, she doesn't. 3rd ps sg -s: She goes to piano class on Monday. He plays baseball on Monday.
3	lexical phrases: Let's get some fruit/snacks/popcorn. SVO: The turkey is behind the chicken. The meat is in front of the chicken. copula verb + S(X): Is that enough? Is the chicken on the cart? Yes, it is. /No, it isn't.
4	*Wh*-word + AUX + SVO: What's she doing? What's he doing? present continuous tense V-ing/SVO: She's sleeping. She's laughing. She isn't eating.
5	formulaic structure: Come on. Gee! Hurry up. possessive determiner/SVO: This is my face. This is his nose. Our school fair is in October.
6	expressions of months: January, February, March, April, May, June, July… copula verb + S(X): Are these two backpacks? Is this a book bag? phrasal plural -s: two ghosts, two ghosts, three witches…
7	formulaic structure: Yippee! SVO: This place is great. I love picnics. AUX + SVO: Did he play football yesterday? Yes, he did. /No, he didn't. simple past -ed: We played football. I washed my face. The dogs played football. possessive determiner: look for your mouse, my face, my teeth…
8	SVO: It's too tight. It is ten forty-five. I wrote a story. *Wh*-word + *do* + SVO: What did you do yesterday? What did you write yesterday?
9	SVO: This is for you. I don't have any cake. Do-fronting: Do you have any mustard? Yes, we do. Do you drink any lemonade? No, I don't.

Appendix Q: Analysed version of focal grammar in *Super Kids*, Book 4

Unit	Grammatical structures
1	country names: Australia, Japan, South Africa, England, France, the U. S. A. *Wh*-word + AUX + SVO: What are you doing now? What are you going to do tonight? present continuous tense V-ing/SVO: We're taking a trip. I'm going to the school.
2	SVO: It's not yours. It's mine. I forgot my handkerchief. copula verb + S(X): Is your handkerchief at home? Is this comb yours?
3	lexical plural -s/SVO: They're next to the mugs. The wallets are behind the fans. copula verb + S(X): Is the wallet here? Is this T-shirt green?
4	single word: Awesome! SVO: They're soft. I like koalas. I don't like winter. AUX + SVO: Did you see a kangaroo? Can you see a platypus?
5	comparative sentences/SVO: A zebra is bigger than an elephant. A giraffe is taller than a zebra.
6	SVO: He was in the store. We were in the post office. copula verb + S(X): Were you in the bookstore? Was he in the toy store?
7	'*go* + gerund': go swimming/go shopping/go fishing. SVO: She wants to go swimming. We want to go fishing. I like to go shopping. *Wh*-word + *do* + SVO: What does she want to do? What does he like to do? 3rd ps sg -s: She wants to go swimming. He likes to go fishing.
8	'There + be' interrogatives: Is there any juice? Yes, there is. phrasal plural -s: some crackers, five sandwiches.
9	SVO: I rode a roller coaster. It's a boomerang. *Wh*-word + *do* + SVO: What did you do in the U. S. A. ? What do you do in the trip? lexical plural -s: postcards, take pictures, souvenirs…

Appendix R: Analysed version of focal grammar in *Join in*, Book 2

Unit	Grammatical structures
1	formulaic structure: good morning/good afternoon/good evening/good night. phrasal plural -s: seven hamsters/two birds. copula verb + S(X): Is Julia's cat black? Is Jeff's fish orange? SVO: Julia's cat is black and white. Jeff's fish is orange. Maria's hamster is white and brown.
2	3rd ps sg -s/SVO: Emma paints a red bridge on Monday. He plays basketball on Tuesday. Emma hates pink. possessive determiner: your favourite day/my favourite colour. copula verb + S(X): Is your favourite colour green? Is your favourite day Monday?

Appendix R: Analysed version of focal grammar in *Join in*, Book 2 (continued)

Unit	Grammatical structures
3	present continuous tense V-ing/SVO: I am wearing a red T-shirt. Sophie is wearing a pink cap. Anna is using makeup. possessive determiner: my favourite T-shirt/your favourite sweater. lexical plural -s: green jeans/black socks/brown shoes. *Wh*-word + AUX + SVO: What am I wearing?
4	present perfect tense V-en/SVO: I've walked three miles. I've finished my homework. possessive determiner: my homework/her schoolbag. present continuous tense V-ing: Anna is wearing a blue T-shirt. Ben is putting on white socks. 3rd ps sg -s: He goes to sleep. A big mouse jumps out. Wh-word + AUX + SVO: How are you feeling today? How is she feeling now?
5	Do-fronting: Do you like apples? Yes, I do. Do you like milk? No, we don't. lexical plural -s: stamps/apples/hamburgers. SVO: I love breakfast. I like chicken. I don't like hamburgers. copula verb + S(X): Is it good for you? Is it bad for me?
6	possessive determiner: touch your feet/its nose. lexical plural -s: shake your legs/your toes/arms. phrasal plural -s: two big eyes/two ears. present perfect tense V-en/SVO: It has got a small mouth. I've got a big mouth. copula verb + S(X): Is it like a monkey? Is this like a mouse?

Appendix S: Analysed version of focal grammar in *Join in*, Book 3

Unit	Grammatical structures
1	words for months: January, February, March, April… SVO: the mouse is tired. The dog is sad. This is the bear. It's in March. Do-fronting: Do you like your yellow T-shirt? Do you love your green skirt? copula verb + S(X): Is Zhaowei's birthday in April? Is Thomas's birthday in May? possessive determiner: your yellow T-shirt/my favourite shirt.
2	words for colours: green, red, yellow, black. SVO: It's on the box. It's behind the box. It's a floor. copula verb + S(X): Is the ball in the box? Is the pen behind the box? phrasal plural -s: six desks/nine chairs/two windows.

Appendix S: Analysed version of focal grammar in *Join in*, Book 3 (continued)

Unit	Grammatical structures
3	formulaic structure: Here you are. Thank you. SVO: His favourite colour is yellow. copula verb + S(X): Is eighteen plus forty-eight sixty-six? Is ninety-nine minus twenty-six seventy-three? phrasal plural -s: two bananas/an ice cream/thirty-three bananas. present perfect tense V-en: I've got a wonderful friend. He's got two bananas. 3rd ps sg -s: He lives at London Zoo. He eats thirty-three bananas for breakfast.
4	SVO: it's small. I often read in the library. She is from Japan. possessive determiner: your schoolbag/her hair. present perfect tense V-en: I have got black hair. She has got brown hair. 3rd ps sg -s: She likes sport. He loves English.
5	SVO: I can play the piano. I can play table tennis. possessive determiner: my brother/her head.
6	AUX + SVO: Can you play the piano? Can I play games? Can you swim? *Wh*-word + AUX + SVO: When will you have your birthday? What will you get for your birthday? copula verb + S(X): Is sixteen plus sixty seventy-six? formulaic structure: What's your name? SVO: They sell their used toys. Most of their parents come to the fete. Do-fronting: Do you like English? Do you study Maths? possessive determiner: their used toys/your birthday. lexical plural -s: their parents/their used toys. phrasal plural -s: four lines/sixteen girls/thirteen boys.

Appendix T: Analysed version of focal grammar in *Join in*, Book 4

Unit	Grammatical structures
1	*Wh*-word + *do* + SVO: What time do you get up? When do you go to school? formulaic structure: What time is it? possessive determiner: my crazy clock/your watch. phrasal plural -s: thirty minutes/four seasons/twelve months/seven days/24 hours. present perfect tense V-en/SVO: I've got a clock. My dad has got a watch. 3rd ps sg -s: My clock starts to sing. My crazy clock strikes two. copula verb + S(X): Is your schoolbag big? Is this your friend?
2	possessive determiner: my favourite subject/his favourite subject. lexical plural -s/SVO: I like tomatoes. We like potatoes. copula verb + S(X): Is your favourite subject Chinese? Is his birthday in May? *Wh*-word + *do* + SVO: What subject does he like? What subject do you like?

Appendix T: Analysed version of focal grammar in *Join in*, Book 4(continued)

Unit	Grammatical structures
3	lexical plural -s: other animals/big ears. phrasal plural -s: four legs/two eyes. AUX + SVO: Does it eat grass? Does it live on farm?
4	possessive determiner: your room/my bedroom. SVO: My bedroom has a bed, a wardrobe, a mirror, a desk and a chair.
5	possessive determiner: my English teacher/our Maths teacher. lexical plural -s: the songs/the lessons/black shoes. phrasal plural -s: eleven boys/four lessons. present continuous tense V-ing/SVO: She is wearing a red cardigan, a blue skirt, a blue tie, black shoes and black socks. He is wearing a black T-shirt. 3rd ps sg -s/SVO: He likes the songs. She likes English class. Do-fronting: Do you like English? Do you want to wear black shoes? *Wh*-word + *do* + SVO: How many English lessons do you have in a week? Which class do you like the most?
6	lexical plural -s: bananas/apples. present continuous tense V-ing/SVO: We're visiting the Great Wall. I'm riding a horse. He is playing basketball. *Wh*-word + AUX + SVO: What are you doing? What is he doing?

Appendix U: Analysed version of focal grammar in *Join in*, Book 5

Unit	Grammatical structures
1	formulaic structure: How are you? Hi/Hello. Thanks/Thank you. SVO: My father is a doctor. He is a taxi driver. I'm her aunt. *Wh*-word + *do* + SVO: What does your father do? What do you do? possessive determiner: your father/your sister/my brother/her aunt. lexical plural -s: your parents/your grandparents.
2	SVO: I like it very much. It's beautiful. AUX + SVO: Are these three pink elephants? Is this a necklace in picture A? phrasal plural -s: three pink elephants/two white cats.
3	SVO: It's twenty to nine. The correct answer is *a*.
4	SVO: They're stamps. It's a sticker. It's an autograph. lexical plural -s: stamps/stickers/autographs. phrasal plural -s: thirty-five autographs/ninety-three stickers. Do-fronting: Do you collect stickers? Do you have stamps? *Wh*-word + *do* + SVO: What do you collect? How many stamps do you collect? *Wh*-word + AUX + SVO: What are you going to do on Sunday? What are the children doing?

Appendix U: Analysed version of focal grammar in *Join in*, Book 5 (continued)

Unit	Grammatical structures
5	AUX + SVO: Are you going to do on Saturday? Can you bring the bread? *Wh*-word + *do* + SVO: What do we need? What do you need? possessive determiner/lexical plural -s: my flowers/your hot dogs. phrasal plural -s: some flowers/three cakes. present continuous tense V-ing/SVO: They are having a garden party at Tony's home. I'm going to my grandparents' home.
6	SVO: I often dream about…I sometimes dream about…

Appendix V: Analysed version of focal grammar in *Join in*, Book 6

Unit	Grammatical structures
1	present continuous tense V-ing/SVO: He's catching a hare. He's swimming across the lake. 3rd ps sg -s/SVO: He jumps in the water. He wants to catch a hare. *Wh*-word + AUX + SVO: What's he catching over there? Where's he swimming?
2	lexical plural -s: cartoons/detective films/sports programmes… SVO: I often watch cartoons and detective films. I always watch cartoons. Cartoons are interesting. *Wh*-word + *do* + SVO: What do you watch, Robert? What do you like the most?
3	formulaic structure: That's OK. SVO: I'll take a taxi. I come to a stop. copula verb + S(X): Is the museum there? Is the train station over there?
4	lexical plural -s: big dogs/horror films… SVO: I'm afraid of cold. I'm not afraid of big dogs.
5	possessive determiner: my favourite beach/our holiday/her horse. lexical plural -s: horses/islands. present continuous tense V-ing: Someone is riding a bike. I am swimming in the warm water. 3rd ps sg -s/SVO: My brother drives on the beach. He likes swimming in the lake.
6	phrasal plural -s: two pencils/three pens. SVO: I like Chinese best. I am afraid of Maths.

Appendix W: Analysed version of focal grammar in *Join in*, Book 7

Unit	Grammatical structures
1	SVO: She will have two new subjects. I like learning new words… Do-fronting: Do the pupils like their teachers? Do you like learning new words? *Wh*-word + *do* + SVO: Which school does Mary Chen go to? What do they often do? What subjects do the children love? *Wh*-word + AUX + SVO: What new subjects will she have this year? What are you learning? possessive determiner: her Drama teacher/their teachers. lexical plural -s: new subjects/sports and games. phrasal plural -s: 23 pupils/many pupils. 3rd ps sg -s: She goes to Lake School on North Island. Alison loves Music. Sue loves Chinese. Sue often learns Chinese language. Simon often works with his computer.
2	SVO: Wuhan is a big city in China. It is a city of rivers. lexical plural -s: rivers/lakes. phrasal plural -s: many lakes/many beautiful parks. 3rd ps sg -s: The Changjiang River runs across the city from west to east. The Han River enters the Changjiang River here.
3	SVO: It is on 31st October. They dress up as witches, monsters or ghosts. They go from house to house. lexical plural -s: witches/monsters/ghosts/chocolates.
4	regular and irregular forms of past tense: He broke his right arm. They called the police. The man wanted to get down the ladder. possessive determiner: his left arm/her right leg. SVO: The children went to Mr. Snow's house. They found a ladder in his garden. AUX + S(X): Did Joel have an accident when he was eight? Did he break his left arm?
5	SVO: He went to the cinema. Li Ping didn't go to the zoo. He didn't play basketball. AUX + S(X): Has it got four legs? Does it eat other animals? simple past -ed: He played football. He watched sports. lexical plural -s: sports/cartoons. phrasal plural -s: four legs/two animals.
6	possessive determiner: my good friend/his guitar/my class. lexical plural -s: photographs/friends. phrasal plural -s: forty-eight pupils/two cameras. 3rd ps sg -s/SVO: Erica loves playing the guitar. She goes to the photo club. He wants to play in a band.

Appendix X: Analysed version of focal grammar in *Join in*, Book 8

Unit	Grammatical structures
1	lexical plural -s: tests/apples/bananas. present perfect tense V-en/SVO: They've got French and History. I've got Chinese and English.
2	phrasal plural -s: four legs/three animals. AUX + SVO: Does it eat other animals? Does it live on a farm? Yes/No.
3	lexical plural -s: films/books. SVO: I'd like to see it very much. I love adventure films. I'll call for you at half past six. Do-fronting: Do you know it? Do you want to see the film? AUX + SVO: Would you like to go with me? Can we watch horror films?
4	possessive determiner: my dreams/their school. lexical plural -s: beautiful gardens/the best schools. phrasal plural -s: a lot of cars/four bikes. SVO: Children have the best schools. Their school must be the best.
5	copula verb + S(X): Is the cinema there? Is their school here? imperatives: go straight ahead/turn left/turn right.
6	3rd ps sg -s/SVO: He likes reading. He doesn't like singing. She likes watching films. Do-fronting: Do you like football? Do you love basketball?

后　记

“课本上所教是否真正适合学习者的语言学习?”这一问题始于笔者在武汉大学文学院攻读硕士研究生时某次与导师的读书会上一位同门师姐的随口一问。之后承蒙澳大利亚导师组的厚爱,笔者幸运地申请上全额奖学金赴澳大利亚国立大学攻读博士研究生学位,主攻方向为语言学(第二语言习得)。2012 年至 2013 年,初入澳大利亚时语言与文化所带来的“休克”体验让我不得不重新对自己的英语学习之路产生反思。自小学三年级始接触和学习英语已长达十几年,但为何当我试图应用从课本上习得的语法与话语表达与澳洲当地英语母语者交流时,却每每遭遇沟通交际障碍?是否是由于以往某些外语教材中所教语法表达并不符合学习者的习得规律?为此我向博士项目导师组的各位导师一一请教,也借此引发了我对博士课题研究问题的深层思考,即从第二语言习得发展进程的角度,“可学性”是否真正被运用结合到小学英语类教材中有关语法教学这部分内容中?

正如澳大利亚国立大学的校训所言“*Naturam Primum Cognoscere Rerum*”(‘First to learn the nature of things’),学术始于学习万物之本。于笔者而言,对于第二语言习得的研究也应从其最基本的问题着手,即学习者本身。在本书涉及的研究过程中,笔者有幸得到了 Dr. Yanyin Zhang, Dr. Louise Jansen, 以及 Dr. Duck－Young Lee 三位师长的悉心指导。在此一并表示感谢。

对于研究“可学性”的理论方法,Dr. Zhang 推荐应用第二语言习得领域的国际前沿理论之一——语言加工性理论(Processability Theory)。从广义上说,语言习得研究着重解决两个核心问题:第一,语言是如何习得的?第二,语言习得是如何进行的?而语言可加工性理论则是着力解决第二个问题。该理论由当代著名的心理语言学及二语习得专家 Manfred Pienemann 于 1998 年提出并于 2005 年得到进一步发展。其以心理语言学为基础,从语言加工及处理的角度,科学描述、阐释并假定二语习得中普遍内在的发展顺序。该理论的重要观点在于:无论学习者处于二语习得发展过程中的哪一个阶段,他们都只能掌握和运用那些能够被当前阶段的语言处理器加工处理的语法结构。因而,学习者掌握和运用语言加工所需的处理程序的依次顺序也决定了二语习得的发展顺序。

关于二语习得顺序的重要研究最早可追溯到 20 世纪 70 年代盛行一时的“语素顺序研究”。其通过大量的实验型调查,观察不同母语背景二语学习者习得几种英语语素的准确率，进而总结和描述二语习得顺序。此后20世纪80年代以德国Zeitspracherwerb Italienischer und Spanischer Arbeiter(简称ZISA)为主的研究学者们将调查重点转向了学习者习得语序及句式上。通过对生活在德国境内的西班牙、意大利及葡萄牙裔劳工的大量实证调查，ZISA研究组描绘并尝试解释德语的语序结构习得过程中所包含的五个发展阶段。然而受制于自身调查范围与理论依据的缺陷，这些研究要么缺乏对不同语言习得情况的概括性以及对所观察到的习得顺序的科学性阐述(如"语素顺序研究")，要么无法从学习者角度阐释二语习得以及对那些超出特定范围的语法结构进入中介语系统提出清晰解释(如ZISA)。进入20世纪90年代，二语习得顺序研究更加重视对不同语言学习规律的普遍性调查，并引入如心理学、认知科学等其他学科来进一步完善其理论框架。其中的重要理论发展之一就是语言加工性理论。

于本书的研究而言，该理论对学习者习得语法规则的普遍性规律提供了科学假定与应用支持。以语言加工性定义"可学性"，对于小学英语类教材的语法教学评估也是一次大胆的尝试。除此之外，笔者将部分英语类教材中"可学性"因素的缺失归结于教材编写过程中贯穿始终的"主题式教学方法"。对于该教学方法以及教材本身的探索得益于导师Dr. Duck－Young Lee的指点。"可学性"仅仅只是教材评估中参考的重要因素之一，而并非单一的决定性的因素。简单来说，语言学习涉及多个方面，例如语法、词汇、语音、功能、交际文化等等。"可学性"一方面的缺失并不意味着教材整体内容的一无是处。小学英语教材中强调"主题"与"功能"两大元素，是侧重培养学生的交际沟通能力，即如何在特定语境中实现有效交流。因而，教材编者在撰写过程中更多考量某一语法结构的出现能否为特定的重要的交际功能服务。例如，某语境强调学生掌握从他人问询及搜集信息的功能，因而实现该功能所需语法结构就包括特殊疑问句*Wh*-questions。因此，笔者对于"可学性"的探索与讨论仅仅是希望能为国内英语教材编写、特别是语法教学方面，提供更为广阔与深刻的思路。要实现语言学习所有方面在教材中的融会贯通仍然任重而道远。

本书在撰写过程中还得到了西悉尼大学Dr. Bruno Di Biase教授对本书参考文献以及内容所提出的真诚而中肯的建议。同时，笔者由衷感谢在澳大利亚国立大学及首都堪培拉学习工作期间的同窗好友与同僚。最为重要的是，笔者对父母数十年如一日的支持与呵护无以回报，唯以拙著面世聊表无限感激。